teach®
yourself

world cultures:
spain

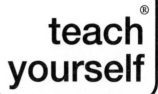

world cultures:
spain
mike zollo
with phil turk

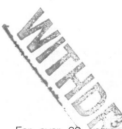

The publisher has used its best endeavours to ensure that the URLs for external websites referred to in this book are correct and active at the time of going to press. However, the publisher has no responsibility for the websites and can make no guarantee that a site will remain live or that the content is or will remain appropriate.

For UK order enquiries: please contact Bookpoint Ltd., 130 Milton Park, Abingdon, Oxon OX14 4SB. Telephone: +44 (0) 1235 827720. Fax: +44 (0) 1235 400454. Lines are open from 09.00–18.00, Monday to Saturday, with a 24-hour message answering service. You can also order through our website www.teachyourself.co.uk

For USA order enquiries: please contact McGraw-Hill Customer Services, PO Box 545, Blacklick, OH 43004-0545, USA. Telephone: 1-800-722-4726. Fax: 1-614-755-5645.

For Canada order enquiries: please contact McGraw-Hill Ryerson Ltd, 300 Water St, Whitby, Ontario L1N 9B6, Canada. Telephone: 905 430 5000. Fax: 905 430 5020.

Long-renowned as the authoritative source for self-guided learning – with more than 30 million copies sold worldwide – the *Teach Yourself* series includes over 300 titles in the fields of languages, crafts, hobbies, business, computing and education.

British Library Cataloguing in Publication Data: a catalogue record for this title is available from The British Library.

Library of Congress Catalog Card Number: on file

First published in UK 2000 by Hodder Headline, 338 Euston Road, London NW1 3BH.

First published in US 2000 by Contemporary Books. a Division of The McGraw-Hill Companies, 1 Prudential Plaza, 130 East Randolph Street, Chicago, IL 60601, USA.

This edition published 2004.

The 'Teach Yourself' name is a registered trade mark of Hodder & Stoughton Ltd.

Copyright ©2000, 2004 Units 1–4 and 7–12 Mike Zollo; Units 5 and 6 Phil Turk

Typeset by Transet Limited, Coventry, England.
Printed in Great Britain for Hodder & Stoughton Educational, a division of Hodder Headline, 338 Euston Road, London NW1 3BH by Cox & Wyman Ltd., Reading, Berkshire.

Papers used in this book are natural, renewable and recyclable products. They are made from wood grown in sustainable forests. The logging and manufacturing processes conform to the environmental regulations of the country of origin.

Impression number   10 9 8 7 6 5 4 3 2 1
Year   2010 2009 2008 2007 2006 2005 2004

contents

introduction

This book is designed to give you as full a basic overview as possible of the main aspects of Spain: the country, its languages, its people, their way of life and culture and what makes them tick.

You will find it a useful foundation if you are studying for examinations which require a knowledge of the background of Spain and its civilization, or if you are learning the language in, for example, an evening class and want to know more about the country and how it works. If your job involves travel and business relations it will provide valuable and practical information about the ways and customs of the people you are working with. Or if you simply have an interest in Spain for whatever reason, it will broaden your knowledge about the country and its inhabitants.

The book is divided into three sections:

- **The making of Spain**
  Units 1 and 2 deal with the forces – historical, geographical, geological, demographical and linguistic – that have brought about the formation of the country we know as Spain and the language we known as Spanish. Unit 2 also takes a look at the role of Spanish outside the immediate frontiers of Spain.

- **Creative Spain**
  Units 3 to 7 deal with the wealth of creative aspects of Spanish culture from the beginnings to the present day. These units take a look at the main areas or works of literature, art and architecture, music, traditions and festivals, science and technology, fashion and food and drink, together with the people who have created and are still creating them.

- **Living in Spain now**
  Units 8 to 11 deal with aspects of contemporary Spanish society and the practicalities of living in present-day Spain: the way the political structure of the country is organized, education, the environment, the workplace and how people spend their leisure time. The final unit looks at the country's political, economic and social relations with the wider world, and takes a glance at the future.

Taking it further
Each unit ends with a section entitled 'Taking it further', where you will find useful addresses, websites, suggested places to visit and things to see and do in order to develop your interest further and increase your knowledge.

The language
Within each chapter you will encounter a number of terms in Spanish, whose meaning is given in English when they are first introduced. If you wish to put your knowledge into practice, we have provided in each unit a list of useful words and phrases to enable you to talk or write about the subject in question. Where English spellings of Spanish places exist, these are generally used.

We have been careful in researching and checking facts, but please be aware that sources sometimes offer differing information. Of course a book of this length cannot contain everything you may need to know on every aspect of Spain. That is why we have provided so many pointers to where you can find further information about any aspect that you may wish to pursue in more depth. We trust that you will enjoy this introductory book, and that it will provide leads to further profitable reading, listening and visiting. *Buen viaje!*

Phil Turk
Series Editor

I would like to thank Virginia Vinuesa Benítez, Cathy Zollo, Tony Zollo and Phil Turk for their help in the preparation of this book.

Grateful thanks to my wife and family for their patience and support.

Mike Zollo

01

the making of Spain

In this unit you will learn
- about the landscape of Spain
- about Spain's climate
- about the people
- about their history

What made Spain what it is? Most people know something about Spain: it is one of the more distinctive countries of the world, and one which has had a great influence on many other countries. Ask anybody about Spain, and almost everyone will be able to mention something they associate with the country, even if it is only something stereotypical like flamenco, castanets or bullfighting. Spain as a country is the result of its geography and its political history, and a look at these will explain what made Spain what it is today.

Spain: the land

Spain occupies most of the Iberian Peninsula, which, with its distinctive shape, sticks out of south-west Europe between the Atlantic and the Mediterranean, and between Europe and Africa. Take away Portugal, which occupies most of the west and south-west of the peninsula, and the outline of Spain looks a bit like the hide of a bull! Its position as an outpost of Europe, tucked away behind the Pyrenees, has been an important factor in the development of Spain as one of the most distinctive countries in Europe. It is sometimes said that 'Africa begins at the Pyrenees' (see Unit 5), and it is certainly true that Spain has undergone influences from the south more than any other country in Europe, as we shall explain later. Indeed, the Peninsula was once joined to Africa, before the Straits of Gibraltar were formed. Although largely surrounded by sea, Spain is a very high country: in average height, it is the second highest country in Europe, with only Switzerland higher. Madrid is situated almost 3000 feet above sea-level, making it one of the highest capital cities of Europe. Much of the peninsula is an enormous high *meseta* (plateau), tilted towards the south-west; more accurately, there are two *mesetas*, one north of Madrid and one to the south. The highest land is in the north-east, and much of the low land is in Portugal. Spain is criss-crossed by *sierras* (mountain ranges). *Sierra* is the Spanish word for 'saw', and indicates the jagged appearance of the mountains when seen from a distance.

The great sierras

The *sierras* mostly run east-west (the Pyrenees form the border with France). Other *sierras* run from north to south, i.e., the Cantabrian mountains, the Sierra de Guadarrama, the Sierra Morena and the Sierra Nevada. These mountain ranges are important because they help to divide Spain up into regions.

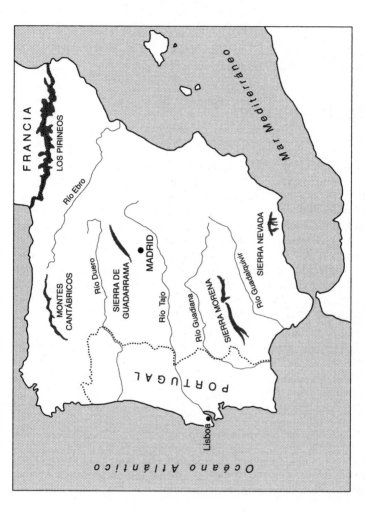

Map of Spain and Portugal

Rivers

Most of the important rivers also flow east-west, except the *Ebro*, which carries water west-east from the Cantabrian Mountains, the Iberian Mountains and the Pyrenees towards the Mediterranean. From north-south, the other rivers are the *Duero* (*Douro* in English), which flows across the northern *meseta*, and across Portugal, reaching the Atlantic at Oporto; the *Tajo* (*Tagus* in English), which flows across the northern part of the southern *meseta*, reaching the Atlantic at Lisbon; the *Guadiana* flows across the southern part of the southern *meseta*, then turns south as it reaches Portugal, finally forming the border between Portugal and Spain as it flows into the Atlantic between the Algarve and Huelva; and the *Guadalquivir*, which flows across the southern region of Andalusia, and into the sea near Seville and Cádiz, forming a huge delta (see pp. 29, 255).

Climate

This country, rich in its variety of landscape, also has a variety of climates. The north coast and particularly the north-west have an Atlantic climate, rather reminiscent of Britain's south-west peninsula or of Britanny: changeable and rather wet, but slightly warmer. The centre of Spain has a typically continental climate: very cold, dry winters and very hot, dry summers. Of Madrid's climate it is said '*Nueve meses de invierno y tres de infierno*' ('Nine months of winter and three of hell') ... which explains why anybody who can, leaves the capital for as long as possible in the summer. The east coast and south-east have a Mediterranean climate: a warm, wet winter and a hot, dry summer. There are, of course, variations and micro-climates: the Pyrenees, the mountains of the north-east and all of the *sierras* mentioned above are snow-capped for much of the year; the far south, especially the southern slopes of the Sierra Nevada – the Alpujarra – have an almost north African climate, evidenced in vegetation not seen elsewhere in Europe. The Cuenca del Ebro (the wide gorge of the *Ebro* around Zaragoza in the north-east) sometimes has a bank of freezing fog which sits in the valley for weeks at a time in winter, when all around is sunshine.

The people of Spain and their history

The earliest inhabitants

The Iberian Peninsula was named after the Ibers, who entered Spain from North Africa. These short, dark people settled mostly in the south and south-east of the peninsula; to an extent they merged with the Celts who, as in France, Britain and Ireland, settled in the westernmost extremities of Europe, arriving in north and north-west Spain around the 5th century BC. Before this time, Phoenician traders had established trading settlements around the Mediterranean coastline; they probably founded Cádiz too, but they had no ambition to colonize the land. The Greeks had also set up trading settlements on the coast centuries before, such as Málaga and Sagunto, one of the oldest towns in Spain, but their influence also spread inland.

The Carthaginians, arriving by 250 BC or so, were more systematic about colonizing, and even used Spain as a base from which to attack Rome by land, fearing that Rome was stealing their supremacy in the Mediterranean. In fact, after their defeat in Italy, it was the Romans pursuing the Carthaginians back into Spain who were the first to conquer the whole of the country, although it took time and effort, owing to the resistance of the Celtiberians.

The Roman era

Roman domination, once complete, brought civilization to Spain in every sense, with the building of cities, roads and aqueducts, and the establishment of Roman law and social structure. Spain became one of the most important of the Roman colonies, and among the many famous Spanish-born Romans were the emperors Hadrian and Trajan and the writers Seneca, Lucan and Martial. Most importantly as far as the modern Hispanic world is concerned, the so-called 'Vulgar Latin' of the Roman legionaries became the language of Roman Spain, later evolving through Romance and splintering into a range of languages and dialects, many of which survive today (see Unit 2). Even the name Spain supposedly derives from the Roman term *Hispalia*, 'land of the rabbits': apparently, when the Romans arrived in Spain, they were struck by the number of rabbits they saw!

The Germanic tribes

The collapse of the Roman Empire, overrun by Germanic hordes, brought the Suevi, Alans and Vandals to Spain in AD 409. They did not respect what the Romans had built up, and the Vandals in particular earned such a reputation for destroying Roman buildings that their name not only survives in the name of *Andalucía*, but also in the term used to describe a particular form of anti-social behaviour! The last Germanic tribe to arrive in Spain – in AD 414 – the Visigoths, were altogether more civilized: they established a Visigothic kingdom in Spain, yet they adopted the language and customs of the Romanized Spaniards. The only Visigothic words which survive in modern Spanish tend to be connected with horses and horsemanship. They were already Christians, as were the Roman Spaniards by the time the Germanic tribes began to invade. Their 300-year rule left little trace other than their ancient system of law, elements of which survive to this day.

Invasion from Africa

In AD 711, when the Visigoths were involved in a squabble over succession to the throne, an Arab army invaded from North Africa keen to conquer new lands and to convert their inhabitants to Islam. Their commander, Tarik, is immortalized in the name of the one of the first parcels of territory he won – Gebel Tarik – the rock of Tarik, now known as Gibraltar. The Arabs, also referred to as Moors because most of their soldiers were from the land we now call Morocco, swept across Spain, such was the weakness of the Visigoths, and by AD 718 they had conquered almost the whole of Spain. The toughest resistance they met was in the region now known as Asturias, where the Christian leader Pelayo and his soldiers were able to defeat a much larger Moorish army against the odds, largely due to the mountainous terrain. The Arabs turned their attention to France, but were eventually pushed back into Spain by the French king Charles Martel (the Hammer) in AD 732.

Muslim Spain

Arab domination in Spain was different from that of the Romans: unlike them the Arabs never managed to impose their language on their Christian subordinates, although many Arabic words have survived in modern-day Spanish. Like the Romans, however, they brought new levels of learning and culture to Spain, they were advanced in medicine, astronomy and mathematics in particular. Elements of Spain's literature, art and architecture show Arab influence, something which is fairly unique in European culture. Some of Spain's oldest universities were founded by the Arabs, and Seville had miles of streets lit by oil lamps while most of Europe was still in the dark ages. Irrigation systems established by them are still in use today, notably in the Huerta de Valencia, the fertile agricultural area south of that city. However, as with the Romans, the most obvious evidence of their almost eight centuries of power in Spain is in place names and buildings: as with other elements of Arab civilization, buildings such as the Alhambra in Granada and the Mezquita in Córdoba are unique to Spain, not found in any other European country.

The period of the *Reconquista*

Soon after the Arab invasion started, the *Reconquista* (Reconquest) began, with the Christians gradually winning back territory and creating new Christian kingdoms, and the Arab side losing control and splitting into small kingdoms. Thus Spain became a patchwork of little kingdoms, some Christian and some Arab; sometimes the religious differences didn't stop Christians seeking help from Arabs to fight against other Christian kingdoms – and vice versa. Some Christians lived as *mozárabes*, under Muslim rule but were allowed to practise their own religion. Similarly, some Arabs lived as *mudéjares*, under Christian rule but practised the Islamic faith. Yet others converted to Christianity, and were known as *conversos*. Many of the kingdoms corresponded to the geographical divisions provided by mountain ranges, and some have survived to this day as autonomous regions, such as the first to establish freedom from the Arabs, the kingdom of Asturias. (It is interesting to note that the Crown Prince, heir to the Spanish throne, has the title *Príncipe de Asturias*, thus being linked to the oldest area of 'free' Spain). With inter-marriages sometimes bringing kingdoms together and others being divided up between heirs to their thrones, along with a succession of alliances and rivalries, gradually larger kingdoms were created; in many cases, however, they 'filled' spaces between mountain ranges in such a way that the **sierras** provided natural boundaries between them.

Reunification: The *Reyes Católicos*

During the many centuries of the Reconquest, there were notable characters and events, prominent among which were the exploits of El Cid in the 11th century (see Unit 3). There were also a few notable monarchs: one was Alfonso X *El Sabio* (the wise), who ruled most of Christian Spain in the 11th century, and established the first chronicles in Spain, also founding Ciudad Real (Royal City, in Castilla-La Mancha, south of Madrid) as his capital in 1255. However, the one thing which would establish Spain as a nation, the final reconquest and reunification of Spain, took a long time coming. Through their marriage in 1469, Fernando, the heir to the throne of Aragón, and Isabel, heiress to that of Castile and León, paved the way for the unification of most of Christian Spain. Uniting their forces, once they had inherited their respective thrones, they set about ejecting the last of the Arabs from Spain: 'mopping up' most of the Arab territory which remained in southern Spain, they often replaced hilltop castles with Christian churches, nowhere more dramatically than at Montefrío in central Andalusia. Then in 1491 they began the siege of Granada, the last remaining outpost of Islam. The base camp for the siege was set up a few miles west of the city: when the camp was destroyed by fire, Isabel ordered a small city of stone to be built, and named it Santa Fe (Holy Faith), the name it bears to this day. The *Reconquista* was duly completed in early 1492 when Granada fell.

The last Moorish ruler of Granada, Boabdil, surrendered the keys of the city to Fernando and Isabel on 2 January, an event commemorated in a painting which can be seen in the sacristy of the cathedral-mosque in Córdoba (see Unit 4). The victorious monarchs occupied the Alhambra, the Moorish castle/palace high above Granada. When Boabdil went off to exile in Africa, he turned back to take a last look at Granada as he crossed the Sierra Nevada to the sea. Seeing him weep at his loss, his mother said to him: 'You do well to weep like a woman for what you were not man enough to defend.' The spot is marked by a plaque on the pass appropriately called Puerto del Suspiro del Moro (Pass of the Moor's Sigh) on the road from Granada to the coast at Motril.

The territory of Spain

It is significant that, with the exception of Gibraltar (seized by the British in 1704 and then ceded to Britain in the Treaty of Utrecht in 1713) the territorial Spain re-established by the *Reyes Católicos* is the same Spain as we know today, still unified in spite of separatist pressures from some regions, and in spite of invasions and civil wars. Symbolic of this unity was the logo often used by Fernando and Isabel – a yoke crossed vertically by a bundle of arrows: the arrows (*flechas*) representing the F of Fernando, and the yoke (*yugo*) representing the Y of Ysabel in the old spelling. This logo has also been used since to symbolize the unity of Spain, most notoriously by General Franco, for whom the *Reyes Católicos* were great heroes.

Religious consolidation

In their religious and imperial zeal, Isabel and Fernando completed the re-establishment of Christianity by expelling all Jews, of whom there had been many in Spain, and by establishing the Inquisition to weed out any religious dissidents. For all of this Pope Alexander VI – himself a Spaniard and the first of the Borgia popes – gave them the title of *Reyes Católicos* (Catholic Monarchs). It was a pity that they failed to realize that by expelling the Jews, they were depriving the new Spain of all the financial expertise which it could so usefully have done with over the next few centuries. The Sephardic Jews (the word *Sepharad* refers to Jewish Spain) mostly went to live around the Mediterranean shores of southern Turkey, where Sephardic Spanish is spoken to this day.

Linguistic consolidation: Spanish or *Castellano*?

It was the language of the conquering Castile which imposed itself over the languages and dialects of other regions of Spain: what we know as 'Spanish' is in fact, more correctly, Castilian: indeed, many Spaniards and most Latin-Americans prefer to refer to their language as *Castellano* rather than *Español*.

A New World and a new age

Having re-established the territorial and religious integrity of Spain as a Christian kingdom, it was logical that the *Reyes Católicos* should now extend their internal religious crusade to far-off shores, and to enlarge their newly consolidated territory to encompass any new ones ready to be discovered. However, it was almost a happy accident that it was the *Reyes Católicos* who became the sponsors of the discovery, exploration and conquest of the New World. The Genoese navigator, Christopher Columbus, had already tried to impress other European monarchs with his 'crazy' plan to establish a westerly route to the spice trade of the East Indies – to rival the new route around Africa recently established and monopolized by the Portuguese – only to be rejected in an age when many still believed the world to be flat.

He had already come to Fernando and Isabel in 1486 and again at Santa Fe in 1491, but at the time they had other things on their minds. He returned to meet them in the Alhambra early in 1492. Influenced by her confessor, the abbot of the Monastery of La Rábida, Huelva, where Columbus had spent some time, Isabel gave Columbus enough jewellery to fund his expedition, making him Admiral of the Ocean and Viceroy of any new lands he might discover. He was just about able to purchase three small *carabelas*: the *Pinta*, the *Niña* and the *Santa María*, the last as his flagship, and to engage a crew of Spaniards and just one Englishman, all of whom expected never to see their families again. On 3 August, they set sail from a little port near Huelva, Palos de la Frontera, the home town of Columbus' two captains, Martín and Vicente Pinzón.

After calling in at the Canary Islands, they set sail south-westwards. Columbus halved the distances he entered in the ship's logbook: some believe it was to fool his sailors, who feared that they would sail off the edge of the (flat) world. In fact it was as a defence against the Portuguese: if arrested for sailing through their waters (they claimed the rights over the South Atlantic), he would claim that the ship's log was not working properly, affecting the accuracy of his navigation.

After many trials and tribulations, on 12 October they finally made land on the island of Guanahaní, renaming it San Salvador. Although he explored much of the Caribbean and the coast of Central America in his three expeditions, he never knew for certain that this was a 'new' continent. The ensuing conquest and colonizing of new lands brought Spain untold wealth and gave her one of the greatest empires of all time, thanks to the foresight of the *Reyes Católicos*. It also took the Spanish language and Spanish culture to new continents, ensuring that

One of Columbus' ships

Spanish would become a true world language, spoken by hundreds of millions of people in many countries and rivalled only by English.

Succession

After all that Isabel and Fernando had accomplished, their remaining ambition was to consolidate their achievements by ensuring succession ... but this was to prove more problematical than their other objectives. They had five children: their only son, Juan, died at the age of 19. One of their daughters, Catalina (Catherine of Aragon) had a similar problem in failing to provide a son and heir for Henry VIII of England. In the end, it was left to their oldest surviving daughter to provide them with a successor: they succeeded in marrying off Juana, known as Juana *la Loca* (the Mad), to Felipe *el Hermoso* (the Handsome), son of Maximilian, the Emperor of the Austro-German Empire. Thus the House of Hapsburg was established, the first of the two great Spanish dynasties. Isabel died in 1504, and Fernando in 1516. Alongside their monumental tomb in the Capilla Real, the Royal Chapel which is an annexe of Granada Cathedral (worth a visit), is that of Juana and Felipe.

The Hapsburg dynasty, or the House of Austria

Monarch	Nickname	Dates	Achievements	Failings
Carlos I (V of Austro-German/ Holy Roman Empire	**El Emperador** (The emperor)	1500–1558 Reign 1516–1556	Energetic; a soldier; bold, ambitious	He knew little about Spain and spoke little Spanish
Felipe II	**El Prudente** (the Prudent)	1527–1598 Reign: 1556–1598	Prudent; good administrator victories at St Quentin 1557 and Battle of Lepanto 1571	Bureaucratic, inflexible; Armada disaster
Felipe III		Reign: 1598–1621		Weak, lazy, unintelligent
Felipe IV		Reign: 1621–1665	Patron of arts	Raised excessive taxes
Carlos II	**El Hechizado** (the Bewitched)	Reign: 1665–1706		Sickly, impotent, weak; neglected Spain

Carlos I, or Carlos V?

The son of Juana and Felipe, Carlos I of Spain, thus inherited not just Spain and its possessions – including those in the New World – but also, through his grandfather, a large part of the Austro-German Empire, making him one of the most powerful monarchs. He was also Carlos V of the Austro-German Empire, and tends to be known as Carlos Quinto – Carlos V. The only snag was that, as he had been brought up largely in Flanders, he knew little about Spain and spoke little Spanish! Thus it was that a 16-year-old foreigner came to Spain to rule, accompanied by garishly dressed Flemish courtiers who also spoke no Spanish and had little interest in Spain. It is sometimes said that the word *flamenco*, the music and dance which tends to be associated with women dressed in bright colours, came from these Flemish courtiers whose brightly coloured clothes contrasted with the sober blacks and greys of the Spanish court.

During Carlos' reign, Spain also controlled much of Italy, Austria, Flanders and parts of France and Germany. His *conquistadores*, among them Cortés and Pizarro, conquered and colonized Mexico, Perú and other countries in the New World, expanding his domains still further. After years of travelling around Europe at the head of his armies, he abdicated in favour of his son in 1556, and died two years later at the monastery of Yuste in Extremadura.

Felipe II

Unlike Carlos, his son was born in Spain; with the throne, Felipe inherited all of his father's Spanish territories and the newly established colonies in the Americas and the Philippines, which were named in his honour. With possessions all around the globe, it was said of Felipe that 'the sun never set on his empire', yet he never left Spain. He was a great, almost fanatical centralizing administrator, and insisted on studying documents from the remotest corners of his empire before making the appropriate decisions. It was Felipe who made a small Moorish village, Magerit, the capital of Spain – because it was pretty well in the centre of the country, while previously the 'capital' had simply been wherever the monarch happened to be. To celebrate the Spanish victory over the French at St Quentin, which took place on St Lawrence's day in 1557, Felipe had the enormous palace/monastery of San Lorenzo designed in the shape of the gridiron on which St Lawrence was martyred, and personally supervised its construction at El Escorial in the foothills of the Sierra de Guadarrama near Madrid. Under the command of his half-brother, Don Juan de Austria, the Christian fleet – Spanish, Genoese, Venetians and Papal States – defeated the Turks at the battle of Lepanto in 1571, thus ending the threat of Turkish power in the Mediterranean.

Having married Mary Tudor in Winchester Cathedral in 1554, Felipe decided to intervene in the religious persecutions which took place decades later in England under Queen Elizabeth I. Unfortunately, he chose the wrong man – the Duke of Medina Sidonia, a self-confessed landlubber – to be admiral of the Armada in 1588. The Spanish fleet fell victim to the English and was scattered by unfavourable winds before it could embark its fighting troops in France. When Felipe heard of its defeat, he replied coolly: 'I sent my ships to fight men, not the elements.' Ten years later, having lost three wives, he died a lonely and sick old man in his cell at El Escorial, overlooking the high altar of the monastery church at the centre of the palace. He is buried there in the royal mausoleum, along with every monarch who has ruled Spain since then.

The decline and fall of the Hapsburgs

In spite of the great territorial and military power of Spain in the 16th century, social and economic conditions in Spain were in a downhill spiral. The country's agriculture and rural areas had been neglected with the loss of so many people, especially from the south and south-west, who left Spain to seek their fortunes in the Americas, or to fight in the various military campaigns abroad. The gold and silver being brought across the Atlantic were largely devoted to paying off the debts incurred by great military campaigns, and the expulsion of the Jews had deprived the Spanish economic system of its most expert financial managers. Felipe had taken Portugal, but Spain lost it again, along with other territories in Europe, and the country was riddled with corruption. Much of the money in the royal coffers was spent on patronage of the arts, and as the political 'Golden Age' drew to a close, the cultural *Edad de Oro* (Golden Age) started (see Units 3, 4 and 5). Felipe II's son and heir, Felipe III left too much power in the hands of his favourite, the Duke of Lerma, and in turn his son Felipe IV similarly entrusted too much to the Count-Duke of Olivares. His son, Carlos II, was a rather pathetic figure compared to his larger-than-life forebears of the 16th century: incapable of ruling, and suffering ill-health (he was epileptic); he also failed to produce an heir. His nickname, *El Hechizado* (the Bewitched), resulted from the popular view of the time that he and Spain were under an evil spell, such was their decline. His death in 1700 brought an end to the Hapsburg dynasty in Spain.

A new dynasty: *Los Borbones*

On the death of Carlos II, the nearest male relative available to take the Spanish throne was Duke Philip of Anjou, a distant French cousin, aged 17, to whom the Spanish throne had been willed. He became king as Felipe V, but not without difficulty, as his claim to the throne was contested in the War of Spanish Succession from 1701–1714. Throughout his reign there was resentment at the presence of Frenchmen in influential positions, and at the many *afrancesados* – Spaniards who allowed themselves to be influenced by, or worse still, curried favour

Monarch	Nickname	Dates	Achievements	Failings
Felipe V		Reign: 1700–1746	Reformed economy and education; established Royal Academy	
Carlos III		Reign: 1759–1788	Intelligent, patriotic; improved administration	
Carlos IV		Reign: 1788–1808		Reversed father's good work; gave way to Napoleon
Fernando VII	El Deseado (the Desired)	Reign: 1808 & 1814–1833		Suspicious insecure, paranoid
María Cristina (Regent)		Reign: 1833–1840		
Isabel II		Reign: 1833–1868		Ruined Spain's economy; very conservative
Amadeo de Saboya		Reign: 1870–1873		Not comfortable on the Spanish throne
Alfonso XII		Reign: 1874–1885	Improved administration; restored prestige	
María Cristina (Regent)		Reign: 1885–1902	A good caretaker	
Alfonso XIII		Reign: 1886–1931		Gave power to military in 1923; abdicated 1931
Juan Carlos I	El Breve (at first); Rey de todos los españoles (since 1981)	Reign: 1976–	Peaceful transition to democracy; earned respect for monarchy; excellent ambassador for Spain	

with the French newcomers. A certain amount of French influence invaded Spain, as did a number of linguistic borrowings from French. Felipe improved Spain's economy by largely weeding out corruption in the tax system, and he introduced reforms in commerce, industry and education, establishing a number of institutions such as the Royal Academy and Academies of Medicine and History.

Although in some ways political decadence continued, cultural life in Spain continued to flourish in the continuing era known as *la Edad de Oro* (the Golden Age) (see Units 3, 4 and 5). His son, Carlos III, largely continued the good work, particularly in rural regeneration and public services, many of which were based on French models, not just in Spain but also in the colonies; Spain's considerable population increase was proof of a greater sense of stability and well-being.

The Napoleonic era: The Peninsular War

The positive aspects of French influence were somewhat mitigated by the fact that the next Bourbon king, Carlos IV, reversed the progress made, placing too much power in the hands of his favourite, the cowardly Manuel Godoy. The French Revolution and then Napoleon's antics therefore came at an awkward time for Spain. Afraid of the revolutionaries, Godoy made peace with them, and later gave the French the use of the Spanish Navy to fight against the British. By 1804 Napoleon was in control of France: after demanding Spanish troops to use in his war against England, he also demanded that Godoy give him control of the Spanish fleet. What ensued was another major disaster for the Spanish: their fleet was all but destroyed with the French fleet at the Battle of Trafalgar in 1805. Carlos IV and Godoy then foolishly allowed Napoleon's troops to enter Spain in 1807, supposedly to attack Portugal (Britain's oldest ally) in order to lure the British out of Britain. In fact Napoleon had Carlos IV and his family taken off to internment in Bayonne in south-western France; he eventually managed to get them to renounce the crown and placed his brother Joseph on the Spanish throne.

Napoleon, however, had reckoned without the Spanish people: on the day of the abduction of the royal family from Madrid on 2 May 1808, the indignant *madrileños*, seeing the cruelty with which they were carrying off the young princes, attacked the French troops. Pitched battles raged throughout the city, civilians fighting with whatever they could lay their hands on, until the French overcame them by sheer brutality. *El Dos de Mayo* (2 May) is celebrated as a day of national heroism, a public holiday, and is the subject of paintings by Goya (see Unit 4). All over Spain, Spaniards rose to the cry '*A las armas!*' ('To

Wellington boots the French
out of Spain

arms!'), and often fought with domestic or agricultural implements, helped also by funds sent from the colonies. A peasant army scored a notable victory against French professional troops at Bailén in northern Andalusia in July 1808. The ensuing Peninsular War brought together Spanish civilians and British troops under the Duke of Wellington: the French armies of occupation were finally ejected from Spain in 1814.

The restoration of the monarchy

In 1811, a new democratic constitution was established at the *Cortes* (Parliament) in Cádiz, in the free part of Spain; it limited the power of the monarchy, upon whom it placed much of the blame for Spain's past problems. Ironically, when Fernando VII returned to Spain to take the throne in 1814, for the Spanish he was *El Deseado* (the Desired), as they hoped he would accept the position of a constitutional monarch in a democratic state. Instead, having been well and truly *afrancesado* under Napoleon's influence, he insisted on absolute power; he set in train the persecution of the Liberals who had masterminded the *Cortes*. The brutal repression of this paranoid king produced a period of economic and political decline, with plummeting national morale. Normally, the application of the Salic Law – according to which a woman cannot inherit if there is a close enough male relative – would have prevented Fernando's young daughter Isabel coming to the throne. However, the law was revoked in favour of Isabel in 1830, eventually giving rise to the Carlist War (1833–1840), in which supporters of Fernando's brother Don Carlos (as heir to the throne), notably in the north of Spain, pressed his claim.

After a period of regency, in which María Cristina, Fernando's widow, attempted to reign, although unpopular, a powerful general, Espartero, was Regent for a time until the very young heiress to the throne, Isabel II, began her troubled reign. Her lavish court was a financial disaster for Spain, and during her reign, much of Spain's wealth, in the form of exploitation of natural resources, was given to foreign banks to pay off horrendous debts. In the end, it was popular resentment which forced her to go into voluntary exile in 1868, having earned herself the ignominious distinction of being probably the most unpopular monarch Spain has ever had.

The second Restoration

Isabel's removal led to a search for a replacement: the only person who was willing to accept the throne, albeit for a short time, was the Italian prince *Amadeo de Saboya* (Savoy). He reluctantly attempted to rule from 1871 until 1873, when the *Cortes* proclaimed Spain a republic. This unleashed a second Carlist War, ending in 1874 when Isabel's son, Alfonso, a young army cadet at the British military academy of Sandhurst, declared his promise to be a good king and was given a rapturous welcome when he arrived in Spain in 1875. It was realized that a policy of reconciliation was what was needed, and a skilful political thinker, Cánovas del Castillo, produced an amended constitution which contrived to allow a continuing period of compromise: the so-called *turno pacífico* gave Spain 20 years of stability, with the Conservatives and Liberals alternating periods of government by means of rigged elections.

Alfonso's second marriage, to María Cristina of Austria, produced a son shortly after his death from tuberculosis in 1885 at the age of 28. In view of the birth of a son and heir to the throne, María Cristina (no relation to Isabel II's mother) was allowed to reign as Regent, which she did tactfully and sensibly, until Alfonso XIII reached the age of 16 in 1902. At the age of 20 he married Victoria Eugenie, a granddaugher of Queen Victoria.

The colonies and 1898

Parallel with economic and political upheaval and decline at home, Spain had also been suffering problems with her colonies. Although in the early years untold wealth in the form of bullion brought to Spain generated considerable prosperity, it had little effect in terms of building up a sound economic base. Trade with the colonies had partly been taken over by other European countries, notably by England as a spin-off of the slave trade. From an early stage the colonies had been quite well managed by means of a system of viceroys, and many towns and cities were similar to those in Spain in many senses. There had also been a considerable level of loyalty to Spain, as evidenced in the funds raised by the colonies to help the Spanish fight the French in the Peninsular War. Increasingly, however, local considerations and interests gave rise to rebellion against Spanish control.

The War of Independence in North America was the inspiration for separatist aspirations, and the instability of the monarchy in the early part of the 19th century did not help. In 1811, Venezuela and Paraguay declared themselves independent, and, thanks to Simón Bolívar, *El Libertador* (the Liberator) and General San Martín, they and neighbouring countries such as Perú and Ecuador actually achieved independence from 1819 to 1825; Mexico became independent in 1821. This colonial decline continued until the ultimate ignominy: after a brief war with the USA, Spain lost her last major colony, Cuba in 1898, the Philippines following suit soon afterwards.

Add this to Spain's own continued decline, and it is easy to understand why this date etched itself in Spain's national psyche as the all-time low point after the greatness of but a few centuries earlier. So much so that it prompted many of the great minds of the day to indulge in a sort of national soul searching; they are known as the 98 Generation (see Unit 3).

The 20th century: From bad to worse

The war left Spain with more crippling debts, but in a way the loss of her colonies cleared the decks for the sorting out of her problems at home. However, this was not before a few decades more of self-destructive turmoil.

Alfonso XIII became king at the age of 16 in 1902 at a difficult time. There was violence brewing among the rural poor in the south, and the Catalans were keen to obtain independence. The *turno pacífico* system was breaking down, and the young king increasingly turned for support to the army, which was top heavy with generals and beginning to have too much power for Spain's good. Anarchists were rampant, even making attempts on the life of the king himself, and anti-clericalism and industrial unrest were rife. The First World War divided Spain, with the powerful supporting Germany and liberals and socialists supporting the Allies, although Spain itself remained neutral.

This neutrality, however, actually boosted Spain's economy, as the country was able to sell goods to the warring countries and recapture some of the South American trade. This created inflation, but as wages did not keep up with prices, industrial unrest intensified, with a general strike in 1917. Social unrest and heavy-handed attempts to control it on the part of the Civil Guard and the Army led to a breakdown of popular trust in these forces and in the regime.

In desperation, Alfonso allowed the establishment of a military government under the dictator, General Miguel Primo de Rivera. He was most concerned to re-establish social order, and he even succeeded in reforming labour relations; under his benevolent regime, Spain actually managed a minor recovery, with improvements to infrastructure – new roads and railways. He tried to achieve some semblance of political respectability, but the world recession of the late 1920s undermined his economic position and the Army deserted him. Primo de Rivera left Spain in 1930, and after failing to form any sort of government, King Alfonso and his family left for Paris, effectively abdicating. His youngest son, Juan de Borbón y Battenberg, was 'rescued' from the Spanish Naval Academy at San Fernando, Cádiz, by a naval gunboat, and reunited with his parents in Paris. They then travelled to London before going into permanent exile in Portugal. While in London they obtained permission from the Admiralty for Juan to continue his naval studies at Britannia Royal Naval College, Dartmouth in Devon. His name appears in the college lists for 1931/32 as Prince John of Spain, and his story continues in Unit 8.

The Republic

The Republic was proclaimed with great joy in most parts of Spain, and, amazingly, in peace. It was supported by the thinkers of the so-called 98 Generation (see Unit 3) and elections were held within months. A socialist majority government under Alcalá Zamora ensured that a period of reform would follow. Some progress was made to reform land tenure by redistributing large estates among landless peasants; controls were imposed on the armed forces, although not enough to prevent a coup being attempted in 1932; education was reformed, and control of schools taken away from the Church; the Church was disestablished, and anti-clerical feelings led to the raiding and burning of churches and convents. Ironically, this had a significant effect on the large numbers of devout women: now that all women had the vote for the first time, the elections of late 1933 saw a swing to the political right. This was also the result of right-wing propaganda emanating from the *Falange*, a sort of fascist political party established by José Primo de Rivera, son of the former dictator. Its ideas were also becoming popular among students.

The *Bienio Negro*

The period of right-wing backlash which ensued has come to be known as the *Bienio Negro* (two black years). The Catalans reacted by declaring independence, and mining communities in Asturias followed suit. The rebellion in Asturias was put down using considerable violence – with over 1300 civilians dead – by a young general called Francisco Franco Bahamonde. He had already made a name for himself as the youngest general in Europe, as a very effective leader of the Spanish troops in North Africa, and as commandant of the army academy in Zaragoza. He had also been courting Hitler and Mussolini ... The right-wing parties were unable to form a solid government, and fresh elections were held in February 1936. The narrow left-wing majority was insufficient once again, and Manuel Azaña, the President, was not strong enough to hold the coalition together, given the squabbling between the various socialist and communist factions. Impatient for agrarian reform, peasants in the south took the law into their own hands, seizing estates owned by rich absentee landlords: government attempts at imposing control led to even more resentment. Political and social unrest intensified, with a sequence of hundreds of political assassinations and reprisals adding to rapidly increasing social disorder.

Civil War

Concerned about the unrest, a group of generals had been plotting a rebellion for some time: aware of this, the government sent them to various far-flung corners of Spanish territory ... but this merely enabled them to hatch their plans far from government surveillance. The date was fixed for 18 July 1936, and a coded message was devised as the signal to act. Francisco Franco Bahamonde was to lead the African contingent of the Army, but he was in the Canary Islands. A British charter pilot was commissioned to fly Franco to Tetuán to take over the military garrison there, although the pilot was not aware of the true purpose of the flight. General Mola was to drive his forces from the north in an advance on Madrid, while other generals were to take over the cities in the south.

The date and hour arrived, and the rebellion was declared, but in some cities the take-over was unsuccessful, notably in Madrid: here, after some initial violence, the city remained under Republican government control. Elements of the Air Force and the Navy remained loyal to the government; naval ships blockaded the Straits of Gibraltar, presenting Franco with a problem: he had duly completed the first part of his role, but the army he controlled was in Africa, whilst the war was in Spain ... which is where his contacts with Hitler and Mussolini came in handy. German and Italian planes bombed the government ships and transported some of Franco's troops to the south of Spain.

Franco quickly joined up with other generals in the south and advanced towards Madrid. On the way, he detoured to Toledo to relieve the garrison of the Alcázar in the centre of the city, which was under siege from the Republican citizens. This delayed his advance on Madrid, and gave the capital time to reinforce itself with Russian military hardware, given by Stalin in exchange for the whole of Spain's gold reserves.

The British, French and American governments insisted on a policy of non-intervention and so refused any help, not wishing to antagonize Hitler. The Spanish Republican government had moved to Valencia, and apart from the Basque Country and Catalonia, which were still Republican, the government controlled the wedge of territory going east and south-east from Madrid. General Mola mopped up the Basque Country after fierce resistance, destroying morale by calling in German aircraft in April 1937 to destroy Guernica, the historic centre of Basque government (see Unit 4). The Germans used the town to practise bombing techniques they would later use against Britain.

Wishing to gain respectability, the Nationalists, which is what the rebels now called themselves, increasingly publicized their campaign at home and abroad as a crusade against Los Rojos (the Reds, i.e. the Communists). However, thousands of anti-fascists, trade unionists and intellectuals from countries like the UK, the USA and France joined to form the International Brigades which fought in support of the Republicans for a while. Included among their number were some names which would later become famous such as George Orwell and Stephen Spender. The brigades were disbanded in good faith in exchange for the German and Italian governments' agreement to pull thousands of their soldiers out of the conflict. (There is a monument to the International Brigades on the Thames Embankment in London, near Waterloo Station.) Deprived of foreign help, the Republican armies began to lose territory, while the Nationalists, aware that Madrid was too tough a nut to crack, decided to isolate Catalonia by driving their troops from Aragon and Castile to the Mediterranean at Castellón de la Plana in June 1938, thus splitting Republican territory in two. Catalonia soon fell, and the bombardment of Barcelona was a particularly vindictive campaign, as had happened in the Basque Country: it was as if revenge was being sought against these two regions with separatist aspirations.

Thousands of Catalan refugees walked to the French border, where they were interned in holding camps by the French government, still unwilling to irritate Hitler by aiding the displaced victims of the Nationalist onslaught.

Militarily, Madrid was never defeated; instead, the Republican government was brought to its knees and in March 1939 it accepted the only terms offered by the Nationalists: unconditional surrender. Franco, who by now had been elected as leader of the rebel generals, swooped into Madrid triumphantly and on 1 April declared the end of the war.

The aftermath

Not only had the Civil War brought about the deaths of well over a million Spaniards, with countless atrocities on both sides, destroyed cities, industry, infrastructures and agriculture, but, more seriously still, it had torn asunder the very fabric of Spanish society in a way that could never have been foreseen in the worst nightmares of the 98 Generation. Fathers had fought against their own sons, and brothers against one another. Although 'peace' had returned, hatred and bitterness was all too common in every community, and it would take generations to restore social cohesion. Besides, Franco's triumphalist policies made matters worse for the surviving Republicans: he declared himself '*Caudillo de España por la Gracia de Dios*' ('Leader of Spain by the grace of God'), and stated that this had been a religious campaign against the threat of Communism. Prominent Republicans and dissidents were rounded up, many being executed by firing squad or imprisoned, while others went into exile abroad. Thousands were used as forced labour, building his monument to the Civil War dead at the *Valle de los Caídos* (Valley of the Fallen) in the foothills of the Sierra de Guadarrama, north-west of Madrid: topped by a huge cross, this cathedral is effectively a hollowed-out mountain, which one day was to become Franco's own mausoleum. In the early years he ruled with an iron fist, and his motto for Spain was '*una, grande, libre*' – (one, great and free)

– revealing his order of priorities. Censorship was imposed, and manifestations of nationalist tendencies, such as the music and dance of Basques, Catalans and even *Gallegos* (he was himself a *Gallego*) were banned (see Unit 5); their languages were prohibited in public gatherings.

Dictatorship

Arguably, Franco did Spain a service in refusing Hitler's request that Spain join him in the Second World War: Spain had suffered enough. Ironically, however, Franco was the one European dictator who survived the war, causing Spain to become a 'pariah' state, ostracized by the United Nations, isolated and refused much needed aid. In the end it was his anti-Communist declarations that lead to a sort of pact with the USA: Spain, with its important strategic position at the mouth of the Mediterranean and with Franco's record of anti-Communist fervour, made a useful ally in the Cold War which began at the end of the 1940s. In exchange for military bases given over to US forces under the terms of a military assistance pact, Spain was given financial aid enabling her to fund economic regeneration. Franco boasted of having over 1000 dams and irrigation schemes constructed, which did indeed provide the essential irrigation for agricultural development and cheap hydro-electric power for new industries.

Franco also had enough foresight to send a group of young businessmen and politicians to the USA to study business and economic management. With their expertise, Spain embarked upon a series of five-year economic plans from the late 1950s onwards, bolstered by income generated by the tourist industry. A spin-off from the Second World War and the development of the jet engine was the availability of rapid, cheap air travel, bringing package holidays within the reach of hordes of northern Europeans, anxious to spend their hard-earned leisure time in the Spanish sunshine. Such was the progress made that over various periods of the 60s and 70s, Spain enjoyed the fastest growth rate in Europe. However, its isolationist, protected market meant that many goods produced for internal consumption were rather shoddy, and would be unable to compete in an open market. Throughout this period much speculative building (which had no proper controls) ruined many areas, especially along the coast and around towns and cities. The policy of attracting workers to industrial cities led to the depopulation of rural areas.

In later years, Franco relaxed his grip to a certain extent, although school pupils still had to undergo the indoctrination of the *Movimiento Nacional*, his political party, in lessons officially called '*formación del espíritu nacional*' ('formation of national spirit') but usually nicknamed '*falange*' after the 1930s political philosophy Franco had espoused. Trade unions were still very much sanitized organizations, and literature on alien political thought was banned in Spain. However, although many opposed his ideas, most Spaniards were more interested in their steadily rising standard of living. One thing Franco would not tolerate, however, was separatism: as a result, frustration and resentment led to the formation in the Basque Country of ETA, the Basque separatist terrorist movement. ETA's most spectacular action was the assassination of Prime Minister Admiral Carrero Blanco in 1973. In August 1975, a few months before his death, and in spite of international appeals for clemency, Franco insisted on going through with the execution by firing squad of a group of terrorists.

Having been for a number of years an increasingly weak old man, Francisco Franco died in November 1975 at the age of 83, in spite of the efforts of the doctors who had managed to keep him alive for weeks against the odds. He is buried in the Valle de los Caídos (see Unit 4).

Whatever view one has of Franco, his achievement as an army man cannot be denied: he always proceeded carefully, yet was an opportunist, always able to turn situations to his own advantage, and was often in the right place at the right time. He fitted the stereotypical image of a *gallego* (native of Galicia): apparently slow-witted and lacking in imagination, he would actually be scheming behind this façade, and was capable of taking canny decisions. If his campaigns took longer than necessary, his victories were more complete ... as a Spaniard opposed to him once said: '*era militar hasta los huesos*' – 'he was a military man to the bone'.

And now?

Considering all that happened up to 1975, it might seem amazing that Spain is now a prosperous, modern, democratic country, rightfully playing her part on the international stage, and a prominent member of the EU and NATO. The story of the smooth and peaceful transition from dictatorship to democracy continues in Unit 8, but it is very largely thanks to King Juan Carlos de Borbón, the current monarch of the Bourbon dynasty.

The regions of Spain

It will now be obvious that the division of Spain into regions is the result not just of its physical geography, but also of its history. The regions were no more and no less than the old kingdoms into which the land became divided during the Reconquest. A major change took place in 1984 when the regions were slighly rejigged to form the *autonomías*, each with its regional government, and a certain amount of independence in various areas of public life. Further detail can be found in Unit 8, but a few regions need to be considered here from the point of view of the Spanish race.

The Spanish race

Like so many other European countries, the Spanish nation is an amalgam of several ancient races and invading nations, and the wide range of physical and genetic make-up of Spaniards reflects this. However, it has undergone little change since the Arab invasion of the 8th century, apart from the influx of French influence in the 18th century and again in Napoleonic times, and the effects of tourism in the second half of the 20th century, both of which are difficult to quantify. In a few areas of Spain there are strong features, often cultural rather than racial, which reveal the diverse origins of the people (see Unit 5 for regional music).

The Basque nation

A very ancient people, the Basques settled in the high valleys of the western Pyrenees at a very early stage, and survived the comings and goings of Romans and Arabs alike. Their language – unlike any other European language (see Unit 2) – and their genes seem to indicate that they are the relics of one of the oldest races in Europe. Basques can now send their children to an *ikastola*, a Basque language school, there are Basque language newspapers, radio and television stations, and the Basque country has its own police force, the *Ertxainxa* (see Unit 8). Basques have the reputation of being energetic and adventurous, and of loving sport and food.

Catalonia

Cataluña in Spanish (Catalunya in the Catalan language) seems in some way to have more in common with France than with the rest of Spain; the language certainly seems to be half-way between the two. Place names are written in Catalan. Many

Catalans refuse to speak *Castellano* to people from other parts of Spain, instead speaking Catalan to make the point that they have their own language.

Galicia

Galicia shows its Celtic connections in place names, its music, which includes the *gaita* (bagpipes) and its ancient religious beliefs and superstitions. *Gallegos* sometimes hold a ritual *queimada*, nowadays for fun, which involves heating up a brew of red wine, brandy and coffee beans and setting fire to it for a few moments before drinking it to ward off the *maigas* – the witches. In the past few decades, the *Gallego* language has been revived and consolidated; it has strong similarities with Portuguese as well as Spanish. Place names nowadays are written in *Gallego*, and various groups keep the language and music alive.

Gitanos

Gitanos are not 'travelling people' as in other European countries, but are the dark-skinned, dark-haired Spanish gypsies who live mostly in Andalusia, often on the fringes of towns and cities. Many are still rather marginalized from mainstream society, a sort of 'Third World' at home, never having been fully integrated. In fact, many Andalusian people are very dark-skinned and dark-haired.

Yet, in spite of these separate and sometimes separatist elements, the Spanish nation as a whole does have a distinctive national character, one which has been passed on to many other Spanish-speaking countries, and which makes Spain stand out from the rest of Europe. In its publicity, the Spanish National Tourist Office used to use the slogan '*España es diferente*' ('Spain is different'). There are certainly distinctive historical and cultural elements peculiar to Spain, which explain its attraction to all who love the country and its people.

Landscape

Owing to its size and its mountainous nature, and the fact that it is bordered by both the Mediterranean and the Atlantic, Spain has a wide range of landscapes, climates and vegetation. The rainy north-west and most of the north coast are very green, and the coast of Asturias is understandably known as the '*Costa Verde*' (the 'green coast'). The north coast itself ranges from rocky coves to sandy beaches. The higher lands of Galicia in the north-west, the *Cordillera Cantábrica* (Cantabrian Mountains) and the *Pirineos* (Pyrenees) are heavily forested in many areas. Moving south-east from these northern mountains, we reach the dry plains of northern Castile and Aragon. While the former typically have vast cereal-growing prairies (the waving wheatfields give rise to the expression used to describe this area: '*el mar de Castilla*', 'the sea of Castile'), some parts of Aragon are so dry and stony that they resemble lunar landscapes, such as the *Monegros* (black mountains) to the east of Zaragoza.

As for the coastline of the north-east, it ranges from the rocky *Costa Brava* (wild coast) to the golden sands of the *Costa Dorada* (gold coast). The river *Ebro* carries the rainwaters of the *Cordillera Cantábrica* and the southern Pyrenees down to its delta, passing through fertile valleys and deep gorges, and the *Cuenca del Ebro* around Zaragoza, a wide, deep canyon. The *Duero* flows across the plains of Castilla y León and into northern Portugal.

The wild and bleak Iberian Mountains to the south of Aragon, with a January average below 0°C, have the lowest ever recorded temperatures in Spain. The Sierra de Guadarrama in central Spain is snowy for part of the year, providing easily accessible skiing for the inhabitants of Madrid, and separating the area which used to be called Old Castile (now Castilla-León) to the north from New Castile (now Castilla-La Mancha) to the south. The north of Castilla-La Mancha has the river *Tajo* or *Tagus*, slicing through it, often flowing through deep canyons (hence the name Tajo which means 'cut' or 'cleft'. The plains of New Castile are similar to those of Old Castile, but usually drier.

In the region of *La Mancha* (meaning 'stain') the ground is reddish in colour, and this whole area is largely used for the production of cereals and wine. To the east of Madrid the land is more mountainous, and there are two particularly interesting features: first, the gorge in Cuenca, famous for the 14th-century *Casas Colgadas* (hanging houses) – once used as the summer residence of the Royal Family – which cling precariously to the top of a cliff; second, just north of Cuenca, an area of weird and wonderful eroded rock formations known as *Ciudad Encantada* (enchanted city).

Moving south and east, the *Levante* – the south-east coast – is largely dry, but quite fertile in irrigated areas. Coastal vegetation is very Mediterranean in nature, with palms and almond and orange trees.

Descending abruptly from the Castilian plateau southwards into Andalusia, one encounters a varied region of fertile '*vegas*' and softly rolling hills, flanked on each side, except the west, by the craggy mountains of the Sierra Morena and Sierra Nevada, the river *Guadalquivir* flowing east to west between the two.

The east of the region is quite mountainous and dry; areas to the north of Almería have been used to shoot 'Western' films, having just the right sorts of landscape. From the Sierra Nevada, snow capped for much of the year, one can look down thousands of feet to the sea. The southern flanks of this range – the Alpujarra – have a benign climate which favours vegetation not found anywhere else in Europe, including some sub-tropical species of flora and fauna; so too does the Serranía de Ronda, south-west of Málaga. The Mediterranean coast of Andalusia ranges from the beaches of Málaga and Marbella to the wilder stretches in Granada province.

Going westwards and north-west from Gibraltar, one leaves behind the wild and windy coast and capes of the Straits of Gibraltar, arriving at the sandy coastal strip which separates the *Guadalquivir* Delta from the Atlantic. This delta is rich in both flora and fauna, much of it being the Coto Doñana nature reserve. Further north, following the Portuguese border, one passes from Andalusia into the region with probably the most difficult agricultural terrain in all of Spain: *Extremadura*, most famous for breeding the toughest fighting bulls and *conquistadores* who made their names in the exploration and conquest of Latin Ameria.

All of this makes Spain a large, wide-open country, fascinating to explore by road.

Flora and fauna

Given Spain's great variety of landscape and climate, it is hardly surprising that this country has a similarly huge and varied abundance of plant and animal life. Within Spain there are animals which are relatively rare elsewhere in Europe, such as storks, vultures and wild boar; it also has some of the last few areas in Europe with brown bears, wolves, lynx and golden eagles, while scorpions, lizards, wild goat and deer, and various species of snake are all quite common. Spain is also home to more exotic species such as the '*quebrantahuesos*' (bone breaker), the bearded vulture which lives on the marrow of the bones of dead animals: carrying the bones in its claws, it dives from a great height, dashing the bones against rock to make the marrow easy to get at.

There are several major *parques naturales* (nature parks) and *parques nacionales* (national parks) (see Unit 11) which can be visited freely. The *Coto Doñana*, which can be toured on safari buses, is a permanent home to rare species such as the Iberian lynx and imperial eagle, deer, wild boar and wild horse; its wetlands are a temporary home to many migrating birds which stop off for up to several weeks at a time for a rest and a feed on their journey between, perhaps, Siberia and South Africa.

The variety and colour of plant life is enormous: vegetation in the north and north-west is typical of the Atlantic climate, and the Mediterranean areas and the south are typical of southern Europe, with vineyards and olive, orange and lemon groves. The far south has species which cannot be found elsewhere in Europe, especially in the Alpujarra and the Serranía de Ronda. Most visible and most striking in much of southern and Mediterranean Spain are the many species of palm, orchid and cactus, including the prickly pear cactus. Cork oak is cultivated in the north-west of Andalusia and Extremadura and the unusual umbrella pine is common around the Coto Doñana, fighting to survive among the sand dunes. Among the exotic fruits cultivated in the Alpujarra is the *chirimoya* (custard apple) and prickly pears and fresh dates are often available in open-air markets in Andalusia and elsewhere.

GLOSSARY

la bandera española	*Spanish flag*
el país	*country*
la nación	*nation*
la raza	*race*
la tierra	*land*
la sierra	*mountain range*
montañoso	*mountainous*
el río	*river*
la meseta	*plateau*
el mar	*sea*
la costa	*coast*
la historia	*history*
descubrir	*to discover*
invadir	*to invade*
la invasión	*invasion*

conquistar	*to conquer*
la conquista	*conquest*
la reconquista	*reconquest*
colonizar	*to colonise*
la colonia	*colony*
fundar	*to found*
establecer	*to establish*
la civilización	*civilisation*
reinar	*to reign*
el reino	*kingdom*
el rey	*king*
la dinastía	*dynasty*
elegir	*to elect*
luchar	*to fight*
la guerra	*war*
rebelar	*to rebel*
la rebelión	*rebellion*
hace ... siglos/años	*... centuries/years ago*
hace poco tiempo	*not long ago*
en el norte/sur/este/oeste/	*in the north/south/east/west/*
centro	*centre*
la región	*region*
el paisaje	*landscape*
el animal	*animal*
la planta	*plant*
cultivar	*cultivate*
crecer	*to grow*

Taking it further

Reading

General history
Background to Spain, B. J. Hill (Longman 1969).

The Hapsburgs
Imperial Spain 1469–1716, J.H. Elliott (Pelican 1963).

Civil War
The Spanish Civil War, David Mitchell (Granada Publishing), ISBN 0246 123206; authoritative and thorough, based on the excellent TV series.

Homage to Catalonia, George Orwell (any edition).

The Spanish Civil War 1936–1939, Paul Preston (Weidenfeld and Nicholson 1986).

Doves of War, Paul Preston (Harper Collins 2002), biographies of four Spanish women.

A Concise History of the Spanish Civil War, Paul Preston (Harper Collins 1996).

Novels: Set during the Civil War

For Whom the Bell Tolls, Ernest Hemingway (any edition).

The Flags of Nada, Michael Barrett.

Adventures of an Innocent in the Spanish Civil War, Antonio Candela (United Writers ISBN 1-852000201).

Franco

Franco, Paul Preston (Harper Collins 1993).

Travelogues

Iberia, James A. Michener (Corgi, ISBN 0-552 987336 + 0-552 987328 – 2 vols).

South from Granada, Gerald Brenan (CUP ISBN 0-521 28029 X).

Spanish Raggle-taggle, Walter Starkie.

As I Walked Out One Midsummer Morning, Laurie Lee (Penguin, ISBN 0-140033181; the period just before the Civil War, and *A Rose for Winter*, Laurie Lee (Penguin, ISBN 0-14003319 X; set in 1950s, a follow-up).

The Spanish

The Spaniards, John Hooper (Penguin, ISBN 0-14-009808-9; a highly respected view of Spain.)

Fire in the Blood, Ian Gibson (Faber & Faber, ISBN 0-563-36194-8; quirky, likes to focus on the less-appealing side of Spain, but entertaining, like the TV series of the same name.

Places to visit

Prehistoric Spain

Las Cuevas de Altamira, near Santillana del Mar/Santander; dolmens at Antequera, Andalusia.

Roman Spain

Aqueduct at Segovia; better still, aqueduct at Tarragona (you can walk across it!).

Moorish Spain
Alhambra, Granada; Mezquita, Córdoba.

Reconquista and *Reyes Católicos*
Montefrío and Santa Fe, Andalusia. The Alhambra and Granada Cathedral.

Columbus
Statue in Plaza de Isabel la Católica and Alhambra, Granada; museum and replica ships at Palos de la Frontera, near Huelva, Andalusia.

Carlos V
Carlos V Palace in the Alhambra.

Felipe II and Hapsburg Spain
El Escorial, Plaza Mayor in Madrid.

Bourbon Spain
El Prado Art Museum, Madrid.

Civil War
Valle de los Caídos.

Mountains
Picos de Europa, Cantabria; Los Mallos de Riglos, Pyrenees; Sierra de Guadarrama; Desfiladero de Despeñaperros (Sierra Morena) on Madrid-Andalusia road; Sierra Nevada from Sacromonte, Granada; Mediterranean from el Pico del Veleta (highest road in Europe, but well worth the drive).

Valleys
Cuenca del Ebro, Zaragoza; Valle de Arán, Pyrenees; Tajo Gorge, Toledo; Ronda Gorge, Andalusia; Pantano de Ebro, south of Santander; Vega de Granada from Sierra Nevada.

Plains
El Mar de Castilla, west of Valladolid; view north from Somosierra pass north of Madrid.

Deserts
Monegros, east of Zaragoza; around Mini-Hollywood, north of Almería.

Estuaries
Santander; Ribadeo (Galicia); Ría de Vigo; Ría de Pontevedra, Ortiguiera, Galicia.

Coastal scenery
Costa Brava; Costa Verde; San Sebastián; Málaga; Algeciras; Tarifa.

Nature parks
Coto Doñana; Picos de Europa; Sierra de Cazorla; Ordesa.

Cityscapes
Barcelona from Montjuich; Granada from Alhambra; Toledo from Parador; Málaga from Gibralfaro; Seville from top of Giralda.

Websites

There are Spanish websites available on many of the historical subjects covered in this unit. A useful site on historical information in Spanish, era by era, is:

http://www.docuweb.ca/SiSpain/spanish/history/html

02

the Spanish language

In this unit you will learn
- about Spanish as a world language
- about the history of the language
- about pronunciation and grammar
- about regional languages and dialects

Spanish: A world language

Like English, Spanish can truly claim to be a world language: it is spoken as a first language by the inhabitants of 23 countries, and these so-called native speakers of Spanish number 350 million or more. Indeed, Spanish will at some stage in the next few years overtake English in terms of the numbers who speak it as their first language. Only Chinese has more speakers, at almost 900 million, but these are mainly concentrated in one huge country.

The reason why Spanish is a world language is that, like English, it was spread around the world as the official language of an enormous empire (see Unit 1): although the countries beyond Spain which made up that empire have long since gained independence, they retain Spanish as their official language. Most countries in Latin America prefer to call their language *Castellano* (Castilian) rather than acknowledge their former colonial masters by using the term *Español*. In fact, Castilian Spanish was the language of Castile, the region which gained military and political control over most of the Iberian Peninsula (see Unit 1), and thus Castilian became the 'national language' of Spain.

The history of Spanish

Prehistory

Although such primitive languages as were probably spoken in Spain have disappeared, some elements of them have survived in place names: it is believed that words like *arroyo* (stream) and *nava* (plain) (as in Navarra) are derived from these ancient languages, but, of course, such connections are difficult to prove. Later racial influxes such as the Celts had a similarly limited effect on modern Spanish, with words such as *briga* (fortification) appearing in some early place names. In addition, many Celtic words may well have been adopted by the Romans in Spain, such as *cerveza* (beer).

Other early languages spoken in the Iberian peninsula were, of course, those of trading nations with settlements along the Mediterranean coasts, such as the Phoenicians and Carthaginians. They are believed to have contributed some place names and the word *mapa* (map). The Greek coastal settlements undoubtedly had a much stronger influence, but it is more difficult to trace conclusively, because so many Greek words were adopted by Latin before passing on into Spanish.

Indo-European: The grandmother of Spanish

Like other languages of Europe, Spanish is descended, via Latin, from Indo-European, a parent language or family of languages spoken in primitive times somewhere in Eastern Europe or south-west Asia, which then spread in every direction in such a way that its descendants are spoken in South-East Asia as well as in Europe.

Latin: The mother of Spanish

One of the early languages which actually developed in Europe was Latin. The Latin we know was probably never spoken in the form which appears in Roman literature: it was too complex, especially for the uneducated and for the peoples conquered by the Romans who had to learn to speak it. The form of Latin spoken by the lower classes and taken by soldiers and mercenaries to Rome's colonies is known as Vulgar Latin – the Latin of the people, as opposed to the more complex Classical Latin of the learned and literary classes. Thus it was the Vulgar Latin of the Roman legionaries and colonists which became the language of Roman Spain. As it developed in the Iberian Peninsula, spoken badly by natives of Spain who 'murdered' the grammar and struggled with the pronunciation, it evolved into Romance, Spain's own dialect of Latin. This in turn splintered into a range of languages and dialects, many of which survive today.

The original languages of Spain disappeared, the only trace of them being, perhaps, in the way that Romance was pronounced. Just as Roman civilization and social structure imposed itself completely over almost all of the peninsula, so too did the Latin language. Among the languages which have come together to form almost all the modern languages and dialects of the Iberian peninsula, Latin imposed itself over the pre-existing languages of Spain, in terms not only of vocabulary but also of structure.

Needless to say, many place names in Spain are derived from Latin, even if in a corrupted form. Here are some examples:

Latin	Spanish
Corduba	Córdoba
Lucus	Lugo
Saguntum	Sagunto
Tarraco	Tarragona
Ardobrica Corunium	La Coruña
Asturica Augusta	Astorga

Emerita Augusta	Mérida
Caesar Augusta	Zaragoza
Betis	Guadalquivir

(Betis is also the name of one of the football teams in Seville.)

As in other languages, a number of Latin expressions are used unchanged. Here are some examples, also used in English, in which the Latin spelling is unchanged apart from the accents:

currículum (vitae)
etcétera
memorándum
per cápita
vademécum
vice versa

Spanish and English: The Latin overlap

It is for this reason that so much Spanish vocabulary is closely related to so many English words: we often forget that around 60 per cent of English vocabulary is derived from Latin, either indirectly – mostly via the Norman French that came to England in 1066 – or directly, usually when new terms were needed in the fields of culture, science and technology. For this reason, thousands of Spanish words are similar to English words, sometimes with the same spelling, but more often with a slightly different spelling.

As you study Spanish, you soon get used to these spelling differences (see pages 39–41) and by making the necessary mental adjustment – almost like switching onto a different linguistic 'wavelength' – you will soon find yourself understanding new words without having to run to the dictionary every time. Most of these so-called 'cognates' (literally words which were 'born together') have the same meanings in both languages; some have partly the same meaning; others have totally changed meanings – these last words are often known as **falsos amigos** (false friends), although the number of similarities which are helpful vastly outweighs those which could be misleading.

Here are some examples:

Spanish	**English**
Same meaning, same spelling	
rural	rural

Same meaning, different spelling

    monumento   monument

Partly the same meaning, same spelling

    local (nearby, premises)   local (only 'nearby')

Partly same meaning, different spelling

    letra   letter (only of alphabet)

False friend, same spelling

    revolver (to turn round)   (not revolver (gun))

False friend, different spelling

    asistir   to be present (not assist)

Significantly, it is often useful when translating from English into Spanish to think of the more 'learned' version of a word: it is most likely derived from the Latin and therefore similar to the Spanish. This is because English often has parallel words of the same or similar meaning, one from the Anglo-Saxon sources and another from Latin.

Here are some examples:

Anglo-Saxon English		'Latinate' English		Spanish
heavenly	=	celestial	=	*celestial*
freedom	=	liberty	=	*libertad*
fatherly	=	paternal	=	*paternal*
enough	=	sufficient	=	*suficiente*

'Spelling quirks' of Spanish

As already mentioned, Spanish spelling has particular 'quirks' which you will soon get used to. It is worth studying them to help you make the mental adjustment which will make it easier for you to guess the meaning of new words accurately ... but remember to beware of *falsos amigos!* Here are the main Spanish spelling quirks comparing Spanish words with the English, and the proof that they work is in the fact that in some cases we don't need to give you a translation!:

'Vowel stretching'

In Spanish, *e* often 'stretches' to *ie* or even changes completely to an *i*; similarly, *o* often stretches and changes to *ue* or just *u*:

e › *ie*: *bien* = well; English 'beneficial' is similar in its area of meaning

o › *ue*: *bueno* = good; English 'bonus' means something good

This can also work the other way round e.g. *precio* = price; *descuento* = discount.

esc-, esp-, est-

Some native Spanish speakers trying to cope with English have problems pronouncing words beginning with *sc*, *sp*, *st*; they tend to begin them with an *e* sound instead, being used to the Spanish words beginning with *esc*, *esp*, *est*. So, to 'guess' new words with these beginnings, simply take off the *e-*, as in these examples: *e* + *sc*: *escuela* = school; *e* = *sp*: *español* = Spanish; *e* + *st*: *estudiante* = student.

i/y

Spanish replaces *y* with an *i* or *-ía* at the end of a word: *sistema* = system; *ritmo* = rhythm; *síntoma* = symptom; *biología* = biology; *farmacia* = pharmacy; *Italia* = Italy.

Double consonants

Spanish has fewer double consonants, and simplifies combinations: *aceptar*, to accept; *efecto*, effect; *psicología*, psychology; *ciencia*, science.

N.B. *ct* combinations in English become *cc*, e.g. *acción*, *diccionario*, *elección*.

f/ph

Spanish does not have ph spellings, using *f* instead: *atmósfera*; *farmacia*; *filosofía*; *geografía*.

ll

Castilian Spanish often used *ll* instead of *cl*, *fl*, and *pl* at the beginning of words: *cl* › *ll*: *llamar* = to call; c.f. exclaim, meaning to 'call out'; *fl* › *ll*: *llama* = flame (also a South American animal, called llama by the explorers because of its colour); *pl* › *ll*: *llano* = flat, plain.

t/th

Spanish does not have *th* spellings, using *t* instead: *teología*, *terapía*, *teatro*, *simpatía*.

Spanish grammar

Spanish grammar is very largely based on Latin grammar. Verb conjugation and the tense structure are derived directly from Latin, and this can be seen in the fact that the subject pronoun, the 'person word' accompanying the verb, is not generally needed; each verb form contains the idea of *who* is doing the action as well as *what* is being done. As an example, it is interesting to compare the present tense of *amare/amar*, (to love):

Latin		Spanish
amare	to love	*amar*
amo	I love	*amo*
amas	you love	*amas*
amat	he/she/it loves	*ama*
amamus	we love	*amamos*
amatis	you (pl) love	*amáis*
amant	they love	*aman*

Note the evolution from the Latin forms to the Spanish: apart from *u* dropping to *o* in *amamos*, the fact that the *t* has disappeared in three forms proves that Roman or early Spanish mums and dads probably told their children off for dropping the weak 't' just as happens in modern English: in the south of England and in Scotland, be..er (better) and in the USA, moun.ain (mountain)!

A rather curious feature of this evolution is that, although the range and structure of some verb tenses is largely similar, other tenses are quite different. The Latin future tense forms (e.g. *amabo* – I will love) were uncomfortably similar to those of the imperfect (*amabam* – I used to love – *amaba* in Spanish), which may have been why the Latin future tense disappeared. As in other Romance (Latin-derived) languages, Spanish developed a new future tense based around the infinitive of the verb with a set of endings added, formed from the present tense of the verb *haber*: thus a form such as *amaré* (I will love) evolved from *amar he* literally 'I have to love = I am to love', logically implying a future tense. Being based on the future tense, the Spanish conditional tense is therefore also different from the Latin, and this follows on to compound tenses based on these two. Other tenses have slightly changed their use and structure, but to anyone who has studied Latin, the correspondence is very noticeable indeed.

In other ways, Spanish grammar has moved away from Latin as the language has evolved. An example is the fact that the case structure of nouns and adjectives has been lost: in place of the complex Latin declension systems, in modern Spanish the only change in nouns is that plurals are formed, quite simply, by adding *s* to the singular form (as in English and French). There are of course many nouns – mostly relating to people or animals – with both masculine and feminine versions such as *chico/chica* (boy/girl), *hermano/hermana* (brother/sister), *actor/actriz* (actor/actress), *perro/perra* (dog/bitch), *gato/gata* (cat).

Of course, with all of these examples, we are concentrating on Castilian Spanish: it must be remembered that other Romance languages and dialects were developing in exactly the same way in various parts of the land we call Spain. However, after a few hundred years of dominating Spain, the language of the Romans, albeit in various heavily modified forms, became firmly established as the language of the Spanish nation.

Visigothic influence

After the collapse of the Roman empire, it was a Germanic tribe called the Visigoths who took control of Spain. Their domination of the Iberian peninsula was short lived, which may be why their language has had relatively little influence on modern Spanish compared to Latin or the language of the Arabs who took Spain over from the Visigoths. However, words such as *ganso* (goose); *guante* (glove); *grupo* (group); *ropa* (clothing); *toalla* (towel) are believed to be of Visigothic origin, along with several words to do with horsemanship, such as *espuela* (spur); *estribo* (stirrup); *trotar* (to trot). There is even a clutch of first names inherited from the Visigoths, among them Federico, Fernando, Julián, Ramiro, Ricardo and Rodrigo, and names of towns like Godos and Vitigudino.

Arab influence

Although Arabs and Moors (from Arab-occupied Morocco) were in Spain for a much longer period than the Romans, the Arabic language had far less influence on modern Spanish than Latin had. Certainly, Arabic did not replace Latin as the 'national' language; this may have been because Latin, or rather the Romance form which was by now developing, was too firmly established, and it may also be because of the *Reconquista* and the widespread attitude that Arabic was the language of the infidel invader who had to be ousted from Christian Spain. However, many place names and a fair number of words survive. Many of the latter relate to fields of knowledge such as medicine, science and technology (some have passed through Spanish to English, such as algebra from Arabic *aljebr* meaning 'reunion of broken parts'!) – and also to plants and plant products introduced to Spain by the Arabs such as *albaricoque*, meaning apricot (from Arabic *al burquq*), and *algodón*, meaning cotton (from Arabic *al qutun*).

Other notable Arabic words in Spanish are:

alcoba	bedroom
alfombra	carpet
aljibe	water tank
almacén	store, warehouse
almirante	admiral
alcázar	castle

The first of these examples even shows how Arabic lifestyle is reflected in the current meaning or use of a word: in English, 'alcove' simply means a recess in a wall – bedrooms in Arab buildings like the Alhambra were merely a large recess off a main room, and closed off only by a curtain.

The expression '*Ojalá!*' is derived from the Arabic *Inchalla*, meaning something like 'if Allah helps me'. You may have noticed that a lot of Arabic words begin with *al-*; this is simply the equivalent of 'the', which tends to get 'stuck' onto Arab words exported to other languages.

Among place names of Arabic origin many also begin with *Al*: examples are Almería, Alicante and Alhama; in addition, many place names include the words *Medina* (city) and *alcázar* (castle), and names of several rivers begin with *Guad-* coming from *wad* (river), as in *Guadalquivir* and *Guadiana*. It was Arabic which adapted the Roman name Caesar Augusta to

Zaragoza. *Ben* appears in places like Benalmadena, Benidorm and Benicasim.

In addition to obvious linguistic influences, Arabic culture and social structure have had an effect on Spanish usage. First, the degree of uncertainty as to the race and religion of the person you were speaking to in the days of the *Reconquista* (see Unit 1), led to use of the expression *vuestra merced* ('your mercy') in addressing strangers; this has contracted and corrupted into the modern Spanish formal term for 'you', *usted(es)*, used for people senior or unknown to you. The other cultural/linguistic feature arising from the Arab occupation is the fact that all Spaniards have two surnames: they take their father's surname first and mother's second. This became the custom during the *Reconquista* as a way of showing people that you were from Christian lineage on both sides of your family – that you were a *Cristiano viejo* (an 'old/pure Christian'!). Women when they marry may add their husband's first surname if they wish. You will recognize this feature in the names of famous Spanish and Latin American people:

Vicente Blasco Ibáñez
Antonio Buero Vallejo
Arantxa Sánchez Vicario
Federico García Lorca
Pablo Ruiz Picasso
Gabriel García Márquez

Notice how the last three are known by their mother's surname, simply because their father's surnames are too commonplace to be memorable! Increasingly, internationally known Spaniards don't bother with their second surname. Do you know the second surnames of Julio Iglesias, Carlos Sainz, Antonio Banderas, Carlos Moyà and Conchita Martínez? We don't!

Castellano → Spanish

As was described in Unit 1, it was the Castilians who proved most successful in fighting against the Arabs, and who eventually dominated all of Christian Spain. Although other dialects and languages survived, the language of the *Reyes Católicos* became the official language of all Spain, and was taken by their *conquistadores* to the colonies of Latin America (see later section); it is now the official language of 21 countries, and is widely spoken in two others. However, 'Spanish' is more often than not called *Castellano* in these other countries because the language was still known as Castellano when the Americas were being explored and settled, and to use the term *Español* would be to acknowledge Spain's former colonial power. Of course, from the time of the *Reyes Católicos* through the ensuing centuries, Spanish developed from what might be termed 'Old Spanish' – up to about 1500 – consolidating all the time in terms of both vocabulary and grammar.

The great scholar Antonio de Nebrija published *Gramática de la Lengua Castellana* in 1492, the first proper, full-scale Spanish grammar, and in 1517, *Reglas de Orthographía* (*Rules for Spelling*), which to a large extent standardized spelling by means of the rules which are followed today.

South American influence

In fact, the form of Spanish taken to the Americas was that of the sailors and explorers who travelled there. A high proportion of them were from Extremadura and Andalusia, so the language of the Americas has some of the features of the accent commonly heard in these parts of Spain (see later). The contact with the new continent had two effects on Spanish: the first was that, in Latin America, a number of nautical terms came to be used for land-based features, such as *mástil* (mast) used for tree in the new lands. Similarly, when the explorers came upon new flora and fauna, they sometimes used the only words they knew to provide approximations for what they were trying to describe, such as using *león* (lion) for any type of large member of the cat family.

The second effect was the influx into Spain, and from there into Europe in some cases, of vocabulary from the native Indian languages of Latin America. These were largely borrowings which accompanied 'new' products brought back to Europe for the first time, such as: *tomate* (tomato), *patata* (potato), *chocolate* and *tobaco* (tobacco). These words all came from Nahuatl, one of the native languages of Mexico, and the final *-tl* sound of the Nahuatl version of the first three was simply changed for the sake of ease of pronunciation in Spanish. In many parts of Latin America the native languages are used for everyday life, Spanish for official purposes.

French influence on Spanish

The influx of French courtiers with Felipe de Anjou in 1700 was bound to have some sort of linguistic influence on Spanish. Words imported are largely connected with changes or additions to lifestyle: thus Spanish gained words like *jaquette*, **chaqueta** (jacket); *gelée*, **jalea** (jelly); *jardin*, **jardín** (garden) and *jambon*, **jamón** (ham). Even popular usage like the terms **mamá** and **papá** became prevalent as a result of this French influence. In any case, Spanish was bound to be influenced linguistically and culturally by its neighbour, and, to an extent, the flow of gallicisms has continued, though long since replaced by anglicisms in volume.

English influence on Spanish

The major influence on the Spanish language in the 20th century was English, either from the UK or from the USA. This is the result of a number of factors: international trade, the mass media, the film industry, popular music, popular culture, foreign travel, international sport, science, fashion, cosmetics, Spain's membership of international bodies such as the EU and NATO, and of course – last but by no means least – computing. Here are some examples of each, in some cases with the 'Spanish' alternative, but with no translation or category provided: you should be able to work those out without any difficulty!

el márketing	*el mercadeo*
el reportero	*el periodista*
el film	*la película*
el clip	*el fotograma*
el single	*el sencillo*
el punki	
el cámping	*el campamento*
chutar	*tirar a gol*
el bluejean	
el champú	
el boicot	
el e-mail	*el correo electrónico* (also affectionately known as *el Emilio!*)

In many cases, the original Spanish word is simply no longer used, having been removed from its nest by a sort of 'linguistic cuckoo' borrowed from English!

In some cases, English borrowings are misused: for example, as well as its proper meaning, *el jogging* can also mean 'tracksuit', while *el footing* is used for 'jogging' even though it does not actually exist in English! The author can remember being totally mystified some years ago by a Spanish student saying '*he comprado un nuevo picú*' ('I've just bought a new record player') ... actually, it must have been a long time ago because **el picú** meant ... 'a record player', being a corruption of 'pickup'), just one part of a record player. The word was popular long before the age of the CD!

One further quirk of English borrowings, of course, is the spellings: Spanish has a very logical system of spelling and pronunciation, diametrically opposed to English. Ask an English speaker to identify the (spoken) word *jersey* in Spanish (sounds like hersei), and he/she will be mystified, whereas in written form it is no problem. And what about *suéter*? Easy if you hear it rather than read it. Of course, both mean sweater/jersey/jumper/pullover, but clearly the former was absorbed into Spanish in written form, presumably on the label of the item of clothing in a shop, while the latter was probably 'borrowed' from English in spoken form, possibly heard from British tourists caught out by colder-than-expected weather on a Spanish coast somewhere ('I wish I had brought my sweater!').

Clearly, the Spanish spelling of a word borrowed from English will depend in part on how it is borrowed; one thing is for certain – Spanish will always adapt the borrowing in such a way that the written word, spoken aloud by a Spaniard will produce the correct sound and vice-versa.

Spanish influence on English

Of course, vocabulary borrowing between Spanish and English is a two-way traffic. As well as the obvious borrowings from Spanish, in the case of words with a cultural or culinary borrowing, such as *siesta*, *fiesta*, *paella*, *sangría* and *tortilla* (Spanish = omelette; Mexican Spanish = maize pancake), there are some unexpected ones. Note how some of the following are associated with 'Wild West' culture: the first 'cowboys' were, in fact, Mexican/Spanish speaking, as proved by the relevant examples:

English	Spanish	Original meaning
buckeroo	*vaquero*	cowboy
calaboose	*calabozo*	dungeon
chaps	*chapas*	(armour) plating (here 'overtrousers')
corral	*corral*	somewhere for animals to run (correr = to run)
lassoo	*lazo*	bow, knot
mosquito	*mosquito*	small fly
tornado	*tronada*	thunderstorm (may also be from tornar = to turn)

Note the 'diminutive' ending on the word *mosca* (fly) adapted with *-ito* to mean 'small'. Diminutive endings appear in other English borrowings from Spanish, as in the name Anita (little Ana). Spanish words and expressions used routinely in the USA include *amigo*, *hombre* and *hasta la vista*.

Finally, beware of mispronouncing borrowed Spanish words: *macho* and *machismo* are well known, but are sometimes mistakenly pronounced with a hard c sound as they would be if they were Italian … but they are not!

Pronunciation and spelling

In spite of its responsibility as the guardian of the standards of Spanish, Spain, and in particular the Spanish Academy, has not stood still. As recently as 1994 it instituted spelling reforms in conjunction with most other Spanish-speaking nations. Prior to 1994, *ch*, *ll* and *ñ* were separate letters in their own right, even having their own sections in the dictionary, listed after all of the *c*s, *l*s and *n*s, respectively, including where they occur in the middle of a word. Bowing to pressure from international organizations and the computing world, the Academy agreed to treat *ch* and *ll* just as they are treated in the rest of the world, and dictionaries had to be rewritten; only *ñ* maintained its independence, there being no real alternative as it is unique.

Pronunciation and spelling remain unchanged, and are totally reliable (compared to English) apart from the following differences, which we have simplified greatly:

Vowels are 'pure' and each essentially has only one possible sound.

Consonants are mostly similar to English, except for: *c* – as English *th* before -*e* and -*i*; but -*s* in southern Spain and Latin America, otherwise normal; *z* – always pronounced *th*, but -*s* in southern Spain and Latin America; *g* – a rough sound from the back of the throat before -*e* and -*i*, otherwise normal; *h* – never pronounced; *r* – rolled briefly in the middle of the word, strongly if at the start or if *rr*.

Note the special term for the *c-th* sound: *ceceo*, supposedly started by Isabel la Católica (see Unit 1) who had a lisp; the alternative -*s*- sound used in southern Spain and the Americas is known as *seseo*.

Spanish is also reliable when it comes to stress patterns – that is, in a word of more than one syllable, one syllable is louder than the other(s). Here are the rules, along with examples:

Words ending in a vowel, -*n* or -*s*

Stress on the penultimate (last but one) syllable: *chico* (boy), *niña* (girl), *agente* (agent), *cantan* (they sing), *sitios* (places).

Words ending in any consonant other than -*n* or -*s*

Stress on the last syllable: *Madrid*, *papel* (paper), *mujer* (woman), *reloj* (watch).

Words which break rules 1 and 2

These need a written accent to show where the stress is: *inglés* (English), *Ramón*, *champú* (shampoo), *exámenes* (exams), *pájaro* (bird).

Grammar

As we have already seen, Spanish grammar is to a certain extent based on Latin, especially in the way verbs are manipulated.

In other ways, however, Spanish is much simpler than Latin; it is also more complex than English. Spanish grammar is unlikely to change much, although some people speak with less respect for the rules than others. Of course, 'grammar' as such is simply a framework you can place over the language to explain how it works – and there are bits that simply don't fit. These irregularities prove that 'rules are made to be broken', and should be learnt alongside the rules themselves. To learn Spanish, you have to get to grips with some grammar; make sure you equip yourself with a good, digestible grammar book which gives you support, not heartburn!

Structures

Word order in Spanish is fairly similar to English, and is generally very flexible; the emphasis in meaning of a sentence is dependent on word order, e.g. *Juan rompío la ventana*, 'Juan broke the window' (not anything else); *la ventana, la rompió Juan*, 'the window was broken by Juan' (emphasis on Juan).

One important difference is that adjectives generally follow the noun described rather than the other way round as in English, e.g. *el caballo negro* (the black horse).

Vocabulary

Much has already been said about vocabulary; Spanish continues to be inventive when necessary. This language is rich in verbs and adjectives, but does not often have the 'duality' available in English (see earlier), where often two words are available for the same concept, one being Anglo-Saxon based, and the other Latin based (the latter more likely to be 'learned').

Spanish is also good at 'multiplying' words, for example by basing a new verb on a borrowing from abroad, usually making it a so-called *-ar* verb, e.g. 'to shoot (football)' → *chutar*.

Abbreviations

Spanish loves abbreviations and acronyms, and dictionaries are quite helpful in listing them. The only thing to watch is that, although similar to English, many appear to be back to front. This is a result of the word order when adjectives and adjectival structures are involved (as just explained). Thus, NATO is *La Organización del Tratado del Atlántico de Norte*, i.e. OTAN; even more tricky is EEUU – *Los Estados Unidos* (USA), the letters being doubled because the expression is plural.

Regional languages

As explained in Unit 1, the dialects and languages of the regions of Spain largely correspond to the old kingdoms. They have generally gained prominence and currency since the end of the repression of the Franco regime: indeed, some are associated with political implications, almost symbolic of the speakers' sense of nationalism and separatist ideals (see Units 8 and 11). Here are the main ones:

Catalan

The language of Catalonia, half-way between Spanish and French in some senses, has strong associations with separatist political ideas. Catalan has far more words ending in consonants than Spanish does, this being one of the features in which it is closer to French. Road signs and place names in Catalan are no major problem as the words are very close to Castilian spelling. In many schools, lessons are all in Catalan, a problem for children of recent immigrants to the region. Catalan people will often insist on speaking only in Catalan, especially to people from other parts of Spain, to make the point that they have their own language and culture; this can be difficult for foreigners. Here are a few examples of Catalan words alongside their Spanish equivalents.

Catalan	Spanish	English
actualment	*actualmente*	actually, currently
altre	*otro*	other
desprès	*después*	afterwards
imatge	*imagen*	image
línia	*línea*	line
nou	*nuevo*	new
successió	*sucesión*	succession
universitat	*universidad*	university

Valenciano (Valencia region) and *Mallorquín* (Balearic Islands)

These are closely related to Catalan.

Gallego/Galego

The language of Galicia, revitalized largely with reference to its close relative, Portuguese, is in fact a sort of half-way house between Spanish and Portuguese. The culture has connections with Welsh (see Unit 1), and signs and notices in Galicia are usually written in *Gallego* and Spanish. To give you a flavour, here are some *Gallego* words alongside their Spanish and English equivalents:

Gallego	Spanish	English
abaixo	*abajo*	below
máis	*más*	more
mesmo	*mismo*	same
onde	*donde*	where
primeiro	*primero*	first
soamente	*solamente*	only
traballo	*trabajo*	work
universidade	*universidad*	university

Vascuence/Basque

Now usually known by the Basque word *Euskera*, it is unlike any other language in Spain, with lots of *Ks* and *Xs*; it has absorbed a lot of modern Spanish vocabulary. A handful of Basque words have entered into use in Spanish, such as *izquierda* (left) and possibly *zurdo* (left handed), and *berri* (new) which appears in place names and surnames, and names like Iñigo and Javier or Xavier. The language is very healthy, partly thanks to the *ikastola* (Basque language schools) and Basque language TV and radio programmes. Signs and notices in the Basque Country are usually given in both Basque and Spanish. Here are a few Basque words from which you can see that some are similar to Spanish, others are quite different:

Basque	Spanish	English
abenturak	*aventura*	adventure
hezkuntza	*educación*	education
iragarkia	*noticia*	notice
lehendakari	*presidente*	president
musika	*música*	music
publikoa	*público*	public
teleberri	*telenoticias*	television news
udala	*ayuntamiento*	town council

Dialects

Bable

This is the old language of Asturias, now all but extinct, although efforts are being made to revive it.

Maño

The most obvious characteristic of this dialect of Aragón is a preference for the diminutive *-ico*; it also shares some characteristics with neighbouring Catalan and Basque.

Andaluz

There are lots of variants around the region and in the Canaries, but its main characteristics are the swapping of *ceceo* for *seseo*, and dropping *-s* and final consonants; this accent, once considered rather slovenly, gained respectability in the 1980s thanks to its being used by President Felipe González and some of his ministers, who were from Seville. The author was once asked by the *portero* (caretaker) of his block of flats: '*Te ingré, ¿no?*'. It took half an hour to work out that he meant: '*Usted es inglés, ¿no?*' ('You are English, aren't you?'). Also typical are what sounds like '*thevija*' for Seville and a car sticker once popular in Granada: '*Zoy de Graná, ¡casi ná!*' for '*Soy de Granada, ¡casi nada!*' ('I'm from Granada – almost nothing!').

Latin American Spanish

Latin American Spanish has even more variants, depending partly on the degree of influence of the local Indian languages, but there is not space to cover them here. A widespread feature is the *seseo* (see earlier), and differences in pronunciation and vocabulary make it about as distant from peninsular Spanish as US English is from British English. There are cases of peninsular Spanish words which are obscene in Latin America and vice-versa, so be warned: a classic case of this is described in Unit 12. If in doubt, consult the dictionary, as most good dictionaries offer Latin American alternatives where they exist.

Typical of the linguistic peculiarities and mismatches are: *guagua* meaning 'car' in the Canaries and Caribbean and 'baby' in most of Latin America; *tinto*, referring to 'red wine' in Spain but to 'black coffee 'in much of Latin America.

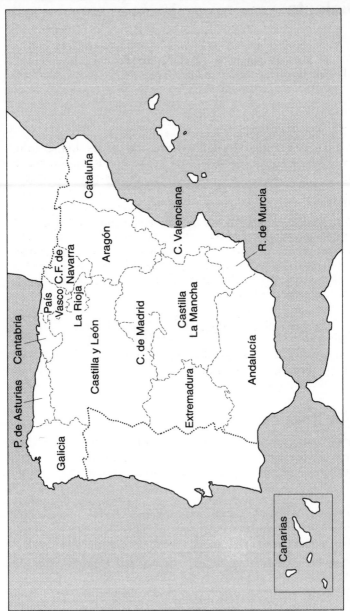

Map of Spain showing regions and languages

In most of Latin America, quite different expressions are used for everyday courtesies, such as '*para servirle*' meaning more or less 'here to please you' added on after the person's name when he/she is asked what his/her name is. Note also the widespread use of *vos* for 'you' (singular), whilst *ustedes* is used for 'you' (plural), and *vosotros* is never used.

Slang

Slang is constantly changing; it mostly arises out of the inventiveness of the young, often as a sort of 'in' language designed to baffle and exclude adults and strangers. Read any cartoon or comic for examples of current slang. Some appear quite quaint, but may in fact have sexual connotations; indeed, sexual swear words are generally not considered as offensive as they are in English, while certain forms of blasphemy are extremely so. Individual slang is a little more enduring, such as the expression *mala leche* (bad milk) used to describe anything or anyone unpleasant, but derived from a colourful curse on your mother's milk!

Spanish around the world

Spanish is spoken in 23 countries around the world, listed here with approximate numbers of speakers:

Spain	39,500,000
Argentina	33,000,000
Bolivia	7,000,000
Chile	14,000,000
Colombia	36,000,000
Costa Rica	3,500,000
Cuba	11,000,000
Dominican Republic	7,500,000
Ecuador	10,000,000
Equatorial Guinea	10,000,000
Guatemala	350,000
Honduras	5,500,000
México	85,000,000
Nicaragua	4,000,000
Panamá	2,500,000
Paraguay	4,500,000
Perú	23,000,000

Map of the Americas showing countries in which Spanish is the main language

Philippines	2,000,000
Puerto Rico	4,500,000
El Salvador	5,500,000
Uruguay	3,500,000
USA	25,500,000
Venezuela	20,000,000

Spanish now and ... in the future?

This major world language seems set to continue gaining influence in the world, and therefore to continue developing. The birthrate in many Spanish-speaking countries is higher than in most of the western world (although Spain's is among the lowest), so the number of Spanish-speakers will inevitably increase. In addition, Spanish is the official language of a large number of countries which are ripe for economic growth, and which are therefore good markets for more developed countries.

Perhaps most crucially, Spanish is the most significant minority language in the USA, but joint official language in California, gaining in number of speakers, and with a rapidly growing political lobbying power. Most of the USA's neighbours are Spanish-speaking countries and Spanish is the most widely taught foreign language in the USA. Meanwhile, Spain itself continues to flourish and gain credibility as a committed player on the European and international stage, and its language is therefore becoming even more valued. With its cultural richness and openness to new ideas, Spain will continue to nurture its language, yet will continue to take the cultural lead in the Spanish-speaking world.

GLOSSARY

la lengua	*language*
el idioma	*language*
hablar	*to speak*
escuchar	*to listen*
oír	*to hear*
escribir	*to write*
bilingüe	*bilingual*
monolingüe	*monolingual*
romano	*Roman*
el latín	*Latin*
los visigodos	*Visigoths*

los árabes	*Arabs*
los moros	*Moors*
el galicismo	*gallicism*
el anglicismo	*anglicism*
el americanismo	*americanism*
la influencia	*influence*
absorber	*to absorb*
aceptar	*to accept*
el argot	*slang*
el dialecto	*dialect*
el sustantivo	*noun*
el verbo	*verb*
el adjetivo	*adjective*
la ortografía	*spelling*
el acento	*stress, accent*
¿Cómo se escribe ...?	*How do you spell ...?*
pronunciar	*to pronounce*
el vocabulario	*vocabulary*
la gramática	*grammar*

Taking it further

Reading

How Spanish Grew, Robert K. Spaulding (University of California Press, 1967); old but thorough. *History of the Spanish Language*, Ralph Perry (CUP, 1991).

Learning

Listen to as much radio/television as you can.

The BBC produces good courses and materials, and good-quality programmes on both television and radio in the UK – look out for them.

The BBC course for adults, '*Sueños*, World Spanish' is particularly good, as it covers Latin American Spanish as well as Peninsular Spanish.

The Open University Spanish courses are now established at all levels. Contact the Centre for Modern Languages, The Open University, Walton Hall, Milton Keynes MK7 6AA, UK.

Watching and listening

Satellite TV is a good investment – in the UK, Televisión Española 2 is available on Eutelsat FII (Hotbird). In some areas, Spanish channels are available on Cable TV. Radio reception on a normal set is variable, but Spanish radio is available on satellite TV.

Places to visit

Travel in Spain or a Spanish-speaking country if you can. Go where the locals go and listen as much as you can, read everything you see and do try to speak: Spaniards will be very appreciative of your efforts and will help if you have problems.

Websites

The web is very popular in Spain and is very widely used; therefore, there is plenty of good material in Spanish available and also a lot from Latin America – all good practice. Choose your subject and do the necessary search, but be prepared to be bombarded with Spanish.

A useful UK site is

www.sgci.mec.es/uk/Pub/tecla.html. Run by the Consejería de Educación (Education Service) of the Spanish Embassy in London, it offers dozens of short articles on various topics, followed by vocabulary lists and exercises in Spanish – all good practice.

Spanish TV and Radio are also available on the internet at:
http://www.comfm.fr/sites/html.

Spanish study websites
www.studyspanish.com
www.bbc.co.uk/education/languages/
www.educationunlimited.co.uk/netclass
www.assk.com/espanol/el/htm
www.geocities.com/Athens/Thebes/6177/
www.lingolex.com/

School language website
rgshw.languages

Verb practice
www.aries17.uwaterloo.ca.lando.verbos/con-jugador.html

Vocabulary learning
www.vokabel.com/spanish.html

Spanish–English dictionary
www.anaya.es/diccionario/diccionar.htm

Dictionary advice/info
www.vox.es/index.htm

Information on learning Spanish
www.cvc.cervantes.es

Help with grammar
www.trentu.ca/academic/modernlanguages/spanish/masarriba

Pronunciation guide
www.geocities.com/Athens/Thebes/6177/ws-pronun.html

Developments in Spanish
www.el-castellano.com/

Spanish search engines
terra.es
www.ole.es/
www.rediris.es/
www.virtualizar.com/buscar/

Argentine search engine
www.brujula.com.ar/

Buying Spanish books
www.spanishbooksellers.com/

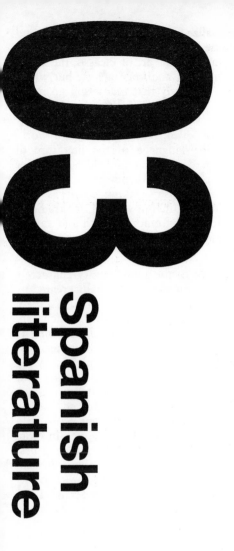

03

Spanish literature

In this unit you will learn
- about the literature of the Romans and Arabs
- about early Spanish literature
- about literature through the centuries
- about literature now

Ask people what they visualize when thinking of Spain, and most will answer with one of the usual stereotypes. Some elements of these will be cultural: the art of Picasso, the music of flamenco, the architecture of Gaudí, perhaps ... but where literature is concerned, it is unlikely that many will go much further than *Don Quijote*. Yet much great literature has been written and continues to be written in the Spanish language. One should not just think of Spain: indeed, as a major world language, Spanish is also the language of the literature of Hispano-America, and writers such as Nobel Prize-winner Gabriel García Márquez and Isabel Allende are popular in English-speaking as well as Spanish-speaking countries. The scope of this book is limited to Spain, but with its rich tradition and long history, Spain offers an enormous wealth and variety of literature, some of the best of it available in English translation.

It is a curious irony that some of the great literary characters which people associate with Spain were not actually created by Spaniards: a Frenchman, Prosper Mérimée, created Carmen, later immortalized in Bizet's opera; it was another Frenchman, Beaumarchais, who created Figaro in his plays *Le Barbier de Seville* (1775) and *Le Mariage de Figaro* (1783): the great potential of this character for opera was later exploited by the Austrian composer Mozart. A parallel irony is the fact that many great stories and characters of Spanish literature have become known around the world by second-hand means, having been taken up and developed in a different genre, in a different medium or even in the works of a foreigner. In more recent times it was Hollywood that produced one of the best epic films ever made; the story of a very Spanish hero, *El Cid*, brought one of the great epics of early Spanish literature to life. *El Cid* was also the subject of a play written by the French 17th-century playwright, Pierre Corneille, in 1636. Other stories and characters which have taken on an existence beyond their original creation are Don Juan and *El Sombrero de Tres Picos* (the Three-cornered Hat); the latter was made into a ballet by the Spanish (at last!) composer, Manuel de Falla.

The character of Don Juan has been an even more prolific traveller: introduced by Tirso de Molina in the 16th century, it was much later taken up by Juan de Zorrilla in Spain, and by Molière in France, Byron, Shaw and many others in England, and by the composers Mozart and Richard Strauss. Why should this be so? It almost seems that the Spanish are great at creating original literary ideas, but not so good at actually promoting them abroad in their own right, leaving it to others to exploit their true potential. Yet the fact is that Spain has an enormous and worthy literary tradition.

Roman, Visigothic and Arab literature in Spain

Among several Spanish-born Romans who became great writers are the poets Martial and Lucan, and Seneca and Quintilian, who wrote about rhetoric – quite a heritage for the Spanish to build on!

It is fair to assume that some sort of literature existed in the Visigothic era, probably the sort of ballad and story-telling traditions which existed elsewhere in Europe. The Visigoths had embraced Christianity before they arrived in Spain, and their culture was in the hands of the clergy, such as San Isidoro de Sevilla, an encyclopaedist, and Orosius, a historian. Arab Spain produced several great writers: Córdoba at the time was the centre of learning in Europe, with many academics and libraries – one with over 400,000 books! The cultured Arabs tolerated Spanish Christians and Jews, and their scholars were responsible for researching and reintroducing Greek literature to western Europe. Arabic love poetry, full of metaphor and symbolism, contributed much to later Spanish love poetry. Perhaps more significantly, the broader cultural influence of Islam is crucial to some of the main threads running through Spanish literature, particularly the theme of honour prevalent in the literature of the Golden Age (see page 71). Similarly, the fatalism of certain elements of Spanish literature, as seen even many centuries later in the drama and poetry of Lorca in the 20th century, partly has its origins in Arab culture.

Early Spanish literature

The Romance period

A direct product of the *Reconquista* (see Unit 1), ballads were recited all over Spain, conveying the stories of great events and adventures to even the remotest parts of the country: Spain rivals Slavonic countries in its great ballad tradition. By coincidence the word used for ballad was *romance*, also used for the language which constituted the half-way stage between Latin and modern Spanish. The exploits of the heroes of the day were a popular theme in those which survive, such as *Bernardo del Carpio*, the *Infantes de Lara, and Durandarte*, the last connected with the great French ballad *La Chanson de Roland*.

These epic poems were a useful way of packaging such stories: poetry made them easier to remember (crucial to wandering *juglares* (minstrels) or *trovadores* (troubadours), earning a living by reciting them). They were often sung, such was the melodic nature of the typical octosyllable line. (See also Unit 5.) To encourage generosity among their audiences, troubadours livened up their stories, embellishing them with drama and human appeal. Although many ballads were written down in *romanceros* – compilations of ballads – this tended to be some time after the event, the story having undergone many years of liberal interpretation and often being incomplete; therefore, as with any literary version of history, they cannot really be considered reliable, historical accounts. King Alfonso X (see Unit 1) however, established the first chronicles, recording history as it happened.

El Poema de Mío Cid

This most famous of Spanish ballads (written in about 1140) tells of the warrior who became the great folk hero of Spain, immortalized in celluloid in the Hollywood epic, featuring Charlton Heston in the role of Rodrigo Díaz de Vivar and Sophia Loren as Doña Jimena. The story epitomizes the *Reconquista* era, during which the Christian Spanish gradually pushed their borders with Arab Spain southwards. The *Poema de Mío Cid* has all the ingredients of a great epic, and is so long that it was usually read or performed in short chunks. However, it remains one of the greatest milestones of Spanish literature, outstanding for its exaltation of virtue, courage and loyalty, and for its vivid characterization.

The story of El Cid

Born in Vivar near Burgos, Rodrigo was the standard-bearer of King Sancho of Castilla. He was famed for his fighting skills, as stated in the ballad: '*en buen ora çinxiestes espada*' – 'it was a great moment when you put on your sword'. Sancho's father, Fernando I, king of Christian Spain, had split his domains between his sons to resolve squabbles as to who should inherit. After his death they fell into war, and Sancho defeated his brother, Alfonso; Rodrigo witnessed the act of treachery by which Alfonso had Sancho murdered. Refusing to pay allegiance to his murderous new king, Rodrigo went into exile, gaining fame and power by his fighting exploits, and becoming ruler of Valencia. He befriended an Arab king, who gave him the nickname *Al Sidi* (the Master), hence *El Cid*. Having eventually made peace with Alfonso, *El Cid* was fatally wounded in battle, but legend says his wife put his corpse on to his horse, Babieca, sending him out to one last battle against the Moors who were threatening Valencia … truly the stuff of legend!

Statue of El Cid in Burgos

El Libro de Buen Amor

Translated as *The Book of Good Love* in 1968, it is not quite what its title suggests. It was written around 1330 by Juan Ruiz, El Arcipreste de Hita (the Archpriest of Hita; hardly the sort of author you might expect to write a bawdy book about love!). It is a collection of many and varied sections with the common thread of love, some religious in nature, others profane, but almost all with some sort of moral intent. *El libro de buen amor* shows many literary influences and views of contemporary society, all conveyed with a sense of humour.

La Celestina

This unique, early, stylized drama, a sort of novel in dialogue, was written by Fernando de Rojas in about 1497. Although in dramatic form, it was never intended for performance. Its strange, haunting story tells of Calisto, who tries to by-pass the usual protracted courtship, enlisting the strange witch-like Celestina, to act as his go-between. After his illicit tryst with Melibea, he falls to his death – a fatalistic punishment for his impatience and his unwise decision to use Celestina's dark powers, compounded by his failure to keep his promises to her. Although scurrilous in terms of its subject, *La Celestina* presents a strong moral, typical of the era: it is dangerous to flirt with the underworld, and those who do come to grief, because they disturb the harmony ordained by the Creator and must be punished. Full of classical references, this 'play' owes much to the Italian 14th-century poet, Petrarch, and has been interpreted in various dramatic media, including film. The theme of the go-between has often been used since in the literature of other European countries.

Early Spanish drama

As in other European countries, the earliest Spanish drama was the performance of scripture stories in churches. Juan del Encina (1492) was the first to develop drama away from churches. Just as in Britain, the tradition of modern drama can be traced back to the performing of short plays and sketches in innyards during the Middle Ages. You can visit an original innyard theatre in Almagro, south of Madrid. The first significant writer who can really be called a playwright is Lope de Rueda (1510–1565) who wrote a series of endearing *pasos*, comic short plays, for performance by travelling troupes of comedy actors.

The novels of chivalry

As in other European countries, these short stories of knights in shining armour, dragons and damsels in distress were very popular in the 16th century, once the advent of printing had made their mass production possible: they were arguably the first form of popular consumer literature. In Spain many involved the heroic exploits of stock heroes and villains against the Arabs, one of the great heroes being Amadís de Gaula. These novels were the natural successor to the ballads of previous centuries, with the same subject matter: being adventurous, escapist literature whose heroes fought against the forces of evil – you could think of them as precursors of James Bond films!

The pastoral novel

Also popular in the 16th century, but contrasting with the chivalresque novel, the pastoral novel idealizes the bucolic life in an idealized countryside populated by shepherds and shepherdesses who while away their time writing love poetry. This very stylized form of sentimental escapism was the vehicle for some worthy love poetry. The most enduring example is the sequence of Jorge de Montemayor's Diana novels, such as *Diana Enamorada*, almost a form of 16th-century soap opera!

The picaresque novel: *Lazarillo de Tormes*

Another strange but very significant literary product of this era is *Lazarillo de Tormes*. Published anonymously in 1554, this is a series of supposedly autobiographical episodes of the life of a young beggar boy who apparently 'makes it good'. Set in the shadiest, seediest layers of Spanish society of the day, it is the first picaresque novel (*pícaro* means a rogue), and in some senses the precursor of the novel as a literary form. Full of often suspect moralizing, the episodes have a common thread: the progress of Lazarillo as he works for one master after another, each representing a sector of society. Each is corrupt or immoral in some way and although Lazarillo comments on this it is only at a superficial level: it is left to the readers to see the true satirizing intent in the story, assisted by the very obvious naivety of Lazarillo and his comments. This influential little book, however, spawned a vogue for picaresque literature, and one author probably inspired by it extended his own interpretation of this genre into the Spanish literary work best known outside Spain: what began life as a picaresque novel with an original slant developed into one of the greatest and best known literary masterpieces of all time. Ironically, Miguel de Cervantes was in prison when he dreamt up and sketched out the first part of none other than *Don Quijote!*

Date	Genre	Subject	Features	Examples
C16	Chivalresque novel	Knights and their exploits	Other stories included	*Amadis de Gaula*
C16	Pastoral novel	Shepherds, shepherdesses	Set in idealized countryside, love poetry	*Diana Enamorada*
C16	Picaresque novel	Rogues and villains	Set in poorer society, pranks and crime	*Lazarillo de Tormes*

La Edad de Oro

This name 'The Golden Age' is given to the period lasting roughly from the beginning of the 16th century to the end of the 17th, following and extending the Renaissance period. It overlaps with Spain's political Golden Age, but starts and ends later, as cultural advancement tends to be a consequence of political development tailing off after political decline. To a certain extent, this cultural boom was inspired by Spain's involvement in the discovery and conquest of lands in the so-called New World. However, its major inspiration was the rediscovery of classical culture: many ideas come from the classics, and reference is often made to classical sources.

Golden Age poetry

Classical inspiration was not always taken directly by Spanish writers, but also came via writers of other European countries, notably Italy. For example, Spanish soldiers returning from Italy, where the kingdom of Naples was under the control of the crown of Aragón, brought to Spain the sonnet and the fashion for courtly poetry. Poets of the time include such names as Garcilaso de la Vega and Juan Boscán. Other great poets followed on: Fray Luís de León wrote mystical poetry; Fernando de Herrera composed patriotic odes; Luis de Góngora and Francisco de Quevedo developed the poetic styles of '*conceptismo*' and '*culteranismo*' in which metaphors are taken to ludicrous lengths.

San Juan de la Cruz and Santa Teresa de Avila

These religious writers, both canonized saints, expressed in poetry and prose, respectively, their love of God and their mystic experiences. St Teresa is also known as founder of many Carmelite convents.

Golden Age prose

Miguel de Cervantes

Best known, of course, for *Don Quijote* (1605), Cervantes actually aspired to be a playwright. Having shown great bravery at the Battle of Lepanto, a sea battle against the Turks, he was kidnapped by North African pirates. The royal letters of recommendation he was carrying were interpreted as indicating that he was from a rich family, so his ransom was set too high for his family. After several years, he eventually returned to

Spain and secured a lowly government job in Seville procuring supplies for the Spanish army. Misfortune struck again: accused of embezzlement, he was imprisoned in Seville. A plaque on the wall of a bank in the Calle Sierpes marks the site of the jail in which the idea for *Don Quijote* was conceived. His short novels, the *novelas ejemplares* – moralizing stories – reassert established values, but include picaresque elements.

Don Quijote began as a short episodic story, but Cervantes' experiment paid off: Book 1 was a runaway success. It was immediately translated into several different languages – published in English as *Don Quixote, The Knight with the Sad Face* (there are modern translations available, too). Such was the popularity of this book that other authors tried to cash in, writing spurious sequels. Cervantes was so incensed that he wrote his own full-length sequel, developing his themes and including subsidiary stories, many being literary gems in their own right.

The story of *Don Quijote*

Alonso Quijano, a minor Castillian nobleman, his head turned by reading too many chivalresque novels, sets out on his horse Rocinante to help those he considers to be in distress:

> *En un lugar de la Mancha de cuyo nombre no quiero acordarme, no ha mucho tiempo que vivía un hidalgo de los de lanza en astillero, adarga antigua, rocín flaco y galgo corredor.*

> (In a place in la Mancha whose name I do not wish to remember, not long ago there lived one of those noblemen with a lance in his weapon-rack, an ancient shield, a skinny horse and a fast greyhound.)

His actions always have unfortunate and usually amusing consequences, yet his crusading ardour – dedicated to his lady love Dulcinea (actually a peasant girl from El Toboso) – is not dimmed. The irony is that his crazy ideals are actually more virtuous than the corrupt motives which drive most of those around him. In Book 2 Don Quijote and his down-to-earth squire, Sancho Panza, have even more amazing and amusing adventures, until finally Don Quijote falls ill: ironically, before dying, he recovers his sanity, but nobody believes him, showing again how we are all a bit crazy. There are many versions available in translation and although set long ago in a foreign country, this story has a lot to offer us today.

Cervantes was never satisfied with his success, always feeling that he had missed his destiny as a playwright. He mismanaged the fortune earned by his masterpiece, dying a sick old man, in relative poverty, in 1616.

Don Quijote, Sancho Panza ... and some windmills

Francisco de Quevedo

Besides poetry, Quevedo produced some of the most incisive satire ever written. His picaresque novel, *La Vida del Buscón*, lambasts certain elements of Spanish society, yet is an entertaining story of a young man in search of a good living, reminiscent of *Lazarillo de Tormes*. Even more incisive is the satire in *Los Sueños* (1627, translated in 1640), a collection of fantasies: in one, the scene is hell – those guilty of corruption in life, from popes to innkeepers, suffer an eternal punishment that fits the crimes they committed on earth. Quevedo evidently had a few axes to grind!

Golden Age drama

Lope de Vega

Lope was the first of three great playwrights who together equal Shakespeare in stature but who individually don't match the Englishman's genius. Lope perfected the Spanish *comedia*, a three-act play which blends comedy and tragedy. Lope wrote plays to be performed by his own company of travelling players. His themes are popular ones: the evil of tyranny in

Fuenteovejuna (1612, translated in 1961) and the monarch as protector of the people in *El Mejor Alcalde, el Rey* (also a theme in *Fuenteovejuna*).

Honour is a common theme, being very important in a Spanish society in which everyone was still obsessively concerned with rank, status and solidity of Christian lineage. However, with Lope we are not talking about the distorted view prevalent among some of his contemporaries and the villains of his plays – that honour goes with rank and privilege. Instead his plays put forward the view that honour has to be earned and deserved by means of good behaviour. Lope was a prolific playwright, writing about 1400, plays and playlets (not all are of good quality), some of which are among the greatest works of Spanish literature. Like other Golden Age playwrights, Lope wrote plays which reflected life in all its richness, combining elements of tragedy and humour, unlike French contemporaries, many of whom considered that to mix these contrasting elements was heresy. Lope's greatest achievement was to take drama to the people with his travelling theatre, and thus to popularize theatre as a genre in Spain.

The story of *Fuenteovejuna*

A village community suffers at the hands of their *comendador*, the nobleman entrusted with control of the village and its people. They are driven to breaking point by his abductions and forced seductions of local girls, and by his habit of imprisoning any men who stand up to him, such as the hero, Frondoso, whose fiancée, Laurencia, falls victim to the *comendador*'s lechery. In spite of the protests of her father, the mayor, she manages to get the villagers to rise against the *comendador*: his home (a castle) is attacked and he meets an untimely end. The king and queen – Fernando and Isabel – investigate this murder of one of their trusted noblemen, but in spite of torture the villagers all refuse to name any individual who might be guilty: instead all assert '*Fuenteovejuna lo hizo*' – 'the whole village was responsible for killing him'. Aware by now of the *comendador*'s crimes, the king and queen grant a pardon to all the village and Frondoso and Laurencia are married. This play was performed regularly in the Soviet Union during the Communist period, epitomizing as it does the struggle of the people against a tyrannical and corrupt ruler; not surprisingly, in the Soviet version there was no final intervention by benevolent monarchs!

Tirso de Molina or Don Juan?

A classic case of the creation being more famous than the author, the Spanish dramatic character best known outside Spain is probably Don Juan, or to give him his full name, Don Juan Tenorio. The original version of what has become a popular story is actually called *El Burlador de Sevilla* (*The Trickster of Seville*, 1630). Tirso wrote many other plays, of course, but this creation of his has become universally known, immortalized by Mozart, in his opera '*Don Giovanni*'. The original story was of a young nobleman who considered any young girl fair game for his lust. As in other previous Spanish literature, the theme is that of a corrupt and vain view of honour versus virtue: because Don Juan goes against what is right, he is given his just deserts. The ingredients of this play were such that they were used by the French playwright Corneille in his play, *Don Juan*, by Mozart, and by the 19th-century Spanish playwright Juan de Zorrilla in *Don Juan Tenorio*. Don Juan has ever since epitomized the womanizer, indeed the name is often used as a nickname for such a person, taking the character far beyond anything Tirso de Molina could ever have dreamt of!

The story of *Don Juan*

He seduces several women one after another, ranging from a fishergirl to a gentlewoman, fooling them with his charms and promises, in one case pretending in the dark to be the girl's fiancé; when discovered he duels with and kills this girl's father, Don Gonzalo, who promises in his dying breath to gain his revenge. Later in the play, Don Juan sees his statue in a church and mockingly invites him to dinner. Every time Don Juan is warned about his conduct, he replies: '*¿Tan largo me lo fiais?*' ('do you give me that long?'). The statue/ghost does indeed appear for dinner and duly invites Don Juan back in his turn. In order not to lose face, Don Juan keeps the appointment, but suddenly the ground opens up and the ghost of Don Gonzalo drags Don Juan down into hell.

Pedro Calderón de la Barca

From some points of view, Calderón was probably the greatest of the three great Golden Age playwrights, at least in terms of his workmanship and the themes he develops. Many of his plays focus strongly on the theme of honour, but Calderón made rather more of his themes than Lope de Vega. Examples of his best known plays are *La Vida es Sueño* (*Life is a Dream*), *El*

Médico de su Honra (*The Doctor of his Honour*) and *El Alcalde de Zalamea* (*The Mayor of Zalamea*, 1642 translated in 1906); the last title was an elaboration of Lope's original play of the same name, but with a more highly developed theme, with a plot not unlike that of *Fuenteovejuna* in portraying a village mayor standing up to a lecherous army officer.

The 18th century: French influence

When Felipe (Philip) de Anjou (see Unit 1) came to Spain to found the Bourbon dynasty with his gaggle of French courtiers, some elements of French culture became popular in Spain. The French influence which came diverted Spanish literature away from the trends which might have developed naturally and towards a pale imitation of things French. One example is the rather shallow sort of court drama popular at this time.

The only writers of note were Bretón de Herreras, whose best play is *El Pelo de la Dehesa* (*The Country Bumpkin*), and Leandro Fernández de Moratín, who wrote *El Sí de las Niñas* (*The Consent of Girls*). These plays are at least witty and gently amusing. Apart from this, there is little Spanish literature of much merit written in this period – quite a contrast to the great literary burgeoning of the Golden Age!

The 19th century

19th-century Romanticism

After the classical era, in which man was seen as a microcosm of the universe, a mere speck at the mercy of all the great forces of nature and the heavens, the Romantic movement of the 19th century portrayed man as the centre of his universe, able to shape events and his own destiny. Thus literature began to look at man and mankind in close-up, and for the first time to take an interest in people and what makes them tick rather than portraying them as mere pawns in the grand design.

The most significant dramatic work which typifies this is *Don Juan Tenorio*, José Zorrilla's re-working of the Don Juan theme from a romantic point of view.

Larra – *novelas costumbristas/regionalistas*

It is not often that anything as ephemeral as newspapers can be associated with literature; however, one of the early contributions to the development of the Spanish novel in the 19th century stemmed from newspapers. Mariano José de Larra's collection of short essay-like narratives for a newspaper set out to portray Spain through its people, covering Spain region by region. What followed was a fashion for novels set in a region with strong characteristics, written in such a way that the region almost becomes a character in the book. One might almost refer to this as the 'geographical' novel.

Realism: The 19th-century novel

This gave way in the second part of the 19th century to the development of an interest in realism, psychology and nature, with the author in control only in a remote sense, portraying characters who are in control of themselves. Thus, with the freedom it allowed the writer, the novel came to the fore as the best medium to convey this new approach. New-found wealth and leisure allowed more people to buy books and read: while Spanish novelists are not as well known internationally as, say, the French novelists Zola and Flaubert, or the English writer Dickens, the best of them are no less worthy. Pereda, Valera, Pardo Bazán and Valdés all focused on regions of Spain, but the following novelists stand out.

Benito Pérez Galdós

Another development in the 19th century was the historical novel. One of the greatest Spanish writers, Galdós, started out writing a series of *episodios nacionales*, novels set around great historical events, viewed through the experiences of a humble participant: a cabin boy on a Spanish ship at the Battle of Trafalgar; a country lad at the Battle of Bailén (see Unit 1), the bloody battle in which a Spanish peasant army scored a significant victory over Napoleon's army in the Peninsular War. Galdós went on to write some of the best novels of the century, largely portraying Madrid society: *Torquemada*, reminiscent of Dickens; *Doña Perfecta*, a story of religious intolerance; *Fortunata y Jacinta*, the lengthy tale of a spoilt *señorito* ('rich kid') trying to divide his love between his wife Jacinta and a captivating gypsy girl Fortunata; *La de Bringas* (translated into English as *The Spendthrifts*), the story of a family living among the hangers-on at the Spanish Royal Court.

Pedro Antonio de Alarcón

This author's story, *El Sombrero de Tres Picos*, is another one better known outside Spain because it was taken up by Manuel de Falla, who based music for a ballet on the story (see Unit 5). This simple story of a local dignitary (the *corregidor*) smitten by love for the local miller's wife is a classic: the ensuing courtship, with the *corregidor* egged on by Tío Lucas and his wife, Frasquita, the humiliation of the suitor and the terrible revenge he attempts to exact on Tío Lucas, all go to make a classic story of passion and intrigue. Yet it is the way in which Alarcón crafted this masterpiece of characterization, caricature and rapid-fire action, depicted in short, snappy chapters, full of humour of various types, and using techniques later developed in film making, that makes this little story a literary gem, well worth reading. (A translation is available in the Everyman series.)

Clarín

This was the pen-name of the literary critic Leopoldo Alas. He used it for the newspaper articles in which he offered critiques of other authors' novels and also his own ideas on how to write a great novel. Eventually he turned his ideas into *La Regenta*, the story of the bored wife of an important official; she is seduced by a younger man, causing her elderly husband to challenge her lover to a duel, which results in the old man's death. In some ways the ingredients and even elements of the plot are reminiscent of Flaubert's *Madame Bovary*, written a few years earlier. This shows how international literary trends had become, but Clarín makes it very much a Spanish novel.

Naturalism

The late 19th-century literary fashion for realism eventually evolved, as in France, into *Naturalismo*, a tendency to examine nature, in the sense of human behaviour, under a literary microscope, with plenty of attention paid to gruesome and intimate details of both a physical and psychological nature.

Blasco Ibáñez

Blasco Ibáñez was probably the greatest exponent of *Naturalismo*. In one of his best novels, *La Barraca*, he studies the interaction of an Aragonese family with their new neighbours, after their move to a *barraca* (Valencian-style farmhouse – see Unit 4). The newcomers have to confront every sort of prejudice, bordering on racism, leading to a sequence of ever more tragic events. In telling the story, Blasco Ibáñez uses literature to a great extent to make political points: in *La Barraca* he is slating intolerance and prejudice and the inaction of officialdom.

The 98 Generation

The close of the 19th century saw Spain's lowest ebb in terms of power and influence, culminating in the loss of her last colony, Cuba, helped in its struggle for independence by the American Navy. The resultant national angst and soul searching gave rise to a great generation of writers, some of whom could be called political philosophers, who attempted to analyse the reasons for Spain's downfall and to point to possible solutions to the low level of national morale. These are the authors of the so-called 98 Generation, followed later by the brilliant poets of the Generation of 27. Among the former are Ortega y Gasset, an intellectual and philosopher whose best known work, *España Invertebrada* (*Spineless Spain*) seeks to explain and rationalize Spanish history; and Miguel de Unamuno, regarded by many as Spain's greatest writer of modern times. A professor of Greek at the University of Salamanca, he is known not just for his literary works, such as the novel *Niebla* (*Mist*) and philosophical works such as *El Sentimiento Trágico de la Vida* (*The Tragic Sense of Life*), but also for his outspoken criticism of virtually every regime in his lifetime.

The 20th century

Angel Ganivet and Menéndez y Pelayo were among the many other philosophers and historians of the day, followed by Ramón Menéndez Pidal, Gregorio Marañón and Salvador de Madariaga, all great names in their own right. Many of them can be read in translation. Pío Baroja wrote *Memorias de un Hombre de Acción* (*Memories of a Man of Action*, 1913–31). The most distinguished dramatist of the Generation of 27 was Jacinto Benavente: his play *Los Intereses Creados* (translated as *Bonds of Interest* in 1917) won him the Nobel Prize for literature in 1922.

Antonio Machado

While the 98 Generation and its second-generation offshoots were indulging in a sort of national navel gazing, other writers, notably the poet Antonio Machado, were evolving a different way of coping with the problem of low national morale. Iinstead of soul searching, they wrote about all that was good about Spain, sometimes in a nostalgic way but often helping to highlight positive qualities of Spain and the Spanish. Antonio Machado, whose life and work bridges the turn of the century, was a schoolmaster: early on in his career, while teaching at the Instituto in Baeza in northern Andalusia, he began to write poetry. His favourite subject was the Spanish landscape, and many of his most famous compositions offer poignant descriptions of Castile (notably in the collection *Campos de Castilla*) written during his time living in Soria in north-eastern Castile. However, he also wrote many delightfully amusing and whimsical poems, such as *Las Moscas*, which tells of the antics of flies. Here are a couple of verses to give you the flavour:

Vosotras, las familiares,	You, the familiar flies,
Inevitables, golosas,	the inevitable, greedy flies
Vosotras, moscas vulgares,	you, the common flies,
Me evocáis todas las cosas	…remind me of … everything …
Y en la aborrecida escuela,	And in the much-hated schoolroom
raudas moscas divertidas	amusing, impetuous flies,
perseguidas	chased around,
por amor de lo que vuela.	for the love of things which fly.

Many of these poems were set to music and sung in the 1970s by the *cantautor* (singer-songwriter) Joan Manuel Serrat on his album '*Dedicado a Antonio Machado*'. Serrat managed to capture beautifully the mood and tone of Machado's poetry, adding his own tribute, '*En Coulliure*': in this moving song, he laments the fact that Antonio Machado, who had to flee from Catalonia during the Spanish Civil War when Franco's Nationalist troops marched on Barcelona, never returned to his beloved homeland, instead dying the lonely death of an exile in the small French town of Collioure. (See Unit 5.)

Federico García Lorca

The other great poet and playwright of the early part of the 20th century is one of the few Spanish writers who has become well known throughout the world. His tragedies have been performed many times on British stages and on television, with notable performances by actresses such as Glenda Jackson, Penelope Keith and Mia Farrow. Indeed, because of his Republican political leanings and his homosexuality, his work was better known and more researched and studied outside Spain during the period of Franco's dictatorship. To an extent, it is only since the return of democracy that Lorca has been given the recognition he deserves in his homeland.

Federico García Lorca was the youngest son of a landowner in Fuentevaqueros in central Andalusia. Having suffered from polio early in his childhood (he had a limp for the rest of his life), he tended to stay at home with the women of the family instead of playing outside with the village lads. He built his own miniature theatre and wrote playlets to perform in it. Lorca studied first in Granada, then in Madrid, where he met other intellectuals of his generation such as the painter Salvador Dalí and the film producer Luis Buñuel. Among his early poetic work was the collection of poetry entitled *Romancero Gitano*: in it he focuses on the poverty and discrimination suffered by the gypsies of Andalusia.

He then went to New York, where he was struck by the plight of the black population of Harlem: in the collection *Poeta en Nueva York* he reflects this concern. Significantly, he was becoming the champion of oppressed minorities. More than for his poetry, Lorca is known for his plays. In the early 1930s, he set up a travelling theatre company called *La Barraca*: he and his friends wished to take drama – particularly the great plays of Lope de Vega – to the simple peasants of rural Spain. He also wrote plays of his own: the best known of his comedies, set in rural Andalusia, is *La Zapatera Prodigiosa*, the tale of an old shoemaker and his concerns at the flirtations of his much younger wife.

However, Lorca's masterpiece is his trilogy of tragedies depicting the problems of women in Spain – another oppressed group. The first is *Yerma*, which tells of the angst of a young wife desperate to have children (*yerma* = barren woman) and whose husband cares only for his animals and property. Her sheer frustration eventually leads her to kill him to end the uncertainty of her future. The second play is *Bodas de Sangre* (*Blood Wedding*), based on a true story of a young bride who runs away from her wedding with a former boyfriend. In the ensuing chase by her bridegroom, the two men fight and stab each other to death. The third and arguably best of these plays is *La Casa de Bernarda Alba* (*The House of Bernarda Alba*).

The story of *La Casa de Bernarda Alba*

Bernarda's second husband has just died, and she is determined to safeguard the family honour and reputation by keeping her five skittish daughters in virtual imprisonment, with the excuse of the obligatory period of several years' mourning. The first word this tyrant utters in the play is '*Silencio!*' and in the first scene with her daughters she announces to them: '*En ocho años que dura el luto, ni el aire de la calle ha de entrar en esta casa*' ('In the eight years the mourning will last, not even the air of the street will enter this house'). Only for the eldest daughter is there a suitable suitor in the village, Pepe el Romano, but while her sisters argue, the youngest daughter, Adela, manages to have a clandestine love affair with him. Significantly for this play, the subtitle of which is *Drama de Mujeres en los Pueblos de España* (*Drama of Women in the Villages of Spain*), no men appear on stage, there is only the unseen presence of Pepe, the catalyst which operates on the women of Bernarda's house with tragic consequences.

Bernarda Alba, the tyrannical Mother in Lorca's play

When her affair is found out and Pepe is chased away by Bernarda with her shot gun, Adela hangs herself, thinking that her mother has killed him. Naturally, faced with this tragedy and with the grief of her other daughters, Bernarda's one concern is to declare hypocritically '*La hija menor de Bernarda Alba ha muerto virgen. ¿Me habéis oído? ¡Silencio, silencio he dicho! ¡Silencio!*' ('The youngest daughter of Bernarda Alba has died a virgin. Did you hear? Silence, silence I said! Silence!').

The most tragic aspect of Lorca is that his promising career came to a sudden and brutal end in 1936: arrested by the Civil Guard for his Republican sympathies only a few months into the Civil War, he was taken away and shot. Many of his plays are available in translation, and the three tragedies are often performed in English.

Literature of the Civil War and dictatorship

The Spanish Civil War was in some strange senses a considerable contributor to 20th-century Spanish literature as well as bringing imprisonment, exile or death to many writers: any writer or intellectual with leftist political leanings had to flee from Spain, and many of those who remained were imprisoned as part of Franco's measures to consolidate his victory by silencing all opposition. One could say that there were two sorts of literature for many years: that of Francoists writing their version of the conflict, and that of Franco's opponents writing in exile, or in code to avoid problems with the censor.

The poet Rafael Alberti was typical of those who could not tolerate Franco's régime: he left Spain and spent years in voluntary exile living and working in Argentina. Among other notable poets, Jorge Guillén had produced a collection of poems called *Cánticos* in 1928; going into exile in 1939, he produced ever more pessimistic poetry, and *Clamor* (1963) has strong social and political themes. Vicente Aleixandre won the Nobel prize in 1977, having produced *Antología Total* in 1975. These poets are sometimes known as the 1936 Generation, and some of the others are characterized by their religious faith. Later poets show social concerns and realism, the most significant perhaps being Blas de Otero and José María Valverde, and, more recently, Lorenzo Gomís, who published a collection called *Poesía* in 1978.

One pro-Franco intellectual and novelist who wrote works which were free of any significant political comment either way was Camilo José Cela: *Viaje a la Alcarria*, for example, is a stylishly written travelogue, in which the 'anonymous' *viajero* (traveller) recounts his journey through La Alcarria, a remote region to the east of Madrid, observing the landscapes and people of his journey and their behaviour, but not passing any comment. His best-known novel, *La familia de Pascual Duarte* (1942, translated into English as *The Family of Pascual Duarte* in 1946), and *Nada* (1944, translated in 1958), by Carmen Laforet, were written in a new type of realism known as *Tremendismo*, featuring an anti-hero and focusing on the ugly, harsh aspects of life, not unlike the work of the French novelist Zola. Cela, by now a member of parliament, won the Nobel Prize for literature in 1989. *La Colmena* (1951, translated as *The Hive* in 1953) is often considered his best novel.

Other Spanish novelists displayed a more traditional type of realism; José María Gironella wrote *Los Cipreses Creen en Dios* (1953, translated as *The Cypresses Believe in God* in 1955), a family saga full of conflict reminiscent of the political tensions that led to the Civil War.

During Franco's regime, some writers produced apparently uncontroversial works which passed the scrutiny of censorship, but which actually commented on Spain's situation between the lines. Two such novelists, Delibes and Castresana, used the device of having children as their central figures, so that the novels would escape censorship on the basis of being apparently children's stories. Miguel Delibes was a journalist who won the Nadal literary prize for his first novel, *La Sombra del Ciprés es Alagarda*, in 1947. He managed to include in books like *Las Ratas* (1962, *The Rats*) some pretty damning implicit criticism of the way Franco's government signally failed to do anything to relieve the poverty of the rural poor, or even to provide any sort of structured help to rural communities to enable them to develop more efficient farming methods.

In addition, what is probably his best and most popular novel, *El Camino* (1950, *The Road*), the story of the pranks and escapades of a group of young boys in a northern Castilian village, portrays a neglected rural underclass in post-Civil War Spain. The road and railway which pass through the village, which could and should provide more of a link to the capital and its prosperity, are perhaps symbolic of how life seems to pass the village by, leaving the villagers standing at the roadside; there is no overt political message, yet there is something ... Another novel, however, is very much for the rural poor and against the landed classes: in *Los Santos Inocentes*, Delibes portrays once again the grinding poverty of peasants working on a large estate owned by absentee landlords, typical of the *latifundio* system of southern and south-western Spain (see Unit 10). One of the peasants in this case gets his revenge on his uncaring boss (this novel has been made into an excellent film by Mario Camus; see Unit 7). Among other novels by Delibes,

Cinco Horas con Mario is perhaps the best known (1966, *Five Hours with Mario*).

Luis de Castresana, yet another journalist by profession, won the Miguel de Cervantes national literary prize in 1967 for *El Otro Arbol de Guernica*: this autobiographical story of young Santi and his sister and friends evacuated to Belgium from a war-torn Bilbao follows these exiles until they are able to return home. Again, there are frequent between-the-lines references – this time not so much anti-regime as anti-war – and the devastating effect it can have on innocent civilians, uprooting innocent children from their environment.

José Fernández Santos is another writer portraying a rural environment in Franco's Spain in which the poor get poorer and the wealthier locals, who undoubtedly support the status quo, are able to exploit their weakness. In one of his best novels, *Los Bravos*, the new local doctor has taken the conscious decision to use his skills to improve the quality of life of the rural poor. He finds himself up against the local establishment in the shape of the wealthiest inhabitant of the village, and he is even confronted by the prejudices of the poorer peasants themselves, many of whom seem to prefer the situation they know rather than to risk becoming even worse off by 'rocking the boat'.

Ana María Matute, writing with exaggerated realism, albeit with lyrical touches, is another author who often uses children as her protagonists, such as in *Los Niños Tontos* (1956, *The Retarded Children*) and *Primera Memoria* (1959, translated as *First Memory*); the latter, set during the Civil War, depicts children trying to come to terms with the conflict tearing their country apart.

Ramón Sender, one of the most important Spanish novelists of his generation, is best known for *Requiem por un Campesino Español* (1962, *Requiem for a Spanish Peasant*), which has very strong political, social and anti-clerical messages. Sender, a US citizen since 1946, wrote a personal account of the Spanish Civil War from the point of view of a counterespionage agent in a novel called *El Superviviente* (1978, translated as *The Survivor*).

Juan Goytisolo's novels also dealt with the social problems of contemporary Spanish society. Among his best-known works are *Juegos de Manos* (1952, translated as *The Young Assassins* in 1959) and *Duelo en el Paraíso* (1955, translated as *Children of Chaos* in 1958).

More recently, Francisco Umbral produced a successful regional novel in *Las Ninfas* (1976, *The Nymphs*), then used the same hero, now situating him in the café world of Madrid, in *La Noche que llegué al Café Gijón* (1977, *The Night that I arrived at the Café Gijón*). This is a combination of reminiscence and 1960's social history.

Post-Civil War drama

There have been far fewer dramatists of merit than novelists since the Civil War. The greatest is undoubtedly Antonio Buero Vallejo, who began writing his realistic plays in the early years of the Franco dictatorship. Like many writers of the time, he felt inclined to criticize the regime, but was inhibited by the strict censorship which was bound to be imposed if he was too overt about it. Typical of his early plays, *Historia de una Escalera* (1949, *Story of a Staircase*) centred on a group of families living on the same floor of a tenement building, followed soon afterwards by *Hoy es Fiesta* (1956, *Today is a Festival*), in which all the characters place their hopes in the ticket they have bought for the national lottery. He chose simply to portray a Spain in which ordinary people lived lives characterized by near poverty, lack of work or prospects and family conflict caused by such external tensions. By implication, Buero Vallejo criticizes the established powers' gross neglect of the plight of the common people. Among later plays *En la Ardiente Oscuridad* tells of a home for the blind whose inmates are mercilessly abused by the director of the institution: the situation is an allegory for Franco's Spain.

Lauro Olmo's plays, such as *La Camisa* (*The Shirt*) deal with social issues later on during Franco's regime, and are not unlike the earlier plays of Buero Vallejo in focusing on the lives of ordinary Spaniards. Other plays of his include *El Cuerpo* (*The Body*), *Inglés Hablado* (*English Spoken*), *Historia de un Pechicidio o la Venganza de don Lauro* (*The Story of the Killing of a Bosom or the Vengeance of Don Lauro*), and *La Pechuga de la Sardina* (*The Sardine's Bosom*).

Post-Franco literature

After the end of the Franco regime, many authors took advantage of the disappearance of censorship to 'catch up' and write their own versions of the Civil War and political events since. A good novel set in the Civil War but which does not favour either side, presenting the trauma of divided loyalties and family divisions, is *La Guerra del General Escobar*, with which José Luis Olaizola won a literary prize in 1983, having already won awards for novels such as *Planicio* (1976) and *Lolo and Cucho*. The novel is the story of a colonel in the Guardia Civil who, following his conscience instead of obeying orders and ignoring his right-wing son, tries to prevent the military uprising in Barcelona.

Who is now writing and reading what

The literary world today is, perhaps, more 'international' than it has ever been before, and there is so much variety that to attempt to describe the current Spanish literary scene comprehensively would be futile. All we can do is try to give you a flavour of what is going on.

Among possible 'great' writers of the present day is Antonio de Villena, whose *La Fascinante Moda de la Vida* (*The Fascinating Fashion of Life*) brings together two books of his short stories: *Para los Dioses Turcos* (*For the Turkish Gods*) and *En el Invierno Romano* (*In the Roman Winter*). Another writer of collections of short stories new on the Spanish literary scene is Félix J. Palma: after a very widely praised first book, he went on to publish *Métodos de Supervivencia* (*Methods of Survival*).

Carmen Martín Gaite is a prize-winning female author of the so-called '50s generation' who has been successful for many years. Her works include the short story *El Balneario* (*The Health Resort*) and the best-sellers *Nubosidad Variable* (*Variable Cloud*) and *Caperucita en Manhattan* (*Red Riding Hood in Manhattan*). She is also a TV scriptwriter. Her novel *La Reina de las Nieves* (*The Snow Queen*) was published in 1999.

Detective novels are popular, as elsewhere, and Manuel Vázquez Montalbán is a popular writer of crime novels, many based on the character of Inspector Pepe Carvalho. A more recent example of a successful crime writer is the award-winning author José Luis Ferris: *Bajarás al Reino de la Tierra* (*You will come down to the Kingdom of the Earth*) is set in 1950s Salamanca.

Within the realms of Spanish literature, one must nowadays include that written in Catalán, Gallego and Basque, bearing in mind the upsurge of use of these languages since the end of the prohibitive Franco era. One of the most notable Catalán authors of the 1990s is Nuria Amat, one of whose novels, *El País del Alma* (*The Land of the Soul*), is set in Barcelona just after the Civil War: it tells of the hard life for a people anxious to preserve their language and culture (and Republican ideals) in times of repression.

The transition to democracy (see Unit 8) was, of course, fertile ground for literary production of a non-fictional nature. Among many other books written about this period is *Papeles de un Cesante* (*The Papers of an Out-of-work Man*) by Leopoldo Calvo Sotelo, president during a short but difficult period in the early days of democracy. In it he describes the political goings-on of the transition, expressing his opinions on people and events, and comments on the present-day situation, particularly with reference to the EU. In a similar non-fictional vein Xavier Rubert de Ventós writes about the *nacionalismos* (the minority Spanish 'nations') in *De la Identidad a la Independencia: una Nueva Transición*) (*From Identity to Independence: a New Transition*).

As with English, Spanish speakers have a tremendously wide choice of literature available to them because their language is spoken – and written – in so many different countries: thus, Latin American authors are popular in Spain. In addition to the well established, such as Gabriel García Márquez, Carlos Fuentes and Isabel Allende, there is a new generation of writers available to the Spanish reader. One example is the Mexican Jorge Volpi, who won the Biblioteca Breve (Short Library) prize in 1999 with a spy novel set in Nazi Germany, *En Busca de Klingsor* (*Looking for Klingsor*).

Fernando Fernán-Gómez is currently one of the most successful playwrights. An early play of his, *Las Bicicletas Son para el Verano* (*Bicycles Are for Summer*), won the Lope de Vega prize and is still performed often. This writer, actor, comedian and film director was made a member of the Spanish Academy in 1998. In that same year he also published a novel, *¡Stop! Novela de Amor* (*Stop! Love Novel*).

Finally, one of the most successful current authors is Antonio Gala, with best-selling books at the Madrid Book Fair in both 1998, with *Más allá del Jardín* (*Beyond the Garden*) and 1999 with *La Regla de Tres* (*The Rule of Three*): this novel tells the story of a bisexual love triangle involving two men and a woman. His first novel, *El Manuscrito Carmesí* (*The Scarlet*

Manuscript) won the Planeta literary prize in 1990. He is a playwright, poet, novelist, essayist and journalist, often writing in the weekly magazine *Cambio16*. His best-known play is probably *Anillos para una Dama* (1973, *Rings for a Lady*). He is also a TV and film scriptwriter. Antonio Gala has the reputation of writing the best Spanish.

At the 1999 Madrid Book Fair the books and authors that sold best were as follows:

La Regla de Tres, by Antonio Gala
La Piel del Tambor (*The Skin of the Drum*),
   by Arturo Pérez Reverte
Lo Raro es Vivir (*The Strange Thing is to Live*),
   by Carmen Martín Gaite
Un Polaco en la Corte del Rey Juan Carlos (*A Pole in the
   Court of King Juan Carlos*), by Manuel Vázquez Montalbán
La Puerta del Sol (*The Gate of the Sun*),
   by Fernándo Fernán-Gómez
Los Rojos no Usaban Sombrero (*The Reds didn't Wear Hats*),
   by Fernando Vizcaíno Casas
Noticia de un Secuestro (*News of a Kidnap*),
   by Gabriel García Márquez

GLOSSARY

la literatura	*literature*
escribir	*to write*
el libro	*book*
(no) me gusta(n) (mucho/poco)	*I (don't like a lot/much)*
me encanta(n)	*I love*
preferir	*to prefer*
leer	*to read*
estudiar	*to study*
ver	*to see, watch (play, film, TV)*
escuchar	*to listen*
el romance	*ballad*
el trovador	*troubadour, balladeer*
el poema	*poem*
la poesía	*poetry, poem*
el poeta, la poetisa	*poet*
el teatro	*theatre (both senses)*
el escenario	*stage*
el actor/la actriz	*actor/actress*
la representación	*performance (play)*

la interpretación	performance (of an actor)
interpretar	to perform
el papel	role
el director	director
la obra	play
la obra de arte	work of art
el drama	drama
el dramaturgo	playwright
la novela	novel
el/la novelista	novelist
el relato/el cuento	short story

Taking it further

Reading

The works of some of the authors mentioned in this unit have been translated into English, and this has been indicated in the text wherever possible. If you do wish to read in Spanish, the best approach is to go for a 'school text' if one is available – that is one which has been set for A level examinations: for many of these there are British editions with a useful introduction, explanatory notes and glossaries.

Listening

For a small handful of the writers mentioned in this unit, there are opportunities to listen to their poetry in the form of song; they should be easily available in Spain, but a specialist music shop in the UK may be able to help. Here are some suggestions: Antonio Machado: Joan Manuel Serrat '*Dedicado a Antonio Machado*', LP of 11 poems set to music. Federico García Lorca: Luar na Lubre *Chove en Santiago*, a poem on 1999 CD 'Cabo do Mondo'; and *Verde*, performed by José Feliciano, taken from García Lorca's *Romance Somnámbulo*, on CD 'Latino'. Rafael Alberti: Joan Manuel Serrat *La Paloma* on LP 'Joan Manuel Serrat'.

Places to visit

There are theatres all over Spain in larger towns and cities. The Corral de Comedias in Almagro has already been mentioned and Almagro as a whole has a great tradition of drama. There is also a school of acting there, so frequent performances are available of Spanish and foreign drama.

Websites

There are some websites which offer information on authors mentioned in this unit, especially the modern ones. One useful UK site is: **www.sgci.mec.es/uk/Pub/tecla.html**. This site, run by the Consejería de Educación (Education Service) of the Spanish Embassy in London, has short articles on dozens of topics, including literature, followed by vocabulary lists and exercises in Spanish.

Extracts from Spanish literature
cvc.cervantes.es/aula/lecturas/

Buying Spanish books
www.spanishbooksellers.com/
www.grantandcutler.com/

04

art and architecture in Spain

In this unit you will learn

- about prehistoric art in Spain
- about early religious art
- about the great Spanish painters
- about Spain's architecture

Ask the average tourist what he/she knows about art and architecture in Spain and the response will probably mention Picasso ('But I don't understand modern art!') and hotels on the Costa del Concrete! Yet, for the tourist prepared to get away from the Costas and, perhaps, to travel around, Spain has to be considered one of the richest countries in the world when it comes to its artistic and architectural patrimony. Curiously enough, Spain is better known for this than for its literary heritage, which is arguably just as worthy. Undoubtedly, with names such as El Greco, Goya, Murillo and Velázquez, Spain has given the world great artists, largely thanks to the wealth contributed by its empire. Ironically, the monarchs who were the greatest patrons of the arts were also the most negligent in the sense of allowing Spain's economic and social structure to fall into decay (see Unit 1). Spain also has a wealth of beautiful and even spectacular architecture, spanning all the main European styles and more besides: uniquely in Europe, Spain has several excellent examples of Arabic architecture.

All of this makes the country ideal for the 'genuine' tourist, willing to travel around independently and explore. Indeed, for some time now the Spanish government has actively been trying to encourage cultural and 'green' tourism in place of the coastal tourism of earlier decades, and thereby attract a better class of tourist – with more money to spend – instead of the traditional package tourists and the notorious lager-louts! Tourist advertising is now focused on Spain's climate and green spaces in the many national parks, and on the artistic and architectural attractions of her towns and villages. Those who have had the courage to explore have been richly rewarded – for reasons which will become apparent in this unit.

Prehistoric art

The cave paintings of Altamira

The earliest known paintings of any sort in Spain (c. 18,000 BC) – indeed among the earliest in the world – are also among the most difficult to get to see. The cave was discovered in 1868 by a hunter whose dog got in through the entrance, buried in undergrowth; in 1879, the daughter of an archaeologist was the first to see the paintings on the low roof of the cave, being short enough to get the view which adults had missed. The ceiling and walls have dozens of paintings of bison and deer depicted in charcoal and the ochres and russetty reds of natural pigments of the time mixed with animal fats. The painters often used the contours of the rock to give a 3D relief effect.

One possible purpose of these paintings was to show young hunters which animals to hunt and how to do so, although some believe there to have been a magical intent: like sticking pins into a wax effigy of one's enemy, to draw an animal with arrows piercing it might have been a way of guaranteeing successful hunting, or of ensuring that the herds would return to the area in numbers as they did the previous year. We shall never know the truth, but the caves of Altamira are a marvel and well worth a visit. A word of warning, however: you have to apply years in advance because the numbers of visitors are strictly limited to avoid the risk of damage caused by the heat and moisture they generate. However, there is a replica of this so-called 'Sistine Chapel' of Quaternary art in the new museum close to the caves, and another in the National Archaeological Museum in Madrid.

Cave paintings

There are also later cave paintings at nearby Remigia, which include humans pursuing animals, and others in the Mediterranean area.

La Dama de Elche

This painted bust of a mysterious woman, the Lady of Elche, dating from about the 4th century BC, was discovered at Elche in the Province of Alicante in south-eastern Spain. Thought to be of Iberian origin, although showing Greek influence, this unique statue is now in the Archaeological Museum of Madrid.

Roman art

Roman painting was almost entirely in the form of the frescoes with which the rich decorated their houses. Although no known examples survive in Spain, it is fair to assume that once there were many; one imagines that they will have been just like those seen today in Pompei or Herculaneum in southern Italy. However, Roman architecture was rather more enduring, and is described later.

Arab art

As with the Romans, Arab art in Spain is to be seen mainly in the decor of the buildings which survive, but unlike Roman art, some Arab art has survived. This tends to be in the form of intricately carved stucco called *atauriques*, wooden and plaster lattice work, *mocárabes* (arch-shaped ornaments), *azulejos*, brightly polychromed tiles and mosaics. The Alhambra in Granada and the *Mezquita* (Mosque) in Cordoba are often visited by the tourist, and both have many examples of these types of art. The most common subjects are elements of nature – flowers and foliage – and geometrical patterns, although the most important elements are the frequent quotations from the Koran. Unusually, there are some actual paintings on leather, depicting hunting scenes, on the ceilings of some of the chambers (*alcobas*, see Unit 2) around the Patio de Los Leones in the Alhambra. One particular attraction in the Mezquita in Córdoba is the beautiful *mihrab*, the holy niche pointing in the direction of Mecca, decorated in gold and stucco.

Early religious art

The Christian religion originally became established in Spain during the Roman era, and from early times, holy figures and scenes from scripture were depicted in churches to support the faith of the congregation, giving them a visual focus for their prayers. Many ancient village churches around Spain have priceless works of art – paintings, carvings and statues – although in recent times some parishes have had to sell such treasures in order to provide the funds necessary to repair the churches themselves. The early works of many of Spain's great artists were painted for churches, and some are renowned specifically for their religious paintings (see, for example, El Greco later in this chapter).

The great Spanish painters

Thanks to the wealth of Spain in the 16th and ensuing centuries, and to the patronage of the monarchy, Madrid became one of the world's foremost centres of culture, attracting artists from abroad and spawning many great Spanish painters. They belonged to a sequence of 'schools' or styles of painting, each generation of painters influencing the next. The first major artistic era we shall deal with is the Renaissance, in which the rediscovery of classical culture led to a new flowering of art, and more sophisticated techniques in painting than the relatively primitive styles of the Middle Ages. This was followed by the Baroque style of the 17th and 18th centuries, using colour to produce graphic and pictorial realism, yet typically elegant and ornate in a balanced way. By gradual evolution, we arrive at the realism and romanticism of the 19th century, before the burgeoning of experimentation and invention of the 20th century.

Here we select a few key Spanish masters from the dozens in each era; there is not space to mention in detail the particularly Spanish art of polychromed wooden statues, so typical of Spanish churches and the Semana Santa and other religious processions (see Unit 6). In some cases, we mention where to find paintings of the following Spanish masters if they are in Spain; the major Spanish galleries are described later in this chapter.

El Greco

El Greco (1541–1614), one of the best-known Spanish painters, was actually born in Crete with the name Domenicos Theotocopoulos. As a young man, he went to Venice, where he worked for Titian and was also influenced by Tintoretto, two great Italian Renaissance painters. From them he learnt the techniques of composition and using colour. He then spent some years in Rome, where he was influenced by Michelangelo's style of depicting human figures. He moved to Spain, settling in Toledo in 1577 because he found the quality of light helped his painting: finding his name something of a mouthful, Spaniards simply called him El Greco (the Greek). He worked to commission, his earliest commissions being religious paintings for churches. He applied to paint frescoes in the royal monastery-palace of El Escorial (see Unit 1), but was turned down by Felipe II himself. El Greco was commissioned to produce *The Disrobing of Christ* for Toledo Cathedral, where it can be seen in the sacristy.

One of his greatest masterpieces, *El Entierro del Conde de Orgaz* (*The Burial of Count Orgaz*), was painted in 1586 for the Church of Santo Tomé in Toledo. In it, El Greco portrays the burial of a 14th-century nobleman of Toledo by two saints, as his soul rises to heaven against a background of angels, saints and important people of the day. You can see clearly the particular style evolved by El Greco, depicting figures with elongated faces, making them look rather gaunt and spiritual: it is said that he modelled them on the inmates of a mental home, their deeply sunken eyes making them look as though they were communicating with heaven.

He also painted very atmospheric views of Toledo and the surrounding landscapes: two other famous paintings of his in the Prado (art museum, Madrid) are the *Baptism of Christ* and *Adoration of the Shepherds*, both characterized by the eerie light generated by the holy figures. He also painted classical subjects, and always signed his paintings in Greek. A wealthy man, El Greco had a large house in Toledo which is now a museum of his paintings and one of the high spots of a visit to that city.

Velázquez

Diego de Velázquez (1599–1660) was born in Seville to a noble family. At first he worked as an apprentice to Francisco Pacheco, a Sevillian painter and married his daughter. During his early years Velázquez was influenced by Flemish and Italian realism, although he is very much a Baroque artist. Many of his early works were 'kitchen pieces' in which human figures are combined with still-life objects. His religious paintings are typified by simple piety, portraying realistic figures for which Velázquez used models from the streets of Seville.

In the *Adoration of the Magi* (1619) which is now in the Prado in Madrid, Velázquez used members of his family (including himself) to model for the holy figures. In 1623 he went to Madrid, and after painting a portrait of the king, Felipe IV, was named his official painter. He produced many portraits of the king, the royal family, and courtiers, although there were a few mythological paintings such as one of Bacchus. He toured Italy to visit the famous art collections, and was influenced by the styles he saw. Back in Madrid, he continued as court painter, but also depicted scenes of battles won by Spanish troops, including the famous *Rendición de Breda* (*The Surrender of Breda*), which is in the Prado. This shows a Spanish general meeting the leader of the defeated enemy after the siege of the Flemish town of Breda in 1624 and combines delicacy of style with visible emotion, bringing this historical event to life.

In later life, Velázquez painted more religious paintings and his renowned *Rokeby Venus*, now in the National Gallery London. His masterpieces, *Las Hilanderas* (*The Weavers*) and *Las Meninas* (*The Maids of Honour*) can be seen in the Prado.

Las Meninas

This intriguing painting of the Infanta (Princess) Margarita and her maids contains several puzzles. For a start, the artist himself appears in it: the left side of the painting is dominated by the partial view of the easel with the artist peeping out from behind, as if in fact he were painting the scene he himself could see through a mirror. Indeed, the painting has in the past been presented to best effect in the Prado: the painting was alone in a room, viewed with the painting behind one's left shoulder, looking into a large mirror on the opposite wall, and with light only coming in at an angle from a partially open window to the left of the painting. This situation is said to have replicated Velazquez' original view accurately, and certainly gave the painting more impact than the more conventional position. The painting has incredible depth, with several 'layers' from foreground to background. In the background, King Felipe IV and Queen Mariana are reflected as shadowy figures in a mirror, such that the whole composition actually portrays the king and queen's own view of the scene ... because they are the subject of the Velázquez in the painting on the easel! Whatever happens, this painting is one of the most influential in Spain, and the inspiration for a series of studies by Picasso (see later).

Murillo

Bartolomé Murillo (1618–1682) was a popular painter of the Baroque period in the 17th century. Born in Seville, he followed in the naturalistic style of his fellow Sevillian painters Velázquez and Zurbarán. His early work was mostly religious, such as the Madonna and the Holy Family. He soon developed his own warm style with his idealized figures lit by soft, luminous tones. This can be seen clearly in Murillos's most frequent subject, *The Immaculate Conception*, of which there are several versions, in the Prado in Madrid (see page 100) and in the Louvre in Paris. He also painted touching scenes of poor children, such as *Young*

Beggar, displayed in the Louvre. Murillo was the founding president of the Seville Academy of Art (1660), and had several students and followers. He had a major influence on later Spanish and European painters.

Goya

Francisco de Goya (1746–1828) was born in the small town of Fuendetodos and went to school in nearby Zaragoza. Later he was apprentice to the painter Luzán and in 1763 went to Madrid. There he was influenced by Bayeu, another artist from Aragón, who was working at the court and who helped him obtain his first important commission, working on frescoes in the Church of the Virgin of El Pilar in Zaragoza. In 1771 Goya went to Italy for a year, and on his return worked on several frescoes. By 1786 Goya was working for King Charles III, being appointed court painter in 1799. He produced cartoon designs for tapestries, which were admired for their realistic views of everyday Spanish life, and which revolutionized the tapestry industry. Also in the 1780s, Goya painted some of his most beautiful portraits of friends, members of the court and the nobility.

His *maja* series, the most famous of which are the *Maja Desnuda* and *Maja Vestida* (*Young Woman Naked* and *Clothed*), are appealing in their warmth and candour. The latter are reputedly of the Duquesa (Duchess) de Alba, with whom Goya is said to have had an affair: the word *maja* almost has the overtones of tarty/flirtatious woman, and the first of these portraits, the reclining nude, supposedly caused something of a scandal. To make amends, Goya produced an almost identical painting, but this time with the woman fully clothed ... he didn't at the time reveal that he had kept the original, and these two charming little paintings are often displayed together in the Prado.

In 1792 a serious disease left Goya totally deaf, a turning point in his career: he became very pessimistic, and this showed in his work. The satirical *Los Caprichos* (*The Caprices*) are prints which mock the social behaviour and beliefs of the time.

Desastres de la Guerra (1810, *Disasters of War*) and later paintings portray the horrors of war, which were of concern to him during the bloody battles of the Napoleonic occupation, in which French soldiers fought Spanish citizens. In 1814 he painted *El Dos de Mayo*, depicting the massacre of unarmed civilians in Madrid (see Unit 1). This famous painting can be viewed in the Prado. Like later paintings, it is composed of lurid colours and black strokes, which heighten the drama of the scene depicted. It was followed up by the similar *El Tres de Mayo*.

Goya's later portraits of the royal family of Charles IV are very homely compared to the more usual formal royal portraits. His self-portraits are appealing in what they show of this very human painter, and are masterpieces in their own right, not just because they are of Goya by Goya. Towards the end of his life, Goya produced the so-called *Black Paintings*, gloomy scenes of witchcraft influenced by his having to leave Spain to escape the oppressive regime of Fernando VII (see Unit 1). He also produced a series of etchings on the art of bullfighting, *Tauromaquía*, and painted many bullfighting scenes. Goya, this most individual of artists, inspired by Velázquez, in turn inspired the next generation of artists in Spain and abroad, including Picasso.

Picasso

Pablo Ruiz Picasso (1881–1973), considered by many to be the greatest artist of the 20th century, and one of the most inventive in terms of styles and techniques was, like Goya, a brilliant exponent of several artistic media. He was incredibly prolific in terms of his output, with more than 20,000 works. Those not familiar with his work often fall into the trap of dismissing it as incomprehensible modern rubbish. A visit to his house in Barcelona, an excellent museum of his art, quickly erases that view, since the brilliance of his technique shines through, starting with his schoolboy sketches. Most unexpected, perhaps, is his excellence in very conventional art forms in his youth.

Picasso was born in Málaga to José Ruiz Blasco, an art teacher, and María Picasso y López. He dropped his father's surname when signing pictures, since his mother's was more memorable (see Chapter 2). Showing his talent early, at 15 he performed brilliantly in the entrance examinations for the Barcelona School of Fine Arts, winning a gold medal with a large painting, *Science and Charity*, depicting a doctor, a nun, and a child at a sick woman's bedside. After three trips to Paris, he moved there in 1904, fascinated by the city's street life: influenced by the French post-impressionists Gauguin and Toulouse Lautrec, he painted people in dance halls and cafés.

From there he evolved the style of his Blue Period, in which the cold tones of his paintings reflected his sadness at the death of his good friend Casagemas: typical is his evocative *Nu de Dos Assis* of 1902 (translated from the French as *Naked Woman Seated, from the Rear*). Many works of this era showed down-and-out elements of society, often with a sort of drawn, haggard look reminiscent of El Greco. From this, he moved on to the Pink Period, from which the most famous picture is *Les Demoiselles d'Avignon*, depicting a group of nudes in pinkish hues in an angular style which already prefigured his Cubist Period. This colouring reflected his happy relationship with Fernande Olivier. He often depicted himself as *Harlequin*. A series of portraits of friends followed, including many of the greats of the Parisian cultural scene of the day.

Inspired by Cézanne and Braques, he developed his Cubist style, applying it mostly to still-life objects. He also developed collage, the technique of sticking objects onto the canvas and incorporating them into a painting. He switched freely – and completely – from one style to another and from one medium to another: *Harlequin* (1915) is a cubist painting, while *Mandolin and Clarinet* (1914) is a sculpture made from odds and ends whilst *La Salchichona* (1917, *the Sausage Lady*) uses an incomplete *pointilliste* technique (little dots of paint) to produce a charming portrait of a young lady wearing her high comb and lacy *mantilla*. His surrealist paintings often have a disturbing quality, such as in *Sleeping Woman in Armchair* (1927). He continued with his Cubist paintings into the 1930s, often of his new ladylove, Marie Thérèse Walter, mother of his daughter Maïa. He also worked on a series of gruesome etchings on bullfight themes, prefiguring the imagery of *Guernica*, the most important work of art of the 20th century.

Guernica (See also Unit 1)

This started as a picture for the Paris International Exposition of 1937. Picasso was lacking ideas and inspiration when he heard of the brutal bombing of the Basque town of Guernica by German planes called in by General Franco. In it, Picasso expresses his outrage at the horror of war, using familiar Spanish imagery such as a bull, a horse, a mother and dead child, a dying soldier, and a woman trapped in a burning building. Its Cubist style and monochrome grey colours make it a most moving portrayal of the horrors of war. For many years it hung in the Museum of Modern Art in New York, until it was returned to Spain in 1981 in fulfilment of a stipulation in

Picasso's will: that it was for the people of Spain, but should not go there until democracy was re-established. It now hangs in the Reina Sofia Art Galley in Madrid.

Picasso's two children by Françoise Gilot, Claude and Paloma, appear in many works. From the 1950s he lived in southern France with the greatest of his loves, Jacqueline. In later life, he based his work on great masters, notably Velázquez: his studies on *Las Meninas* hang in his Barcelona musuem, as does a series of engravings, some rather erotic, which were his last major works before his death.

Miró

Joan Miró (1893–1983) was born in Barcelona and studied at the Barcelona School of Fine Arts. Although his early work shows many influences and styles, he is known as a very original surrealist painter. Often dreamlike and whimsically humorous, his paintings are full of brightly coloured distorted forms: animals, people and geometric shapes, often against plain, greyish backgrounds. He experimented in other media, notably etchings and lithographs, although he also worked in watercolour, pastel, various types of collage, and ceramics.

Dalí

Salvador Dalí (1904–1989) was one of the great eccentrics of the 20th century, and, as with others, there is the danger that in failing to understand him, we miss out on his often amazing genius. He was born in Figueres, Catalonia, and suffered psychological problems due to his awareness of his parents having lost a son before him … also called Salvador. He attended the School of Fine Arts in Madrid in the 1920s where he had many notable friends, such as Lorca (see Unit 3). His paintings from this period mostly depict dream imagery, full of mundane objects in unexpected forms, such as the famous oozing watches in *The Persistence of Memory* (1931). He became the archetypal self-publicizing surrealist painter, exaggerated and often controversial in his own life. Living in the USA in the 1940s, his art became more commercialized, but his later paintings are often on classical religious themes. The most stunningly beautiful is the *Crucifixion* (1954), in which the crucified Christ is seen from above, as though by God, while below his feet lies the world which is redeemed by his sacrifice.

In later life, after years of eccentricity, he settled down, devoted to his wife Gala, formerly the wife of his French poet friend Paul Elouard. He worked in many other artistic fields such as book illustration, jewellery, ballet, films and theatrical sets and costumes.

Much of his work can be seen in the Teatro-Museo Dalí in Figueres, Catalonia. Dalí should be remembered not for his eccentricity, but for his art: to write him off as an artistic idiot is to miss the meticulous and realistic artistry of his paintings.

Where to see them

Spain has many great art galleries, and the houses of several artists have been turned into museums of their work, as already mentioned where relevant. In addition, here is a selection of the best galleries.

Madrid

El Prado

El Palacio del Prado, to give it its correct name, was formerly a royal palace, given to the Spanish nation to use as an art gallery. This huge building houses a collection many times greater than it can display, so there is an almost constant rotation of paintings. It has an excellent selection covering all the European schools of painting.

Centro de Arte Reina Sofía

This gallery, opened in 1992, contains one of the foremost collections of modern art, with works by Picasso, Miró, Dalí and other notable 20th-century artists such as Ponce de León and Gutiérrez Solana. Picasso's *Guernica*, is displayed here – previously it was in an annexe of the Prado.

Museo Thyssen-Bornemisza

This museum contains one of the most important private collections in the world.

Barcelona

This most artistic of cities has many museums, among them the Museu Nacional d'Art de Catalunya, containing one of the world's finest collections of frescoes, and the Fundació Joan

Miró, designed by the artist's friend Josep Lluis Sert to display Miró's work in the most suitable surroundings. The Picasso museum should not be missed.

Bilbao

The recently completed Guggenheim Museum is dedicated to modern art, but the building itself is likely to be the main attraction.

The Guggenheim Museum, Bilbao

Architecture

Spain has an abundance of fine architecture to match its artistic richness, and every major European style is well represented. In addition, two great occupying civilizations, both accomplished in architecture, left their mark in the form of surviving buildings, and have influenced the styles developed in Spain. In the case of its Arab heritage, Spain is unique among European countries.

The ancients

Apart from the caves mentioned earlier, cave dwellings have been found at the Sierra de Atapuerca in northern Spain, and at Nerja in the far south, among others; the latter is open to visitors. Near Nerja, outside Antequera, are the large dolmens, burial chambers of tribal leaders of around 2000 BC.

The Romans

Although most Roman buildings fell victim to the destructive instincts of the Germanic invaders (see Unit 1), others survived, such was the strength of the construction technique used for public building, using massive stone blocks. Imposing aqueducts survive at Segovia and Tarragona. The former still carries water (now in pipes) and one can walk over the latter. Tarragona also still has the ruins of a Roman arena and like many other towns its walls were originally constructed by the Romans. Near Seville, a Roman road can be seen at Itálica. The ruins at Mérida are spectacular.

Romanesque architecture

In Christian areas freed early on from Moorish rule, Romanesque churches flourished, some being built as early as the 8th century, the style continuing to the 13th. The best groupings of Romanesque churches, with their typical ornate, round arched doorways, massive walls and elegant towers are in the cities of Segovia and Zamora. The 11th-century Benedictine monastery of Santo Domingo de Silos, near Burgos, contains an excellent example of Romanesque cloisters.

Moorish architecture

Even before the Arabs invaded, watchtowers were built along the southern and eastern coasts of Spain, including the one immortalized in the name of Torremolinos, whose name literally means tower/windmills. Among the many impressive structures built during eight centuries of occupation, the following stand out.

La Alhambra

The name means 'red palace', and reddish-pink is the colour of the walls of the palace within this massive fortress on a hill overlooking Granada. It was built by the Nasrid dynasty mostly from 1236 onwards, with palaces and *patios* (courtyards) being added at various intervals. The most beautiful parts are the Patio de los Arrayanes (Court of the Myrtles), the Patio de los Leones (The Court of the Lions) and the Jardines del Partal (Gardens of the Partal), although smaller features such as the Mirador de Lindaraja (Lindaraja's balcony) and other *miradores*, the harem baths and so much more make this a veritable treasure.

Just up the hill is the Generalife, a more delicate palace set in yet more beautiful gardens: orange and lemon trees abound, and the sound of the trickling water of streams, pools and fountains is everywhere, a sort of elementary air conditioning.

In the centre of the Alhambra is a massive palace, built for Charles V, contrasting with the elegance and delicacy of the rest. The Alhambra as a whole is best viewed from the old Arab quarter (the Albaicín) on the next hill: from there at certain times of year, it can be seen against the backdrop of the snows of the Sierra Nevada.

Mezquita

The great Mosque of Córdoba was originally built in 787 by Abd al Rahman I, and added to later, including the addition of a Gothic cathedral in the centre in the 16th century. Over 850 columns, many from the Roman temple on this site, and from Visigothic buildings, support a unique double tier of red and white-painted arches (see earlier mention of Mihrab). This is still regarded as a mosque by Muslims, the second largest in the world.

Los Reales Alcázares

The courtyards of this Moorish palace in Seville rival those of the Alhambra, but the setting is less spectacular, being in the heart of the city. On the banks of the Guadalquivir stands the Torre del Oro (Tower of Gold), the surviving one of a pair of defensive towers between which a chain used to stretch across the river to prevent enemy ships sailing upstream. Its name may arise from the gold unloaded here from the galleons, or from the gilt tiles which once clad its walls. Another Arab structure of note is the tower of the cathedral, La Giralda, the only remaining part of a mosque on the same site – originally it was a minaret with the unusual feature of having a continuous ramp rather than stairs, supposedly to allow the ruler to ride his horse to the top of the tower.

There are hundreds more Moorish buildings in Spain, including countless *alcázares* (castles) in the south, such as at Málaga, Almería, Tarifa and Gibraltar. The commanding position of the Gibralfaro high above Málaga, offers a panorama of the city and the coastline for miles beyond.

Architecture of the *Reconquista*

The struggles between Moors and Christians resulted in the building of hundreds of castles and fortifications, especially in the region of Castile, which owes its very name to its castles. Very often, the Christians rebuilt or modified Moorish structures. The most spectacular are:

- The medieval walls and turrets of Avila, constructed in the 11th century and the best preserved in Europe.
- The walled town at Santa Fe, originally a military encampment for the siege of Granada (see Unit 1).
- The church at Montefrío, Andalusia, built by the *Reyes Católicos* to replace the Moorish castle on top of the spectacular crag which rises in the middle of the town.
- The Alcázar at Segovia, originally built in the 12th century, rebuilt in the 15th, and finally again in the 19th after a major fire. Viewed from the valley below, this is truly a fairy-tale castle in Spain.
- The spectacularly solid 15th-century Mudéjar castle at Coca; the Mudéjar style was the work of Moorish craftsmen living under Christian rule, and they evolved a style of ornate brickwork seen in many churches and public buildings, especially in the north and north-east of Spain. Meanwhile, the 10th-century church of San Miguel de Escalada in León is typical of the style known as Mozárabe, that of Christians influenced by Moors.

European styles

Gothic architecture was imported from France and Germany around the 12th century, with its typical pointed arches and soaring, vaulted roofs, supported externally by buttresses. The best examples of Spanish Gothic are in the cathedrals of Burgos with its lacy spires; Toledo, León (all 13th century) and Barcelona (14th century) with strong vertical lines similar to French Gothic, and the latter with beautiful stained-glass windows, while those of Segovia and Salamanca are late Gothic, with a softer, more rounded silhouette. Another famous building in Salamanca is the Casa de las Conchas, a mansion built in the 16th century for a member of the Order of Santiago, whose symbol was a seashell: the main façades of the house are adorned with carved stone shells. The area in Barcelona around the cathedral is known as the Barrio Gótico, and this style is seen in many of its buildings.

The Renaissance brought a return in the 16th century to severe Roman styles of architecture, such as seen in the Carlos V Palace in the Alhambra and El Escorial, whose architect was Juan de Herrera. A disciple of his, Juan Gómez de la Mora designed the Plaza Mayor in Madrid, softening the style to make one of the most magnificent squares in Europe. Meanwhile, an adaptation of the Gothic and classical forms, influenced by Spain's love of decoration and the influence of Arab styles of ornate woodwork and plaster-work, became known as Isabelline style. A highly decorative form of this developed: known as Plateresque, based on the word *platero* (silversmith) because of the finely traced detail, this style tended to be used for interior decor of churches, such as the cathedral of Toledo and the 'new' cathedral of Salamanca and for the facades of public buildings such as the Colegio de Santa Cruz in Valladolid.

The Baroque movement of the 17th and 18th centuries reacted against the severity of the Renaissance in favour of an extremely ornate and exuberant style, full of movement and extravagance of detail. The style was originally developed in Italy, where examples can be seen in the High Altar of St Peter's in Rome. Elements of this, such as the twisted columns, are incorporated into the unbelievably ornate sacristy of the Monastery of la Cartuja in Granada. The Baroque style was developed in an extremely individual way in Spain, where, for instance, Andalusia had its own style. A good example of this is the facade of Granada Cathedral, designed by Alonso Cano, while another new style of Baroque, Churrigueresque, was named after the family of architects who developed it. Other fine Baroque works include the cathedral at Santiago de Compostela, the entrance to the University of Valladolid and the facade of the Municipal Museum in Madrid. Some of the buildings in another great square in Madrid, the Puerta del Sol, were built in this era.

It is appropriate to mention the multiplicity of royal palaces, built mostly in the 18th century for the earlier Bourbon monarchs. The Palacio Real in Madrid, commissioned by Felipe V in 1734, is enormous, ornate, full of exuberant décor and works of art. La Granja de San Ildefonso, on the north side of the Sierra de Guadarrama near Segovia, was started in 1720 by the same monarch, attempting to rival Versailles with the sumptuousness of the palace and the scale of the gardens and fountains. The 'humbler' summer palace at Aranjuez, south of Madrid, was built to replace an earlier palace destroyed by fire.

20th-century architecture

By far the most important name in 20th-century architecture is Antoni Gaudí, a son of Catalonia at the time of its great artistic resurgence in the 19th century. Born in 1852 in Reus, he studied in Barcelona and soon developed his own style. 'Adopted' by the wealthy Count of Güell, he was given total freedom to design a series of buildings and a park – the Park Güell – all of which manifest Gaudí's originality, treating each element as a work of art. The shapes and colours are startlingly alive and fresh, whether in houses such as the Palacio Güell and the Casa Milá, or in his masterpiece, the Sagrada Familia (Holy Family). This as yet unfinished cathedral is of a totally original style: perhaps it could be described as a sort of organic modernist Baroque Gothic, combining as it does so many other elements, yet adding Gaudí's own originality. He was, unfortunately, knocked down and killed by a tram in 1926. His plans and models for the Sagrada Familia were largely destroyed during the Spanish Civil War, but in spite of problems, construction continues. Controversy was sparked by the Fachada de la Pasión (Passion Facade) completed in the late 1980s by the sculptor Josep Subirachs: the weird, sinister figures seem out of place, yet Gaudí would have been the first to say that a cathedral takes generations to build, each adding its own unique styles.

General Franco can be said to have left an architectural heritage: the Valle de los Caídos (see Unit 1) has rather sombre

The Sagrada Familia Cathedral

associations; the hundreds of dams built for hydro-electric and irrigation schemes are testament to what is possible with absolute power. In Madrid, the Plaza de España acquired its current appearance with the massive Edificio de España (1948) and the Torre de Madrid (1957) (see also later). However, the impact of his regime in town suburbs and on the Costa areas has been less edifying, with unregulated property speculation producing truly awful slums of badly designed housing, and ecologically disastrous tourist development.

The architecture of the last decades of the 20th century, however, shows Spain in a much better light. Several major projects were all completed in 1992: the imaginative and sensitive remodelling of the station at Atocha in Madrid, the development of the port area of Barcelona for the Olympic Games, the new airport and station in Seville for the AVE (high-speed train). Madrid has, among others, the dramatic KIO Towers, Bilbao has the eye-catching Guggenheim Museum, and Barcelona and other major cities have benefited from high-quality redevelopment.

Where the Spanish live

Modern-day Spaniards live mostly in apartment blocks, although a striking feature of the late 1990s is the amount of development around large cities of areas of individual housing. Fortunately, one can still see the traditional types of rural housing in the regions of Spain. In the north, one often sees houses with wooden *galerías* (galleries), completely enclosed balconies; enclosed by glass in the case of those in Galicia, the most striking examples being in Coruña.

In Aragón, Catalonia and the Basque Country, rural communities still feature the *masía*, large stone houses in which the animals are stabled on the ground floor and the families live above. In the mountainous areas of the Basque Country the partly wooden chalets are reminiscent of Switzerland. The thatched and whitewashed *barraca* of the Valencia region is not unlike the *teito* of Asturias, while in the remoter settlements of the Coto Doñana there are cottages entirely of thatch: only a few are lived in now, but middle-aged locals remember when most people used to live in them.

The stone houses of Castilla León and the whitewashed houses of Castilla-La Mancha give way to the *pueblos blancos* (white towns) of Andalusia, especially in the Alpujarra, and the area bordered by Málaga, Seville and Ronda, where they cling to the mountainsides or sit atop hills. The Barrio de Santa Cruz in Seville is the best urban manifestation of this style of architecture, with charming, cool patios glimpsed through open doors. The Casas Colgadas of Cuenca perch precariously at the top of a cliff, while at Alagón near Zaragoza, at Guadix near Granada, and in the Sacromonte in Granada itself there are still a few people who prefer to live in cave dwellings ... although these are well constructed, with all mod-cons, cheaper to buy and maintain than a conventional house.

Agricultural architecture in Spain is also fascinating: the *hórreos* of Asturias are square wooden storehouses with tiled roofs, constructed on four mushroom-shaped stilts to prevent rats getting at the produce within. Galicia has a smaller rectangular version built of local granite. The windmills of Campo de Criptana, and the hillside above Consuegra were immortalized by Don Quijote.

Public buildings

Paradores

These are high-quality, state-owned hotels, often occupying a refurbished palace (Ubeda), convent (Alhambra), monastery (Alcañiz) or castle (Jaén), while others are modern (Toledo).

Theatres

The medieval Corral de Comedias in Almagro was built in the style of the innyards where drama was first performed. Among other notable theatres are the Teatro Real and the Opera in Madrid; Palau de Música, Valencia; the Liceo in Barcelona, which reopened in 1999 after being rebuilt. Other buildings of note in Madrid are the Real Academia, Cortes and Biblioteca Nacional.

Stadia

The best known are Nou Camp (Barcelona) and Santiago Bernabeu (Real Madrid). The Olympic stadia built in Barcelona for the 1992 Olympic Games are striking yet elegant.

Bullrings

The best known are the huge Ventas bullring in Madrid, the elegant bullring in Ronda and la Maestranza in Seville; rural communities often have a simple wooden structure.

Bridges

Roman bridges still carry traffic in Córdoba, Seville, Ronda, Toledo and Salamanca, while elegant modern bridges grace Ribadeo, Vigo, Seville and the road from Huelva into Portugal.

Industrial architecture

The cigar factory associated with Carmen still exists in Seville, while sherry *bodegas* (wine factories/cellars) contribute to the elegance of Jerez de la Frontera; that of González Byass has an elegant wrought iron *bodega* designed by Gustave Eiffell.

Monuments

Among the most famous in Madrid are the Bourbon Puerta de Alcalá (Alcalá Gate), the Cervantes monument in the Plaza de España with Don Quijote, Sancho Panza and Cervantes himself, the statue of the goddess Cibeles in front of the elegant Palacio de Comunicaciones, the Alfonso XII monument in front of the *estanque* (lake) in the Parque del Retiro and el Oso y el Madroño (the bear and the strawberry tree, symbol of Madrid in the Puerta del Sol). In Barcelona, the Columbus monument, in which the explorer stands on top of a column overlooking the harbour; in Granada the statue of Columbus talking to the seated Isabel la Católica and in Burgos the statue of El Cid charging his enemy are the most famous.

GLOSSARY

(see Unit 3 for expressions of liking etc.)

el arte	*art*
las bellas artes	*fine arts*
pintar	*to paint*
el pintor	*painter*
el cuadro	*picture, painting*
el retrato	*portrait*
el paisaje	*landscape*

el color	colour
el estilo	style
imitar	to imitate
ser influido por	to be influenced by
la influencia	influence
inventar	to invent
el renacimiento	Renaissance
el romanticismo	Romanticism
el realismo	Realism
el impresionismo	Impressionism
el cubismo	Cubism
el surrealismo	Surrealism
el surrealista	Surrealist
el escultor	sculptor
escultar	to sculpt
la escultura	sculpture
la estatua	statue
la arquitectura	architecture
el arquitecto	architect
diseñar	to design
romano	Roman, Romanesque
árabe	Arabic
moro	Moorish
renacentista	Renaissance (adjective)
gótico	Gothic
barroco	Baroque
moderno	modern

Taking it further

Reading

Spain, Eyewitness Travel Guides (Dorling Kindersley, ISBN 0 7513 0106 X) packed with information and beautiful illustrations of architecture, paintings and plans of important buildings.

Specific painters, Galley Press (*The Masters Collection*), e.g. Spanish painting in general, e.g. *Arts of Spain*, José Gudiol (Thames & Hudson), but thorough, *Treasures of Spanish Art* (Internos, ISBN 848804544X).

Places to visit

Museums, art galleries, buildings and monuments of architectural interest worth visiting are mentioned in this unit. Almost all are open to visitors, entry fees are very reasonable. But beware ... most museums are CLOSED on MONDAYS!

Websites

There are many web sites available on the painters and architects covered in this unit. One useful site is **www.sgci.mec.es/uk/Pub.tecla.html**; in the USA, information is available from the Spanish Embassy Education Office, Washington DC:

www.links2go.com/more/ or
www.spainemb.org/information/ indexin.html.

05

Spanish music

In this unit you will learn
- about traditional Spanish music and instruments
- about Spanish religious festivals and classical music and composers
- about Spanish pop music

Spanish music? What music?

Chabrier's *España*, Rimsky-Korsakov's *Capriccio Espagnol*, Debussy's *Ibéria*, Ravel's *Alborada del Gracioso*, *Rapsodie Espagnole* and, of course, *Bolero*, not forgetting the most famous of all, Bizet's *Carmen*: you could almost be forgiven for thinking that the 'best' of Spanish music was written by foreigners. Splendid though these pieces are, you will see in this chapter that this allegation is patently not true. Nevertheless, it remains a fact that many composers from outside Spain have been deeply attracted to, and influenced by, the rhythms and harmonies of Spanish music. But what about the genuine 'native' stuff?

Modern, Europe-orientated Spaniards will baulk at the old adage that 'Africa begins at the Pyrenees', but where Spanish music is concerned, there is more than an element of truth in the saying. Much of the colour, rhythms and harmonies of 'traditional' Spanish music – particularly that of the south – owe at least something to the eight centuries of Arab presence in the Peninsula. This, mixed with the Mediterranean or 'Latin' characteristics of its inhabitants gives much Spanish music a character distinct from that of other European countries to the north. Even formal religious music tends to look to Italy rather than further north for its inspiration.

While it is true to say that Spain has never produced Bach, Beethoven or the Beatles, over the centuries it has produced a wealth of interesting and enjoyable music, in which there is something for every taste.

Traditional music

Ballads and troubadours

Reference has already been made in Unit 3 to the *romances* (ballads), mainly on historical themes and events, that were sung by *trovadores* (troubadours) or *juglares* (minstrels) during the late Middle Ages. These were both a popular and a court entertainment, and were later taken up and developed by educated writers and composers. At this time the singer was usually accompanied on the *vihuela*. They were included in plays by Lope de Vega and other writers of the Golden Age, and the tradition has been followed through the centuries right down to García Lorca in the 20th century.

Traditional musical instrument, the *vihuela*

Traditional folk music

Because of the diversity of regions and the varied history of so many parts of Spain, it is hardly surprising that nearly every region has its own distinct style of traditional folk music. By this we mean the sort of song that would be sung by the peasants in the fields or sung and danced at the many diverse festivals throughout the year and the country. They are too many to list here in detail, but it is worth drawing your attention to some of the more striking characteristics of certain regions.

On the whole, the music of the north coast, the one region which is separated from the rest of Spain by the Cantabrian Mountains, does not have the rhythms typical of the more southerly areas. The Celtic inheritance of the north-west is evident in the sometimes melancholy tone of the music, emphasized by the softness of the *gallego* language and the fact that it is accompanied by the *gaita*, or bagpipe. More about this later.

The *gaita*, or bagpipe

Ya se van los pastores

Ya se van los pastores

You can even find social history illustrated in some of the folk songs of the north and centre: '*Ya se van los pastores a la Extremadura*' laments the departure of the shepherds driving their flocks south-west in the autumn, leaving the *sierra* '*triste y oscura*' (sad and dark), and, more to the point, the girls without their shepherd boyfriends! (Sheep are in fact still seasonally transported or herded across the Spanish peninsula.)

Ya se van los pastores	The shepherds are off
a la Extremadura (x2)	to Extremadura (x2)
Ya se queda la sierra	And the sierra
triste y oscura (x2)	is sad and dark (x2)
Ya se van los pastores,	The shepherds are off,
ya se van marchando (x2)	they're going away (x2)
más de cuatro zagalas	and more than four lasses
se quedan llorando (x2)	are left behind, weeping (x2)
Ya se van los pastores	The shepherds are off to
hacia la majada (x2)	the fold (x2)
Ya se queda la sierra	And the sierra is left sad
triste y callada (x2)	and silent (x2)

Needless, to say, the Basques have something original to offer. Their music is often accompanied by the *txistu* (a sort of small flute) and *tamboril* (drum). One of their traditional dances is the *zortzico*, notable for its unusual 5/8 rhythm.

In the square outside Barcelona Cathedral any Sunday at midday you will find people gathered in large circles dancing the traditional Catalan *sardana*. Any number of people can take part, in a large circle, and you form another one (concentric if space dictates) when the first has become too big. The music is very distinctive in its rhythm and in the *cobla* or ensemble of instruments which accompany it. The most immediately noticeable of these is the *flabiol*, a kind of piccolo, which always plays the *introit* (introduction). You will also hear the *cornetí* (rather like a bugle), a *tenora* (like an oboe), a *contrabaix* (double bass) and *tamborí* (drum) played by the *flabiol*-player's free hand.

Many traditional songs are performed by *tuna* groups. These are groups of usually male university students who perform in their academic robes and brightly coloured ribbons, either to amuse themselves and their girlfriends, or possibly at a function such as a wedding. Several groups are available on CD and are well worth the outlay.

In Aragon and Valencia the traditional dance is the lively triple-time *jota*, but the region with perhaps the greatest variety of music is Andalusia, with its *fandangos*, *seguidillas*, *sevillanas* and *malagueñas*, all elements of *flamenco*.

Flamenco

Flamenco is perhaps the best-known Spanish music, but at the same time least understood by the non-Spaniard. There is some uncertainty as to its exact origins, but there is clear North African influence, and it has become very much the musical expression of the Andalusian gipsies.

Basically, there are two types of *flamenco*, both accompanied by the guitar. The *cante chico*, which is the vehicle of light entertainment, is played by professional flamenco groups, such as Paco Peña's, both in Spain and around the world. Besides the guitar, rhythmic accompaniment is added by *castañuelas* (castanets) and syncopated hand clapping by *jaleadores*, and the female dancers dress in typical Andalusian costume with bright colours and swirling skirts. On the outer fringes of this type of *flamenco* is the lively and popular *sevillana* dance from, obviously, the Seville area, and the *malagueña* from Málaga.

The *cante jondo*, or 'deep song', as its name suggests, is much more profound. The subject matter is serious, usually about love or death. The words are economical, often just two or three lines, although the song may last for several minutes, usually accompanied by the guitar only and usually sung by the *cantaor/a* (singer). There is a pattern of basic rhythms and *rasgueado* (strummed guitar chords). In a recent interview for the Spanish magazine *Cambio16*, José Menese, a major *cante jondo* performer, remarked about communicating this type of music: '*Para transmitirlo hay que sufrir: si no se sufre, no se dice nada*' ('To communicate it you have to suffer: if you don't suffer, you don't say anything.')

An 'offshoot' of the *cante jondo* is the religious *saeta*, a song of adoration usually to the Virgin Mary. You hear it during the *Semana Santa* (Holy Week) processions in Andalusian towns. When the procession pauses, a lone voice from the crowd or from a balcony will be heard, with all the modulations of the *cante jondo* singer, but without a guitar accompaniment. It is called *saeta* (arrow), perhaps because it pierces the air above the silent crowd. It is one of the most atmospheric experiences of Holy Week in southern Spain!

The Spanish Guitar

Villancicos

Another partly popular, partly 'composer-developed' form worthy of attention is the *villancico*. This kind of song with an *estribillo* (refrain) was developed by Juan del Encina (1468–1529) at the court of the Duque de Alba. Some of Encina's *villancicos* and other songs were of a quite bawdy nature. Many *villancicos*, however, took on a religious theme

Campana sobre campana

and became the nearest Spanish equivalent to the Anglo-Saxon Christmas carol, celebrating various aspects of the Nativity. But be prepared for surprises: no sedate 'Away in a Manger' here – they range from the lyrical to the positively lively! A popular one of the latter type is '*Campana sobre campana*'. Some even have quite earthy and, to Anglo-Saxon ears, irreverent words. In: '*Hacia Belén va una burra, rin-rin*'; a donkey is going to Bethlehem laden with chocolate, and Mary is told to hurry up as thieves have stolen the Baby Jesus's *pañales* (nappies/diapers) and mice have been gnawing Joseph's breeches! (Irreverent but not wholly irrelevant, if you think about it, as the event did, after all, take place in a stable!). These *villancicos* are traditionally accompanied by *zambombas* (a kind of drum with a stretched skin across the top into which a stick is rubbed, making a sort of '*foom*' noise), *matracas* (wooden rattles) and *panderetas* (tambourines).

Villancico: '*Campana sobre campana*'

(*Note*: the English version is only intended as an approximate guide to the Spanish, which is sometimes not easily translatable, and it is not intended to fit the music.)

Campana sobre campana,
y sobre campana una
asómate a la ventana
verás al Niño en la cuna.
(*Estribillo*)
Belén, campanas de Belén,
que los ángeles tocan
¿Qué nuevas me traéis?

Recogido tu rebaño
¿a dónde vas, pastorcito?
Voy a llevar al portal,
requesón, manteca y vino.
Belén ...

Campana sobre campana,
y sobre campanas dos,
asómate a la ventana,
verás al Hijo de Dios.
Belén ...

(Bell upon bell
and one bell more,
look out of the window,
you'll see the Baby in the cradle.
(*Refrain*)
Bethlehem, bells of Bethlehem
which the angels are ringing
what news do you bring?

Having gathered in your flock
where are you going, little shepherd?
I'm taking to the door
curds, butter and wine.
Bethlehem ...

Bell upon bell
and two bells more
look out of the window
and you'll see the Son of God.
Bethlehem ...)

War songs

Another interesting branch of the folk song are the songs which were sung by soldiers during the various wars which have ravaged the Peninsula. The 1936–1939 Civil War gave rise to a number of these. Sometimes traditional songs such as '*No hay quien pueda*' had their words adapted to the circumstances. One of the best known, thanks to Carlos Saura's film of the same name is '*¡Ay Carmela!*' (See Unit 7) This began life sung by the Spanish guerrillas in the Napoleonic Wars.

Classical music

Plainchant and polyphony

Throughout the Middle Ages the main type of music sung in churches and monasteries was plainchant, consisting of one musical line, 'the tune'. It is interesting how the relaxed and soothing tones of plainchant have become popular as an antidote to the stress of the modern world, including the success on CD of the monks of the Monastery of Santo Domingo de Silos in Castile.

With the Renaissance came the change to polyphonic music, that is, the interweaving of a number of independent 'lines' to create harmony. At this time, music for organ was developing, and one of the significant exponents of organ music was Antonio de Cabezón (1510–1566), organist to Carlos V and Felipe II: in fact he played at the latter's marriage to Mary Tudor in England. Cristóbal de Morales (c. 1500–1553) composed a number of polyphonic masses; indeed his '*Magnificat cum quattuor vocibus*' (Magnificat for Four Voices) earned him wide recognition. Another of his works is his '*Missa "Mille Regretz"*', probably written to be performed during Lent. Francisco Guerrero (1528–1599), although living and working in Italy, kept in constant touch with his native Seville. All these composers of church music of the time worked at least for a period either in Rome or elsewhere in Italy, including Tomás Luis de Victoria (c. 1548–1611). They were therefore in touch both with the developments at the centre of the Catholic church and its music and with their native Spain. Victoria wrote motets for anything from four to eight voices and various masses, including '*Missa: O quam gloriosum*'. All these religious composers, of course, set Latin words to music.

This flowering of religious music corresponded approximately to the other aspects of Spain's *Edad de Oro* (Golden Age) of New World discoveries and literary outpourings described in Units 1 and 3. These composers were also contemporaries of Giovanni Palestrina in Italy and Thomas Tallis and William Byrd in England. They are well worth further exploration if your musical interests lie in that direction.

The 18th century

If the music of the Church was heavily influenced from Rome in the 16th and early 17th centuries, popular and court music had continued the Spanish traditions established previously. However, the advent of the Bourbon dynasty in Spain, as already mentioned in Chapters 1 and 3, led to a much greater influence of current European fashion on both literature and music. Two composers of this period are well worth a mention.

Soler

Antonio Soler (1729–1783) was a pupil of the Italian, Domenico Scarlatti, who was resident in and around Madrid. Soler wrote 130 sonatas for harpsichord, similar in form to Scarlatti's, and a number of concerti for keyboard: harpsichord or organ or a combination of both. He was also a prolific musical theorist, explaining among other things, the quickest way to change from one key to another. In spite of this rather academic-sounding CV, his music is lively and compelling.

Arriaga

Juan Crisóstomo Jacobo Antonio de Arriaga y Balzola, or simply Arriaga in the CD catalogue, was born on 27 January 1806, 50 years to the day after Mozart, and was to live barely more than half of the latter's short span. He died of consumption before he was 20, another victim of the apparent short-lived composer syndrome of around this time. Food for thought as to what might have been had medical science been more advanced. Incredibly enough, he produced an opera '*Los Esclavos Felices*' ('The Happy Slaves'), three string quartets, and a '*Sinfonía a Gran Orquesta* ('Symphony for Large Orchestra'). The orchestra for the latter is not particularly large by modern standards, although the score does include trumpets and drums. Seemingly one of Spain's best-kept secrets, there is in fact nothing particularly Spanish sounding about his music, since Arriaga had gone to Paris to study at the Conservatoire there. The symphony sounds rather like Schubert, who was a contemporary, after all, with its restless outer movements and a slow movement that has two glorious song-like melodies, with interplay between strings and woodwind.

The Romantic Impressionists

The second half of the 19th century and the early part of the 20th saw the arrival of a group of composers who were Romantic in the sense that their music was a representation of their personal feelings, and Impressionist in that in much of their music they endeavour to conjure up impressions of aspects of Spanish history, culture and ambience.

Albéniz

Although Isaac Albéniz (1860–1909) was a Catalan, most of his entire work is devoted to his reactions to other parts of Spain, and in particular Andalusia. Much of it is written for the piano, and his '*Rapsodía española*' contains a range of traditional Spanish dances, such as the *jota* and the *malagueña*. His most notable composition is '*Iberia*', also for piano, consisting of four books of 'impressions' of Spain. They are full of colour, vitality, rhythm and technical difficulty, to the point that Albéniz once considered destroying the score as being unplayable. Fortunately, the Spanish pianist Alicia de Larrocha has proved him wrong. The 'impressions' include '*Puerto de Santa María*', '*Corpus Christi en Sevilla*', '*Rondeña*' (i.e., Ronda), '*Almería*', '*Triana*', the Seville gypsy quarter: the pieces become increasingly virtuoso in the fourth book.

Granados

Enrique Granados (1867–1916) was a concert pianist, whose most important work, '*Goyescas*', is the only work for piano to have been converted into an opera. Both piano and operatic versions are based on and around the works of the painter Goya (see Unit 4), and the best-known piece is the aria '*La Maja y Ruiseñor*' ('The Girl and the Nightingale'). Most of his work was for either piano or voice. He actually wrote seven operas, of which at least one was a *zarzuela* (see later). Granados and his wife lost their lives when their British ship was torpedoed as they were returning from the successful staging of '*Goyescas*' in New York in 1916.

Tárrega

Francisco Tárrega (1852–1909) is mainly known for his contribution to the re-establishment of the guitar as a significant classical instrument in 19th-century Spain. Besides writing music himself, he adapted works of classical composers, for example, Beethoven, for the guitar, thus expanding its repertoire.

De Falla

Manuel de Falla (1876–1946) is probably the Spanish composer best known outside Spain, since several of his works figure frequently in the concert repertoire of many orchestras. Maybe it is because he wrote for orchestra, rather than just for piano, that his works have reached a wider audience. Ironically, it was only after living in Paris and coming into contact with the French composers Debussy and Ravel that de Falla realized the potential of his Spanish background. His '*Noches en los Jardines de España*' ('Nights in the Gardens of Spain') for piano and orchestra is to some extent in a similar evocative, impressionistic vein to Albéniz and Granados, in which you can sense the shimmering warmth of an Andalusian evening. De Falla also uses Spanish literature as an inspiration: his ballet '*El sombrero de Tres Picos*' ('The Three-Cornered Hat') is based on the famous short novel by Pedro Antonio de Alarcón (see Unit 3), which in turn was inspired by a folk story of the beautiful wife of the hunchback *molinero* (miller) being seduced by the old and highly unattractive local *corregidor* (mayor-cum-magistrate). It is a complete ballet, although more commonly performed is the 'orchestral suite' which includes '*Los vecinos*' ('The Neighbours'), '*La Danza del Molinero*' ('Miller's Dance') and '*Danza final*' ('Final Dance'). De Falla also wrote a one-act opera, '*El Retablo de Maese Pedro*' ('Master Peter's Puppet Show'), based on the episode of the same title in *Don Quijote*. Other works worth exploring are the opera '*La Vida Breve*', another one-act ballet, '*El Amor Brujo*' ('Love the Magician'), which contains the famous ritual fire dance, and '*Siete Canciones Populares Españoles*' – de Falla's arrangements of some well-known folk songs and some of his own invention.

Turina

The reviewer of a recent CD of a representative selection of the music of Joaquín Turina (1882–1949) described it as: 'An hour's worth of musical sunshine, with the occasional cloud drifting by just for tonal contrast.' Turina was a *sevillano*, who like de Falla, studied in Paris, and came under the influence of Debussy, before returning to Spain. His best-known compositions are '*Danzas fantásticas*', '*La Procesión del Rocío*', '*Sinfonía Sevillana*' and '*Ritmos*'. Although his work is inspired by his native Spain, especially Andalusia, he did incorporate this in rather more European forms, for example the symphony, than his contemporaries. He is not as well known as they are, but worth exploration, nevertheless!

Rodrigo

Joaquín Rodrigo (1901–1999) was another composer who sought inspiration in his Spanish roots. Although quite prolific, he is mainly known for his '*Concierto de Aranjuez*' (another historic Spanish palace and garden, 50 km south of Madrid) for guitar. This piece is not only deservedly famous for the attractiveness of the music, especially the long, langorous tune of the slow movement, but also for the composer's sheer feat of balancing an unamplified classical guitar against the modern orchestra. This is done by accompanying the guitar mainly with woodwind and reserving the heavier strings for the rhythmic undercurrent. You should also look out for his '*Fantasía para un Gentilhombre*' (again for guitar) and his much later '*Concierto Pastoral*' this time for flute, and written in 1972 specially for the Irish flautist James Galway. Rodrigo is an odd mixture of the Romantic, to some extent Impressionist, and yet with a style that has perhaps a more classical 'feel' than those described earlier. He could at any rate be described as the last in the tradition begun by Albéniz and Granados.

TEN SPANISH PERFORMERS ON THE WORLD STAGE

During the 20th century Spain produced a range of musical performers who made their mark worldwide:

Pau (Pablo) Casals	cellist
Victoria de los Angeles	soprano
Teresa Berganza	soprano
Plácido Domingo and José Carreras	tenors (i.e. two-thirds of the 'Three Tenors' – Pavarotti is Italian)
Montserrat Caballé	soprano
Andrés Segovia	guitarist
Narciso Yepes	guitarist
Alicia de Larrocha	pianist
Julio Iglesias	popular singer

Zarzuela

Zarzuela is roughly to Spain what 'Gilbert and Sullivan' is to Britain, *opéra comique* is to France, or to some extent the 'West Side Story' type of musical is to America. It is a sort of light opera, operetta or a 'musical'.

It had its origins in the 16th century, as the first piece to be called a *zarzuela* was '*El golfo de las Sirenas*' ('Mermaid Bay') in 1657. It gets its name from the royal palace outside Madrid, where the present royal family lives, and where the first *zarzuela* was performed. Rather like its English and French counterparts, it had its heyday as an entertainment during the second half of the 19th and early 20th century. There was the *género chico* (one-act *zarzuela*) or *género grande* (operetta of three or more acts). Usually the plot and setting were Spanish, often indeed *madrileño* (in Madrid). Rather like the 16th-century playwright, Lope de Vega, composers had to compose quickly and prolifically to satisfy customer demand. It has in fact been said that some excellent composers were prevented from producing works of a more profound nature by the demands for more *zarzuelas* and the financial rewards available from them. One of the most prolific composers was Federico Chueca, who wrote, among others, '*La Gran Vía*' (the name of one of the main streets in Madrid) (1886), '*Agua, Azucarillos y Aguardiente*' (1897, 'Water, Sweets and Liquor') and '*La Alegría de la Huerta*' (1890, 'Joy in the *Huerta*' – the fertile region of Valencia). These operettas and those of other composers are good entertainment, and many of them contain memorable tunes, e.g. '*Pobre chica, la que tiene que servir*' ('Poor Servant Girl') from '*La Gran Vía*'. They are still performed today, not least at the Teatro de la Zarzuela in Madrid. Many are available on CD, both inside and outside Spain.

Spanish pop music

An inherent problem in writing about pop music in any country is its tendency to be here today and gone tomorrow. It is therefore not easy to highlight the more enduring music and performers. Also the predominant use of English as the common language of pop can have a distorting effect. This predominance is hardly surprising since the original inspiration and marketing have largely been in the USA and to a lesser extent the UK. In fact, one of the early Spanish terms for 'pop' music was *música yeyé*, presumably inspired by the 1960s Beatles' song 'She loves you, yeah, yeah, yeah'. Spanish pop music has, however, developed a character of its own, with, in most cases, Spanish lyrics, and often with the additional backing of instruments such as Spanish guitars and *gaitas* (bagpipes) more recently.

Since the beginnings of amplified pop music in the 1960s, Spain has produced a number of personalities and groups who have made their mark, certainly within the Spanish-speaking world, and sometimes beyond. In the 1960s, the group *Los Bravos* achieved recognition abroad, probably because they sang in English, and *Los Brincos* became known as *Los Beatles españoles*. In the same decade, Raphael, who is still performing, had a crack at both the 1966 and 1967 Eurovision Song

Contest, without success, but at least it helped to make him known abroad. And then in 1968 the female singer Massiel won the Contest with '*La, La, La.*' Some critics said it was as a result of the song's meaningless words in no particular language, but Massiel did deserve at least some of the credit! One of the best known names internationally is Julio Iglesias, whose career as a professional footballer was curtailed by injury, so he became a singer, another Eurovision winner for Spain with '*Gwendolynne*', and heartthrob of the late 1970s and early 1980s.

A special mention should be made of Joan (Catalán for Juan) Manuel Serrat. This *cantautor* (singer-songwriter) began in the late 1960s with records like '*La Paloma*' ('The Dove'), a poem by Rafael Alberti (see Unit 3) set to a haunting tune, and compositions of his own such as '*Penelope*' and '*Tiempo de lluvia*' ('Rainy Days'). In 1973 he published his LP '*Dedicado a Antonio Machado*', featuring many of Machado's poems (see Unit 3) set to music composed by him in a variety of styles. Serrat's own song '*En Coulliure*' commemorates the poet's death in exile in France and its sentiment and nostalgia are worthy of Machado himself.

Although Latin America is not within the remit of this book, the common language has meant that there is a great deal of musical traffic between the countries of the Spanish-speaking world, just as there is between, say, the USA, the UK and Australia. Many of the musical successes in Spain have been equally successful in Latin America, and vice-versa. Songs of political protest by, for example, *Quilapayún*, were particularly in vogue after Pinochet's Chilean coup in 1973, and the rise in the popularity of *salsa*, *merengue* and related music from the Caribbean in recent times has by no means been confined to Spain.

A phenomenon since the 1990s, in Spain as elsewhere, has been the success of female performers. Marta y Marilia sold a million discs in 1996 with their first effort '*Ella baila sola*' ('She dances alone'). Rosario Flores made her first disc in 1992 and in 1999 produced '*Jugar a la Locura*' ('Playing at madness').

Flamenco and Celtic pop

It was perhaps inevitable that there would eventually be a fusion of the very popular *flamenco*-type music and modern 'pop'. In the mid-1970s the flamenco guitarist Paco de Lucía produced '*Entre Dos Aguas*', and Manolo Sanlúcar came out with LPs such as '*Caballo Negro*' and '*Sentimiento*'. *Sevillanas* (see earlier) became a popular music form, with topical themes such as squeezing everyone into the family *seílla* (Seat 600 car) for a day at the seaside. The *flamenco* trend intensified in the mid-1980s when the *sevillano* Felipe González became Prime Minister. Through the 1990s flamenco groups such as *Ketama* fused *flamenco* and jazz in a new style of *flamenco* pop, with even stronger north African influence than before. In the mid-1990s, another style peculiar to Spain was the fusion of harps, Andean pipes and ocarina by Diego Modena and Jean-Philippe Audin. An even more striking Celtic pipe phenomenon is the Asturian musician José Angel Hevia, who had huge sales with his first CD in 1998.

Originally a manifestation of separatist aspirations, regional music has now acquired a following as a result of its own merits and those of its performers, for example, *Luar na Lubre* and other neo-Celtic groups in Galicia. Many Galician groups attend the Welsh Eisteddfod and other Celtic music festivals. The British pop composer Mike Oldfield has used not only Celtic instruments and melodies, but also *Luar na Lubre*'s female singer in 'Tubular Bells 3'. When he was 18, the Galician *gaitero* (bagpiper) Carlos Núñez played in the Irish group The Chieftains: his 1999 disc '*Os Amores libres*' ('Free Loves') combined Celtic and *flamenco* elements. He has also collaborated with the Catalan Joan Manuel Serrat in '*Princesa*'. As he says: '*La música no tiene fronteras*' ('Music has no frontiers').

If you look back over this unit, you may conclude that it never did have frontiers, but that Spanish sources and inspiration from whatever region of Spain do impart something special to the music in question, whether it be written by Spaniards, or non-Spaniards, including Debussy, Rimsky-Korsakov and their associates as we saw in the opening of this chapter.

GLOSSARY

me gusta (mucho)	... I (very much) like
no me gusta (nada) ...	I don't like (at all)
prefiero la música de ...	I prefer ...'s music
asistir a un concierto	to attend a concert
bailar	to dance, perform (i.e. a dance)
tocar (estupendamente)	to play, perform (superbly)
tocar un instrumento, música, un CD	to play an instrument, music, a CD (NB you can't use **jugar** 'to play' in this sense: keep it for games!)
la canción	song
cantar	to sing, perform (a song)
la actuación	performance
la música clásica	classical music
la sala de conciertos	concert hall
oír música	to listen to music
la ópera	opera
un aria (f.) operática	operatic aria
la melodía	melody, tune
la sinfonía	symphony
el concierto para piano/guitarra	piano/guitar concerto
la orquesta	orchestra
el compositor/la compositora	composer
el/la guitarrista	guitarist
las cuerdas	strings
el violín	violin
el violonchelo	cello
el órgano	organ
el tambor	drum
la flauta	flute
el clarinete	clarinet
el oboe	oboe
la trompeta	trumpet
la música pop	pop music
el jazz	jazz
el saxófono	saxophone
el rock	rock
el rockero/la rockera	rock singer/musician/fan
la zampoña	panpipes
la gaita	bagpipes
la batería	drums

el compás	beat, time (in that sense)
el ritmo	rhythm
el baile	dance
el CD (ce-dé), el compacto	CD, compact disc
el elepé	LP, long-playing record

Taking it further

Classical music: a basic Spanish collection

It is not practical to recommend specific recordings, since these would be a subjective choice on the part of the authors, they may be withdrawn with little notice by the issuing company, and in any case catalogue numbers may well not correspond in all countries. Also, of course, the price of CDs varies as do the financial resources of our readers. So choose your recording to suit your taste and pocket out of:

- Albéniz: '*Ibéria*', 'Iberia' (complete or selection)
- Arriaga: '*Sinfonía a Gran Orquesta*', 'Symphony for a Large Orchestra'
- Chueca: '*La Gran Vía*' (or any other of his zarzuelas)
- de Falla: '*El Sombrero de Tres Picos*', 'The Three-cornered Hat' (either complete or 'Three dances from …')
- de Falla: '*Noches en los Jardines de España*', 'Nights in the Gardens of Spain'
- Guitar music: any selection by Segovia or Narciso Yepes; the British guitarist Julian Bream and the Australian John Williams are also highly recommendable exponents of Spanish guitar music
- Rodrigo: '*Concierto de Aranjuez*', 'Aranjuez Concerto' (for guitar)
- Rodrigo: '*Fantasía para un Gentilhombre*', 'Fantasia for a Gentleman' (for guitar)
- Santo Domingo de Silos (Monks of the Monastery of Silos) Plainchant
- Soler: any selection of his sonatas
- Turina: '*La Procesión del Rocío*', '*The El Rocío Procession*'
- Victoria: '*Misa: O quam gloriosum*'

Selections of Spanish and other music by the performers mentioned in this unit are also easily available. Outside Spain, you may need to go to a specialist dealer to obtain a reasonable selection of *zarzuelas* or religious music. The CD departments of El Corte Inglés, the large department store with branches in the main Spanish cities, have a wide choice of most kinds of Spanish music. Their music website: **www.musica.elcorteingles.es** is a wonderful source of information on all types of Spanish music, groups and performers, often giving comments on the CDs. Just type what you need to know in the *buscador rápido* (quick search).

Spanish pop/rock performers

Some further successful performers to look out for in the record shops (mainly from the late 1980s to the present):

- *Groups*
- Duncan Dhu
- Mecano
- Celtas Cortos
- La Oreja de Van Gogh
- Platero y Tú
- Hombres G
- Cabra Mecánica
- Mojinos Escocíos
- Extromoduro
- Marca
- M Clan
- Extrechivato y Tú
- Los Rodríguez
- Seguridad Social
- Triana   }
- Camarón de la Isla } *flamenco* influence
- Ketama   }
- Luar na Lubre   } Celtic (Galician) influence
- Berrogüetto   }

- *Soloists*
- Miguel Bosé
- Miguel Ríos
- Joaquín Sabina
- Tamara
- Alex Ubago
- Jaime Urrutia
- Lole y Manuel
- Rosendo
- Ana Torruja
- Rosario Flores
- Marta y Marilia

Reading

Further details about Spanish classical composers, their lives and works, and other aspects of classical music can be found in: *The New Oxford Companion to Music* (Oxford University Press, 2 volumes); *New Groves' Dictionary of Music and Musicians* (Macmillan (UK) Groves Dictionaries (USA), 20 volumes); *Spanish Music*, Ann Livermore (Duckworth, 1972): gives a full and thorough account of the development of all areas of Spanish music, except pop, up to the early 1970s; *The Gramophone Good CD Guide* (General Gramophone Publications, Harrow, UK), published annually, gives biographical and other useful information about classical composers and their music, besides critical evaluations of particular CDs; *¡Sólo para fans! La Música yeyé y pop de los Años 60*, Gerardo Irles (Alianza Editorial, 1997): in Spanish, it looks back over the early pop years with portraits and details of Spanish groups and performers.

06

Spanish traditions, festivals and customs

In this unit you will learn
- about Spain's annual festivals
- about bullfighting
- about the Spanish lifecycle from birth to death
- about other customs peculiar to Spain

Spain, like any other modern society, is in a constant state of evolution, as some old cultural traditions change and new ones emerge. It may be that given Spain's rapid modernization in the quarter century since the death of Franco, some traditions have fallen by the wayside more quickly than others. There are few countries that are not subject to creeping, or sometimes rampant, americanization, and Spain is no exception. Given its desire to be seen as an enthusiastic participant in modern Europe, it is also subject to 'europeanization' in the sense of catching up with and behaving in the same way as the rest of the affluent western part of the continent. However, with its long and profound Catholic history, mingled with the influence of seven centuries of Arab presence, and not forgetting its warm and reliable climate, Spain offers an intriguing assortment of cultural attitudes and events, some of which have certainly changed little over the centuries and show few signs of doing so, in spite of all the external influences.

Every day a saint's day

As you might expect in a country with such a visible Catholic heritage, there are, if not a festival for every single day of the year, many days where there is a festival somewhere which has its origin in some religious celebration or commemoration.

Almost every day of the year is dedicated to a saint, although not all of them manage what might be deemed 'first team' status. Spanish people traditionally celebrate the day associated with the Saint whose name they bear: so, for example, Miguel (Michael) would celebrate his *santo* (Saint's Day) on 29 September (Michaelmas in English). Although celebration of the *santo* is perhaps not so prevalent as in the past, it does provide an opportunity for a kind of second birthday, complete with good wishes and gifts.

There are also many locally celebrated Saints and Virgins, on whose 'day' there is some sort of festivity in the village, often at the end of a *romería* (pilgrimage or procession), bearing the statue of the Saint or Virgin to his/her *santuario* (shrine). In some cases this may be on the top of a nearby hill, the climb up to it forming part of the homage, and the consequent celebration – usually with food and free-flowing wine – a reward for the effort.

SOME OF THE MORE SIGNIFICANT SAINTS' DAYS		
19 de marzo	San José	St Joseph
23 de abril	Sant Jordi/San Jorge	St George
24 de junio	San Juan	St John
29 de junio	San Pedro	St Peter
7 de julio	San Fermín	St Firmin
25 de julio	Santiago	St James
16 de agosto	San Roque	St Roque
29 de septiembre	San Miguel	St Michael
15 de octubre	Santa Teresa	St Theresa
1 de noviembre	Todos los Santos	All Saints
28 de diciembre	Los Santos Inocentes	Holy Innocents

A whole year of *fiestas*

Let's make a 'tour' of the main festivals through the year, some national, others local. By starting the cycle in February, we won't have to split the Christmas and New Year festivities into two.

Carnaval

febrero

Carnaval takes place in February in the days leading up to *miércoles de ceniza* (Ash Wednesday), the beginning of *Cuaresma* (Lent) and six weeks' penitence and abstinence. Its name means 'goodbye to meat'. The name has, of course, in Spanish as in other languages, come to mean a 'carnival' often involving processions and good fun for all, and this is certainly the way in which it is celebrated all over Spain. Over the centuries, this festival met with mixed approval from the authorities, owing to the tendency of the populace to have a final fling and rather overdo things before the privations of Lent. The actual form of celebration varies, but in places both large and small it often involves some form of fancy dress. In Madrid's Plaza Mayor, there is a fancy dress competition; in Barcelona's municipal markets the stallholders dress up. The greatest spectacles are in Tenerife and Cádiz. In the village of Cogolludo, north-east of Madrid, a man in a white mask anoints ladies with chocolate. Ciudad Rodrigo, in Salamanca province, holds an *encierro*, or bullrun, and the main square is boarded up to make a bullring.

Las Fallas de Valencia

18 de marzo

The word *falla* in Valencian simply means 'bonfire'. The origins may have been a previous Moorish festivity, or may simply have developed from people spring cleaning in mid-March and making a bonfire of unwanted junk: there could well be elements of both. Whatever the precise origin, the festival was established formally in the 16th century by the *Gremio de los Carpinteros* (Carpenters' Guild) in honour of their patron saint, San José (St Joseph), who was, of course, a carpenter. Nowadays the festival consists of processions of tableaux of enormous effigies and figures of wood and cardboard, often satirizing politicians and other public figures or making a comment on social conditions. The festival lasts a couple of weeks, until midnight on 18 March, the eve of San José, when all the effigies, except the one which is judged to be the best, are set alight in an enormous conflagration. The winning one is kept in *el Museo del Ninot*, a museum dedicated to the *fallas*. The figures take months to assemble, and it is said that the work of construction lasts from 29 September (San Miguel) to a few days before the burning of San José on 19 March: a literally constructive way to while away the long winter evenings, but a large amount of both effort and expense goes up in smoke at the end of it!

A falla

Semana Santa

marzo/
abril

Cuaresma culminates in *Semana Santa* (Holy Week). The week begins with *Domingo de Ramos* (Palm Sunday), when in many towns and villages children and grown-ups process through the streets to the church carrying palm fronds. *Semana Santa* is observed in all parts of Spain, but it is in Andalusia where the religious experience is the most profound and the spectacle the most striking. In Seville, Córdoba, Granada, Málaga and other smaller towns, all week long there are nightly processions of penitents dressed in long cloaks and tall pointed *capuchas* (hoods), with slits for the eyes, accompanied by eerie music on trumpets and drums. These *penitentes* (penitents), *encapuchados* (literally 'hooded penitents') or *nazarenos* (literally 'Nazarenes') belong to a *cofradía* (brotherhood) usually associated with a particular *parroquia* (parish church), each with its own coloured cloak. The penitents accompany the *paso* (tableau) depicting a scene from the Passion, *Dolorosa* (grieving Virgin) or Christ on the Cross. These are usually figures carved in wood, often many years old, and very richly ornamented and surrounded by flowers and many large *cirios* (candles) – wax ones, with naked flames, not electrically powered bulbs. This weighty tableau is borne by men four or five abreast underneath: it is not on wheels, as this is a penance! The slow and literally painful progress is regulated by *el capataz* (the man in charge), whose responsibility it is to guide the tableau and procession round some very awkward corners often with overhanging *rejas* (balconies) or *faroles* (lamps). Obviously the procession needs to make frequent stops for the bearers to have a rest and a swig of liquid refreshments. This may provide the opportunity for a *saeta* singer (see page 117) in the crowd to perform. The processions set out from their churches at nightfall for the cathedral, and continue well into the small hours. Each *cofradía* has its particular night to process.

The climax of all this, when all of the *cofradías* are on the move, is the night of *jueves santo* (Maundy Thursday) into the early hours of *viernes santo* (Good Friday).

There are variations on these scenarios in other parts of Spain: in Murcia, in the south-east, the *penitentes'* cloaks have a pouch filled with sweets which they throw to the watching crowds: the religious experience in this part of Spain may be less profound

Penitents

and the festive atmosphere more in evidence. In Seville and Córdoba, nevertheless, the bars do a roaring all-night trade with both residents and tourists.

In spite of the reduced influence of the Catholic Church in modern Spain, and the huge influx of foreign tourists who have little knowledge of the religious background to the spectacle, *Semana Santa* is still celebrated by a large proportion of the population, whether they are practising Christians or not. Shops and offices close at lunchtime on *jueves santo* and remain closed for all of *viernes santo*.

Note that the phrase *Semana Santa* is the expression you would use to indicate the period around Easter, and in schools *las vacaciones de Semana Santa* are what the Anglo-Saxons call the Easter holidays/vacation.

Domingo de Gloria, Pascua Florida or Pascua de Resurrección (Easter Sunday)

After the solemnity of *Semana Santa*, Easter Sunday marks not only the Resurrection usually with *Misa Mayor* (High Mass) in the cathedrals and churches, but the new beginning of normal life: it is traditional to put on *estrenos* (first performances) of new films, plays, etc., also to *estrenar* (wear for the first time) new clothes; traditionally Easter Sunday is the opening of the new bullfighting season. Shops, offices and other workplaces resume normal operations on Easter Monday, which is not a holiday and has no special Spanish name.

La Feria de Sevilla (Seville Fair)

This fair, which has no religious significance, takes place towards the end of April, about two weeks after *Semana Santa*. It originated in the middle of the 19th century as a horse and cattle fair and although this element still exists, the attraction of the modern *feria* is the spectacle of horsemanship, *flamenco* and *sevillana* dancing, and costume: the women in their traditional colourful swirling dresses and the men in their black suits and hats. It is a chance to celebrate the spring, and a notable contrast to the solemnity of *Semana Santa*.

Moros y Cristianos (Moors and Christians)

There are *Moros y cristianos* festivals in a number of towns and villages in south-eastern Spain, but the most famous is celebrated in Alcoy (Alicante province) around the festival on 23 April of Sant Jordi (in Valencian) or San Jorge (in Castilian): i.e. St George, also the patron saint of England, although dragons do not figure in the Spanish context! In Alcoy, the 'contest' is organized on the basis of more than 20 *filaes*, all-male societies, rather like the *Semana Santa cofradías*, although there is no connection with the Church. Indeed their organization with its secrecy bears some resemblance to masonic lodges, and it is said that the *filá* provided opportunities for discussion of forbidden topics in times of political oppression. About half the *filaes* are *Cristianos* and the other half are *Moros*. Dressed in bright and elaborate costumes, they stage processions and mock battles between Christians and Moors. A great deal of money is spent by the members of each *filá* in an attempt to make the best show.

El día del trabajo (Labour Day)

This is a holiday, as it is in most European countries. *Los sindicatos* (trade unions) hold processions in many Spanish towns.

1 de mayo

El dos de mayo

This is also a public holiday, and commemorates the uprising of Madrid against the forces of Napoleon on 2 May 1808. This uprising is the subject of one

2 de mayo

of a pair of famous paintings by Goya. The other depicts the reprisals of the French on the next day, 3 May (which, for obvious reasons, is not a holiday). (See Units 1 and 4.)

Pentecostés (Whitsun)

This is celebrated in churches all over Spain, but the most notable event is *La Romería de la Virgen del Rocío*, which takes place at Whitsun in the village of El Rocío, in Huelva province in the extreme south-west, very close to the Coto Doñana wildlife reserve. The tableau of *la Virgen de la Paloma Blanca* (The Virgin of the White Dove) is carried to the shrine on the shoulders of local men. This is the largest *romería* (see page 134) in Spain, and attracts over a million followers and visitors each year.

mayo

San Fermines

This festival takes place in Pamplona in Navarra over seven days beginning on 7 July. It commemorates *San Fermín* (St Firmin), of Toulouse, who went to convert Pamplona and met his end, tied to and dragged along behind a bull. Hence the association with Pamplona (whose patron saint he became) and with bulls. The particular attraction of the modern festival is the *encierro*, or bullrun, when at seven each morning, bulls are let loose down the boarded *calle Sotelo* leading to the bullring, where they will be fought later in the day. What started as a 'rite of passage' for the young males of the city attired in their traditional white shirt and trousers with bright red sash and neckerchief, has become a major attraction and challenge for large numbers of young foreigners who also wish to try their luck. Needless to say there are casualties every year, and occasional fatalities, since many of the 'bullrunners', especially the inexperienced foreigners, are high on alcohol and consequently low on fleetness of foot. Should you feel tempted, read the small print of your holiday insurance before jumping the barrier! Besides the *encierro* and the bullfights, the city is in *fiesta* mode with all the usual trappings for the whole week.

7 de julio

El Camino de Santiago (The Road to Santiago or St James)

The Pilgrims' Way across the north of Spain from Puente La Reina, where all the routes through France meet, to Santiago de Compostela in Galicia has been in existence since the early Middle Ages.

25 de julio

Tradition has it that the mortal remains of St James the Apostle had been brought to Galicia and were rediscovered in the 10th century. A star is reputed to have led to the resting place in a field, hence *campus stellae*, Latin for 'the field of the star', or 'Compostela'. A shrine was built, which became an immediate focus of pilgrimage and repentance for the many who believed that the world would end in AD 1000. The present cathedral stands on that site. The *Camino* is nowadays well-trodden both by genuine pilgrims and by tourists, and many people do make the pilgrimage on foot or by bicycle on well-marked paths and roads. Besides splendid countryside, there is a wealth of interesting architecture along the route, most of it connected with the *Camino*. The amount of literature on the subject is huge (see the end of this chapter for a selection). St James, or *Santiago*, is the patron saint of Spain, and the war cry during the medieval *Reconquista* from the Moors was '*¡Santiago y cierra España!*' ('St James, and Spain close in!'). St James' Day is 25 July, and a year when this day falls on a Sunday, as for example in 1993, 1999 (a handy coincidence for those who believed the world would end with the second millennium, not the first), 2004 and 2010, is known as an *Año Xacobeo* (*Año Jacobeo* in Castilian). In these years many pilgrims make a special point of arriving in Santiago for that day, and the *Camino* can become very congested, some would say too much so for its own preservation. Those who complete the pilgrimage receive a certificate in Latin as a confirmation of their effort and endurance.

El día de la Asunción

15 de agosto

As in all Catholic countries, the Assumption of the Virgin Mary is a public holiday and most workplaces are closed: make sure you have changed your travellers' cheques on the 14th unless you have a card which will work the *cajero automático* (cash machine). Some regions manage to extend the holiday by also celebrating *San Roque* on the following day, 16 August.

El día de la Hispanidad

12 de octubre

'The Day of Hispanicity (or 'Spanishness')': Spain's National Day, and the anniversary of Columbus setting out on the voyage on which he 'discovered' America. There is a military parade and the King takes the salute.

Todos los Santos (All Saints)

The Spanish do not make a point of Hallowe'en on 31 October, but *Todos los Santos* is observed by placing flowers at the graves of one's relatives who have

1 de noviembre

passed on. An interesting curiosity are the bone-shaped and bone-coloured marzipan sweets called *huesos de santo* (saints' bones) that you can buy in the *confiterías* (confectioners).

La Navidad y el Año Nuevo (Christmas and New Year)

In the Anglo-Saxon world commerce has dictated that Christmas should begin no later than when the Hallowe'en masks and Guy Fawkes fireworks have disappeared from the shops in early November at the latest. Spain, happily, seems not to suffer to such an extent from

24 de diciembre

6 de enero

these commercial pressures, and the shops begin to fill with Christmas goods only around the end of November.

The Spanish celebrate Christmas as any other western country, but there are significant differences from the north European and American ways. Although what might be termed 'universal' Christmas decorations can be bought in El Corte Inglés (the department store chain) and similar outlets, the traditional decoration in the Spanish home is the *belén* (crib, literally 'Bethlehem'), with its manger, *María* (Mary), *José* (Joseph) and *Niño Jesús* (Child Jesus), *Reyes Magos* (Three Kings) and sundry stable animals, shepherds and angels. Christmas trees, although available (usually plastic ones), are not really part of Spanish culture: Norwegian spruces belong to Norway and northern countries of Europe and America! Similarly *Papá Noël* (Father Christmas/Santa Claus), although he figures increasingly on the Christmas scene, owing to the pervasive influence of largely American culture, is not a genuine part of the Spanish tradition. You need to jump to 6 January to see what children traditionally do to receive their gifts. Even Christmas carols are very different (there is mention of them on pages 117–20).

Christmas food, as in all countries, is rich, and many families do cook a *pavo* (turkey), but tend to have it for supper on Christmas Eve, rather than as a Christmas Day lunch. Other goodies are *turrón*, a kind of very sweet nougat made from almonds or other nuts and honey from Xixona, in south-east Spain. You can choose either hard or soft types according to your dental capacity, from a wide variety of flavours. Also popular are *mazapanes* (marzipan sweets and cakes).

Christmas and New Year, day-by-day:

- *24 de diciembre: Nochebuena*, Christmas Eve: special supper: *Misa del Gallo*, Midnight Mass.
- *25 de diciembre: Día de Navidad*, Christmas Day: a holiday, at home with friends or family.
- *28 de diciembre: Los Santos Inocentes*, Holy Innocents' Day: equivalent of April Fool's Day, when you play tricks on your friends and family.
- *31 de diciembre: Nochevieja*, New Year's Eve: *Las doce uvas de la suerte* (the 12 lucky grapes) – in Madrid, crowds gather in the Puerta del Sol, and when the clock on the *Ministerio del Interior* (Home Office) strikes 12, you are supposed to swallow a grape for each of the chimes, and if you finish before or with the clock, you will have good luck in the coming year. You then wish your friends ¡*Feliz Año Nuevo!* (Happy New year!). There are similar celebrations elsewhere in Spain, and of course, many people watch this on television and eat their grapes at home.
- *1 de enero: Día del Año Nuevo*, New Year's Day: a holiday to do what you like. The Christmas festivities have not yet finished.
- *6 de enero: Día de los Reyes Magos* or simply *Reyes*, literally the Kings' Day (Twelfth Night or Epiphany): the Spanish tradition is that in the afternoon of 5 January, the *Reyes Magos* (Three Kings) parade through the town, and that night children leave their shoes on the balcony for the Kings to put their presents in. It is also traditional to leave a carrot or something similar for the Kings' horses! It is maybe worth noting that the majority of Spaniards live in flats, without separate chimneys, so even if Santa Claus were to supersede the *Reyes* he would have to adapt his means of delivery. A further food item traditional of this time is the *roscón de Reyes*, a kind of cake in the form of a ring, containing *sorpresas* (lucky charms).

If you forget to send your Spanish friends *un chrismas* (a Christmas card) before the last Christmas mailing, do not fret. The card industry has not penetrated Spain to the extent it has the English-speaking world, and if you do justifiably wish to convey your seasonal greetings, most Spaniards time it for New Year rather than for Christmas itself, which explains why your Spanish friends' card did not arrive before Christmas!

La corrida (the bullfight)

You will have observed that several of the *fiestas* described in this unit involve the bull, that potent symbol of strength, and to some foreigners, Spain itself. Indeed, the bullfight is known as *la fiesta nacional*. In this sense, the word *fiesta* defies translation, since none of the usual equivalents, 'feast', 'holiday', 'festival', fits, and 'national sport' puts a perverse Anglo-Saxon 'bloodsport' twist on the translation, since the Spaniards do not regard bullfighting as a sport. In the *Anuario El País*, the annual compendium of reports and statistics published by the newspaper of the same name, *la lidia* (another term for bullfighting), appears in the section dedicated to *Arte*.

Whole books have been written on this subject, and it is not our intention to go deeply into the moral pros and cons of bullfighting in the space available here. Suffice it to say that many Spaniards do follow and attend bullfights, and that many of the finer points appreciated by the *aficionado* are totally lost on the casual foreign observer (to that extent, at least, it may resemble cricket or baseball). *La corrida* (another word for it) is regularly featured live on television, and 'results' are given in regular news bulletins. A well-known bullfighter is as much a national household name and hero as his footballing equivalent. (The Spanish for bullfighter is *matador* or *torero* and not *'toreador'*, a term invented by Bizet, composer of the opera 'Carmen', a Frenchman with poor Spanish). One of the latest is the young star El Juli, who went to fight in Mexico until he was legally old enough to do so in Spain. All this is not to say that all Spaniards are avid *aficionados al toreo* (bullfighting fans). Many are indifferent, and a fair proportion disapprove, but are not anti-bullfight activists. *ADDA – La Asociación para la Defensa de los Derechos de los Animales –* (The Association for the Defence of Animal Rights), and other non-Spanish animal protection societies are of course actively opposed. In spite of disapproving noises, however, emanating from the European Union and animal-loving Anglo-Saxons, it seems unlikely that there will be much change to *la lidia* in the foreseeable future. Even an attempt to pioneer the way for women bullfighters bit the dust with the resignation at the end of the 1999 season of

Cristina Sánchez, who had made her name as a successful female *torero*, complaining that the *macho* image and lack of cooperation from the male-dominated organization did not allow her to progress as she should.

Cómo torear (How to fight a bull)

- You will have had several years' training in a special school, e.g. the *Escuela taurina* in Madrid.

- Your opponent, *el toro* (the bull), will ideally be four to five years old, having lived his life on a *finca* (ranch) dedicated to rearing *toros bravos* (fighting bulls), and will doubtless be feeling disgruntled at his sudden removal to the cramped quarters behind the bullring.

- On the day of the *corrida* (bullfight), make sure you arrive in good time at the *plaza de toros* (bullring), since the bullfight always begins on time.

- You put on your *traje de luces* (brightly coloured bullfighting costume)

- You will hear the *clarín* (bugle) which announces the start of the *corrida* (bullfight) and you and other *toreros* lead the *cuadrilla* (parade) which marches into the ring to the accompaniment of the band.

- Then you salute the *presidente* of the *corrida* in his *palco* (box) and march off with the *cuadrilla*.

- The *clarín* sounds again and on comes the bull, followed by the *peones* (assistants on foot) who taunt the bull with cloaks to test his movements; and *picadores*, mounted on horses with protective padding, who prod the bull with their *picas* (pikes).

- If yours is the first fight (usually of six), you then go on with the *banderilleros*, whose task it is to place four *banderillas* (sticks with barbed points and coloured streamers) into the shoulders of the bull to weaken him.

- Time for you now really to do your stuff, making *pases* and *véronicas* (different types of passes), daringly dodging the bull's horns, to the satisfaction of the crowd.

- Then comes the moment of truth, with your *capa* (cloak) and *estoque* (sword), you virtually make the bull bow before you, before plunging your *estoque* into the nape of his neck, and felling him with one stroke.

- If, during this time, you haven't suffered a *cogida*, i.e. the bull hasn't got you first, you have won, and may be awarded *las orejas* (the ears) and/or *el rabo* (the tail) of the bull in recognition of your talent.

The Spanish lifecycle

The Spanish lifecycle is much the same as anyone else's, but there are a number of points of interest. As elsewhere in the western world, many of these institutions are in a state of flux. The following are the traditions, but obviously they will not be observed by the whole population.

El bautizo

Some weeks after birth, you undergo *el bautizo* (baptism, christening). A Spanish person's name includes the mother's surname. So if Manuel's father is Sr Gómez, and his mother's name is Pérez, his formal full name would be Manuel Gómez Pérez. Similarly, a wife traditionally retains her maiden name and hitches her husband's on to the end: hence, Manuel's mother would be Teresa Pérez de Gómez. There is the (surely apocryphal) story of the young lady called Dolores, a common first name, but which also means 'pains', whose *apellido* (surname) was Fuertes (strong). She married a Sr Barriga (a word of about the same level on the crudity scale as its equivalent 'belly'), so she started her married life as *Dolores Fuertes de Barriga* (Severe Belly Ache).

Primera comunión

The next stage in one's life in a traditional family is the *primera comunión* (first communion), when the girls put on a white dress like a bride and the boys a white suit, and there is always a photo to display thereafter in the family album.

Marriage

You can get married *por la iglesia* (in church) or at the *ayuntamiento* (town hall). Afterwards there is a reception, with a many-course meal, a wedding cake, usually an iced sponge of several tiers, which serves as the dessert. You may be entertained at some point by a *tuna* group (see Unit 5).

Death

When someone dies, you offer your *pésame* (condolences) to the bereaved, and if the person is important enough, there will be a black-bordered announcement in one of the national or regional newspapers. Although there are some crematoria, the majority of people are still buried in a graveyard.

'España es diferente' ('Spain is different')

This was the slogan used to attract tourists during the Franco years, when Spain was, indeed, different in many ways from the majority of other western European countries. In spite of subsequent europeanization and americanization, there still remain a number of Spanish customs which make it different from the countries in which the majority of readers of this book are likely to live.

El sereno

You won't see them around nowadays, but you are likely to come across references to *el sereno*. This was the man who patrolled your street-block during the night after the *portero* (doorman) had locked up your block of flats and gone to bed. To get in you clapped your hands loudly in the street and the *sereno* would come along with his bunch of keys and open the outer door for you in exchange for a small *propina* (tip). The *sereno's* original job was to be a kind of nightwatchman and to call the hour and the weather: '*Las tres y todo sereno*' ('Three o'clock and all calm'): hence his name. They died out in the 1970s with fuller employment in Spain and the subsequent installation of electronic entry devices, although some Spanish people might claim they felt more secure in their beds when they were around.

Heating

Still used, although to some extent superseded by central heating, is the *brasero* and the *mesa camilla*. The former was originally a large metal bowl which fitted into a sort of cradle under a small round table of about one metre's diameter. The *brasero* was filled with red hot charcoal and you sat around the *mesa camilla* (table) with your legs and feet under the flap of the thick tablecloth. You can still get electric ones and you often see the *mesa camilla* in the living rooms of older flats and houses.

Drinking vessels

Many tourists return from Spain with one of the traditional drinking vessels as a souvenir. The *porrón* is a glass vessel with a narrow spout used for drinking wine. The *bota* is a goatskin bag also used for wine, and the *botijo* is an earthenware vessel for water, whose porousness helps to keep the water cool. The advantage all three have in common is that you can pass them around, pouring the liquid down your throat, without the spout touching anyone's lips. A great aid to conviviality, perhaps not used so much in the age of fast food outlets and plastic cups, but again traditional vessels to which you will find many references.

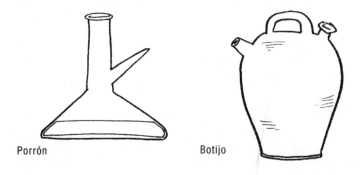

Porrón   Botijo

Bota

Meal times

In spite of various attempts, especially by industry, to europeanize Spanish meal times, little progress has been made, and the Spanish stick doggedly to their traditional times: a very light breakfast when you get up (even taken by some working people in the café near their workplace); *el almuerzo* or *la comida* (lunch) seldom before 1.30 pm and more likely 2 or 2.30, the later the further south you go. Lunch still tends to be regarded as the main meal of the day in many parts of Spain, although commuters into the big cities may settle for something lighter. *La cena* (dinner/supper) is seldom eaten before 8.30 pm and often at 10 or later.

This meal schedule goes a long way towards explaining why the word *tarde* translates into English as 'afternoon' or 'evening', since it represents the period between lunch and nightfall. Also during this interval is the time of *el paseo* (promenade), when many Spaniards go out *a la calle* (literally, 'into the street', but meaning 'out of doors') for a walk and perhaps to have a drink in a bar or on a café terrace with friends or family before returning home to supper.

La siesta

Ask a modern Spaniard if he takes a *siesta*, and he'll probably wonder what you are talking about, as he hasn't time for that sort of thing! Nevertheless, Spain gave the world the word for forty winks after lunch, and the lunch 'hour' of up to, in fact, three and a half hours, still allows in theory for this admirable institution. The word derives from *sexta*, i.e. the sixth hour of the working day. The author Camilo José Cela (see Unit 3) describes an authentic *siesta* as '*en cama, con pijama, y orinal*' ('in bed, with pyjamas, and a chamber pot').

GLOSSARY

festejar or **celebrar**	*to celebrate*
conmemorar	*to commemorate*
el regalo	*gift, present*
regalar	*to give (as a gift)*
la procesión or **el desfile**	*procession*
el baile	*dance*
bailar	*to dance*
la juerga	*binge, 'fling'*
divertirse	*to enjoy oneself*
pasarlo bien	*to have a good time*
el disfraz	*disguise, fancy dress*
disfrazarse	*to disguise oneself, dress up*
la máscara	*mask*
el baile de máscaras	*masked ball*
quemar	*to burn*
la hoguera	*bonfire*
el fuego	*fire (in general sense)*
alegre	*happy, joyful*
solemne	*solemn*
cantar	*to sing*
la canción	*song*
el himno	*hymn*
herir	*to wound, injure*
herido	*wounded, injured; casualty*
correr	*to run*
saltar (por encima de)	*to jump (over)*
el peregrino/la peregrina	*pilgrim*
el peregrinaje	*pilgrimage*
caminar	*to walk, hike*
torear or **lidiar**	*to fight (a bull), to 'bullfight'*
la corrida	*bullfight (i.e. the actual fight)*
la lidia or **el toreo**	*bullfighting (i.e. the art/skill)*
matar	*to kill*
morir	*to die*
la muerte	*death*
la arena	*sand*

nacer	to be born
bautizar	to baptize, christen
casarse (con)	to get married (to)
la boda	wedding
dar el pésame	to offer one's condolences
el entierro	burial, funeral
enterrar	to bury
hacer or dar la siesta	to have or take a siesta

A number of specialized vocabulary items have been introduced at the relevant points in the text of this unit: please refer back to them.

Taking it further

Places to visit

Visit any of the places mentioned in the text at the appropriate time: but remember that during the more popular festivals, accommodation is at a premium, and prices rise significantly. Book early!

Elsewhere you will find that even the smallest village will have its *fiesta* or *romería* at some point of the calendar, and not always necessarily in the summer months.

Your first point of contact may well be the Spanish National Tourist Office in your own country. They should be able to supply you with postal addresses, telephone/fax numbers or e-mail addresses of the relevant local tourist offices in Spain, from whom you should be able to obtain more detailed information, including lists of accommodation.

Outside the actual date or season of the festival in question, there is sometimes a museum or other place where you can get some idea of the activity and the atmosphere. The local *oficina de turismo* will normally be able to help.

Fallas de Valencia

El Museo del Ninot (The *Falla* Museum) in Valencia, in the calle Monteolivete. The official website **www.fallas.com** gives a great deal of useful information.

Holy Week

In the *tesoro* (treasury) of the church of La Macarena in Seville it is possible to see the processional tableaux.

Camino de Santiago

The Cathedral in Santiago de Compostela is open during normal hours, and it is easy to obtain maps and information about the towns and villages along the *Camino* from the relevant *oficina de turismo*. The *Camino* is fully waymarked throughout its length.

Bull-fighting

Most Spanish towns and large villages have their bullring, which it is usually possible to visit when there is no *corrida*. You don't actually have to attend a bullfight to visit them! The bullring at Ronda, in Andalusia, built in 1785, is interesting for both its architecture and the bullfighting that has taken place in it over more than two centuries. Also *La Maestranza*, the bullring in Sevilla, alongside the river Guadalquivir, is one of the more famous ones and will give a fair indication of the atmosphere.

Reading

Because Spain and its traditions and customs are, and continue to be, such a fascinating subject, there is a wealth of literature which deals with the various aspects of the subject. These take the form of travel books of various descriptions, some of which have become classics.

Most guidebooks, especially those devoted to specific regions, will usually give at least basic information about local traditions, *fiestas*, etc.

An up-to-date and often very amusing, tongue-in-cheek, but sympathetic account of some of the more obscure goings-on in 'modern' Spain is Paul Richardson's *Our Lady of the Sewers, and Other Adventures in Deep Spain* (Little, Brown & Company 1998; Abacus 1999).

El Camino de Santiago

There is a huge library about this fascinating subject, since the recurring *Año Xacobeo* (see earlier in this unit) usually gives rise to a new outpouring of literature (and also newspaper and magazine articles and television programmes). A useful selection would include:

The Road to Santiago, Walter Starkie (John Murray, 1957), the classic: Starkie travelled gypsy-style around many parts of Spain, and 'did' the *Camino* four times. He gives a very full account of many aspects of the Way and the people he met along it. *The Pilgrimage to Santiago*, Edward Mullins (Secker & Warburg, 1974): concentrates on the architecture along the *Camino*. *The Pilgrim Route to Santiago*, Brian and Maurice Tate (Phaidon, 1987): for the history of the Way and the traces that can be found along it.

Books in Spanish include:

El Camino de Santiago, J. Mora, J.I. Tamargo and N. Catalán (El País Aguilar, 1993): a particularly useful guide for the walker, published for the 1993 *Año Xacobeo*; and if your Spanish is up to it, two novels based on the history and ambiance of the Camino: *Compostela y su Ángel* (*Compostela and its Angel*), Torrente Ballester (Alianza Editorial, 1999) and *El Peregrino* (*The Pilgrim*), Jesús Torbado (Planeta, 1999).

There are also many interesting and useful websites: just type *Camino de Santiago* into a search engine.

Bullfighting

Bulls, Bullfighting and Spanish Identities, Carrie B. Douglass (Tucson: University of Arizona Press, 1997); *Women and Bullfighting: Gender, Sex and the Consumption*, Sarah Pink; *Blood Sport: A Social History of Spanish bullfighting*, Timothy J. Michell (Philadephia: University of Pennsylvania Press, 1991); *Bullfighting: Art, Technique and Spanish Society*, John McCormick (London: Transaction Publishers, 1998).

Also of interest: *Death in the Afternoon*, Ernest Hemingway (a fictional account by a famous foreign *aficionado*).

The website **www.red2000.com/spain/toros/1index.html** provides useful information on the history and origins of the bullfight, with links to other sites. There are also a good number of sites dedicated to the *San Fermines* in Pamplona: try it in a search engine!

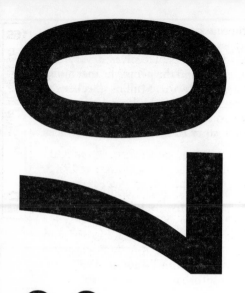

07

creativity in other spheres

In this unit you will learn
- about science and technology in Spain
- about 20th century industry
- about Spain's infrastructure
- about media, fashion, food and drink

When they think of Spain, those who don't know the country will often resort to stereotypes and misapprehensions, and most lack any authentic information about Spain. You have seen in the preceding units how Spain has been responsible for more than its fair share of creativity, and certainly more than most people realize. However, in areas other than the arts, Spain's creativity is not so well known even though Spaniards have been very inventive and productive in certain areas.

Spain has embraced modern technology and ideas readily and enthusiastically; in terms of 'getting things done', the year 1992 was a high spot, with several major events taking place in Spain, all of which needed a great deal of preparation including construction of the necessary infrastructure. These events went so well that many foreign commentators waxed lyrical in praising Spain's organizing ability. But what other highlights of creativity have there been beyond Spain's distinguished heritage in the fine arts?

Science and technology: The legacy

The Arabs

Perhaps even more than the Romans, the Arabs and Moors (see Unit 1) were technologically very advanced for their day, and it is interesting to contrast Moorish Spain with the rest of Europe in the Dark Ages: while life in Europe had largely returned to a relatively primitive state since the collapse of the Roman Empire, the arts, sciences and technology were thriving in Spain (see Unit 1) under the Arabs. Medicine and astronomy were quite advanced; certain areas of mathematics were too, as evidenced for example, in our own use of the Arabic word algebra; the Arabs refined the ancient Persian game *shatranj* (possibly invented originally in India) and introduced it to Europe via Spain as *ajedrez* (chess). Seville had miles of street lights at a time of gloom in the rest of Europe.

The often intricate and delicate architecture and decor seen in Moorish *alcázares* (castles) and palaces is a further example of their ingenuity, especially the techniques of producing *atauriques*, intricately carved stucco and plaster lattice work, and *azulejos*, brightly polychromed tiles. The traditional ceramics industry in some parts of Spain still uses techniques and even kilns first established in Arab times.

Perhaps the most enduring element of Moorish technology is that of irrigation: all over southern and south-eastern Spain schemes were set up, and water flowed from canals into smaller and smaller branching channels, until finally it flowed into the fields to irrigate crops such as cotton – *algodón* in Spanish, derived from the Arabic – introduced into Spain by the Arabs. If they could not use gravity to take the water where it was wanted, they would use giant waterwheels turned by a river to lift water up and into irrigation channels; there is just such a wheel on the riverbank near the Mosque in *Córdoba* (see Unit 4), restored many times, of course, but originally constructed by the Arabs; there are two more near Murcia.

In the Huerta de Valencia, a fertile farming area near Valencia, not only does the irrigation system established by the Moors survive, so too does the ancient *Tribunal de las Aguas*, the water court which sits on Thursdays to judge and punish farmers who misuse the water or draw it off the canals at the wrong times. Other irrigation schemes were set up purely for the sake of earthly pleasure, watering gardens and providing a sort of cooling system as in the burbling water channels and fountains of the Alhambra and its gardens (see Unit 4).

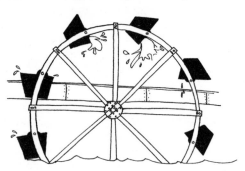

Una noria (a waterwheel)

The navigators

Both Cristóbal Colón (Columbus), who needs no introduction, and the first map maker to make maps of the New World, Amerigo Vespucci (America is named after him), were from what is now Italy. However, several great names stand out from the hundreds of Spanish sailors and navigators involved in the age of discovery. First among them were the Pinzón brothers from Palos de la Frontera (see Unit 1) who were captains of two of Columbus's ships. For these three men and their crews to sail into the unknown was difficult enough, but to manage to sail back to Spain and repeat their voyage proved their competence as navigators. Martín Alonso Pinzón commanded the *Pinta*, and his brother Vicente Yáñez Pinzón was captain of the *Niña*. The latter also led an expedition to Brazil, discovered the mouth of the Amazon, and explored the coasts of what is now Mexico and Venezuela. Their surname has lived on over generations of Spanish sailors as one of the most respected names in Spanish maritime tradition; significantly, the first ever young woman cadet to be admitted to the Escuela Naval Militar (Spanish Naval College) at Marín in Galicia in 1990 was Ester Yáñez, a descendent of this great naval family.

The Spanish navigator who is best known outside Spain is Fernando de Magallanes, usually known as Magellan. Actually born in Portugal, he led the first expedition to circumnavigate the globe by sailing westwards from Europe to reach the East Indies; like Columbus before him, he could not be sure that this was actually possible. He became Spanish having renounced his Portuguese nationality after a quarrel with his king, and in 1517 went to Spain to 'sell' his plan to Charles V. He was successful, and having won support for his voyage, he set sail in 1519 with a fleet of five vessels from Sanlúcar de Barrameda in Andalusia with 50 men. After searching for a passage through South America, he eventually discovered Tierra del Fuego ('Land of Fire', so called because of the fires lit by the natives to keep warm because the climate is so cold!) and what we know as the Straits of Magellan in 1520.

Poor Magellan was killed in a battle in the islands which soon after became known as the Philippines, after the Emperor Felipe II. Even though Magellan did not finish his intended voyage, he is still credited with being the first person to sail around the world.

However, after the death of Magellan, the Basque Juan Sebastián de Elcano took command, to complete the voyage, including stopping off to load up with spices in the Moluccas islands, which had been Magellan's aim. His ship, the *Victoria*, with only 18 crew members left, reached Sanlúcar de Barrameda in 1522, nearly three years after setting sail. Although he is hardly known outside Spain, he is another great hero of the Spanish Navy, and the elegant sail-training ship in which all of their young officers do a sixth-month training cruise is called the *Juan Sebastián de Elcano*. Significantly, this cruise often takes the ship and her crew on a voyage around the world, and its motto, set on a banner over the globe, is *Primus circumdedisti me* which in Latin means 'You were the first to sail around me'.

The significance of this historic voyage is not always appreciated: at last these intrepid Spaniards had proved that the earth is round, and they had been able to measure its circumference, thus defining the meaning of a degree of latitude in terms of distance ... and that one could indeed sail from one ocean to another because the oceans were connected. They even realized that in sailing westwards they had lost a day as a result of crossing what we now call the International Dateline!

Past masters: Spanish craftsmanship

It goes without saying, indeed it is self-evident from the last couple of paragraphs, that the Spanish were excellent and innovative shipbuilders; indeed they still are, but more of that later. Other smaller scale products of Spain were famous centuries ago, and indeed, much sought after. Here we shall mention just three which reflect a high degree of skillful artisanship. Toledo was, and is, renowned for its high-quality steel swords and other cutlery. Other skills and products have largely taken the limelight in recent years, but in past centuries, Toledo swords were considered among the best, if not the best available, and one can still buy miniature Toledo steel swords – souvenir paper-knives – but the beautiful and intricate inlaid gold *damasquinado* jewellery is a more popular purchase nowadays. Highly worked, strong leather from Córdoba was similarly sought after all over Europe, to such an extent that the English language even has its own name for these goods: cordwain, a corruption of *cordoban*. Again, this is a popular purchase among tourists in Córdoba.

Finally, while we are probably all familiar with the lacy black *mantillas* (headscarves) so typical and traditional a part of women's national dress, few of us realize that in past centuries Spanish lace was almost as much sought after outside Spain as were Toledo swords and leather goods from Córdoba.

20th-century industry

Spanish industry has never had an easy time: first, the industrial revolution arrived relatively late in Spain, and then the Civil War largely devasted it (see Unit 1). The isolationist economic policies of the Franco regime gave Spanish industry a protected status, but this actually made matters worse, allowing low-quality goods to be sold at home without competition from abroad. There was dramatic economic growth in the 1960s and 1970s, and industry progressed a great deal. When finally the markets opened up, particularly with Spain's entry into the European Economic Community (now the European Union) in 1986, Spanish industry suddenly had to compete with better quality, often cheaper products from abroad. However, it has survived and prospered, as can be seen in some of the following examples.

The motor industry

Nowadays, although a high proportion of cars sold in Spain are imported, many are actually manufactured in Spain, although in almost every case they bear foreign names. Renault, GM, Ford and others have factories in Spain; indeed, the original Ford Fiesta was produced in a specially built factory in Valencia, and General Motors constructed a factory in Zaragoza specifically to build the Vauxhall Nova/Opel Corsa. There have been great Spanish names in car manufacturing history: Hispano Suiza (literally Spanish-Swiss) and Pegaso were famed for large, elegant cars with powerful engines, but as far as car making is concerned these names have all but disappeared. Pegaso, however, is still one of the leading makes of lorry seen on Spanish roads, known for power and ruggedness.

The nearest Spain has come to having its own mass-market manufacturer is the SEAT company: originally set up by the Spanish government and the Italian Fiat company on the basis of joint ownership, it used to construct Fiat models under licence. In the 1980s, Fiat sold its shares and the German Volkswagen company eventually took it over completely. SEAT used to be known abroad mostly for small cars, but now it has a full range of modern cars which have a lot of engineering features in common with Volkswagen. SEAT cars came out very well in a recent world survey of reliability and quality, being declared the second best manufacturer in Europe. It is interesting that the Volkswagen/Audi design centre is situated on the Costa Brava in north-east Spain.

One Spanish name linked with the motor industry is a rather curious one, associated with one of the world's great prestige vehicles even though the car is not actually Spanish. We are all familiar with the Mercedes, or Mercedes Benz, to give it its full name, yet few people know the reason for its name. Herr Benz

Mercedes Benz admires her father's car!

had married a Spanish woman, and they called their daughter by a Spanish girl's name: Mercedes. Then when Herr Benz created his motoring masterpiece, he named it after his daughter, Mercedes Benz.

Spaniards on two wheels

Italian-made scooters used to be the only affordable means of transport for many Spanish families in the 1950s and 1960s, but Spain has for a long time had its own successful motorcycle industry, with names like Derbi, Bultaco and Montesa. The first of these is best known for small-engined motorbikes, raced with great success on the international motorcycle racing scene in the 1980s by the Spanish ace, Angel Nieto, who was World Champion on Derbi motorcycles in both the 50cc and 125cc classes. Angel Nieto now manages the successful Repsol Honda racing team, using Japanese motorcycles, but sponsored by the Spanish petrol company Repsol (see Units 9 and 10). Montesa and Bultaco produce rugged all-terrain trailbikes, used by shepherds and police to cover rough ground in remote areas, and now popular among off-road bikers elsewhere in Europe. More recently in 1999 Alex Crivillé won the 500cc World Championship and Emilio Alzamora won the 125cc championship.

In the air

Few people realize that the forerunner of the helicopter, the *autogiro*, was invented in the early 1920s by a Spanish aeronautical engineer Juan de la Cierva. The *autogiro* relied on forward speed to make its helicopter-type rotor-blade rotate and thus provide the lift instead of wings. Its conventional engine and propeller provided forward motion, but were not connected to the rotor at all, unlike that of a helicopter. To make the *autogiro* easier to manoeuvre, de la Cierva also mounted a small rotor at the tail, like that of the modern helicopter. Because *autogiros* could climb or descend very steeply on extremely small airfields, they were used during the 1930s for military liaison, crop spraying, mail delivery, and even exploration. Essentially descended from the *autogiro*, the helicopter has now replaced it, its powered rotors giving it the added ability to hover and to climb and descend vertically.

In more recent times, the Spanish aviation company CASA has been a member of the European Airbus consortium, building sections of the various passenger airliners in the Airbus range. The Spanish aircraft industry is also a partner in the Typhoon/Eurofighter project with the UK, Italy and Germany.

On the water

In the middle of a roundabout in the port of Cartagena in south-east Spain, there is a curious sight: a submarine. In fact this is no less than the world's first proper submarine, designed and built by a local engineer Isaac Peral between 1884 and 1887. Unfortunately, when he demonstrated it to the senior staff of the Spanish navy, they refused to back the project.

However, this great maritime nation has had great success in shipbuilding: in the 1970s and 1980s, Spain was one of the world's leading constructors of merchant shipping, particularly supertankers. The nationalized company Bazán, which builds most of Spain's naval warships, has developed an excellent reputation for shipbuilding. In the early 1990s it became the first company in the world to build an aircraft carrier for a foreign navy, winning the contract against fierce competition from Germany and Great Britain: tailor-made for the Royal Thai Navy, the *Chakri-Naruebet* is a slightly scaled-down version of the Spanish Navy's own aircraft carrier, the *Príncipe de Asturias* (named after the Crown Prince). Bazán's computer design facilities and modular construction methods have also produced two of the most modern amphibious support ships in the world, jointly developed with the Dutch.

Infrastructure

On the rails

In the early 1940s another Spanish inventor, Basque engineer Alejandro Goicoechea, provided a practical solution to a physical problem with the financial backing of a businessman, José Luis Oriol. Since this train was introduced to service in the early 1950s generations of tourists may have wondered about the name of one of the fastest Spanish trains, the Talgo. In fact, the name of the company which has built and maintained these unique trains ever since is an acronym: *Tren Articulado Ligero Goicoechea y Oriol* – 'articulated light train (designed by) Goicoechea and Oriol'. The original Talgo trains were low-slung and lightweight and ultra modern for their age, each coach being much shorter than normal and articulated into the next, there being only one bogey per coach: the purpose of this was to enable the trains to travel much faster than conventional trains on Spain's twisting mountainous tracks.

The Talgo company even pioneered a system of hydraulically adjustable axles to allow the train to 'adjust' from Spain's wide gauge to the narrower European track as it moves through a special section of track at the French border: this design has been used throughout the world where neighbouring countries have incompatible track gauges. The innovative design principles of the axles, allowing greater stability and flexibility at speed, have been used in high-speed trains throughout the world. In the 1970s a new version was developed, the *Talgo pendular*, or tilting Talgo. The company has built trains for the USA, Canada, Germany, and several other European countries, while its designs have been used under licence to build trains in Finland, Australia and Japan.

Both types of Spanish Talgo are still in operation, but in 1992 the new AVE train was inaugurated on specially built tracks of conventional European gauge from Madrid to Seville: this high-speed train based on the French TGV (AVE = *tren de alta velocidad*,

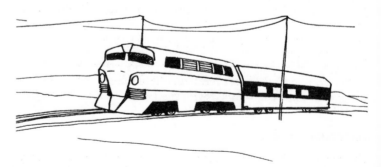

An early Talgo train

high speed train) will soon run on new tracks between Madrid and the Mediterranean at Valencia and Barcelona, from there linking up with the European high-speed network.

On the roads

Spain's roads used to be among the worst in Europe, but not any more. After considerable improvements in the 1970s and 1980s, including the building of the first *autopistas* (motorways) in the north, enormous funds were pumped into road building, much of it grants from the European Community: in the late 1980s and early 1990s, the network was improved in time for the boom year of 1992. This was the year in which Spain hosted the Olympic Games in Barcelona, the EXPO was held in Seville, and Madrid was the European Capital of Culture. Now some of the motorways and *autovías* (dual carriageways), especially in the north where dramatic viaducts sweep across deep valleys, are among the most spectacular in Europe.

The media

The press

While newspapers have been an important aspect of Spanish society, in the past often the vehicle for literary talents, the development of the press in the 20th century has been dominated by the changing political situation. Needless to say, the dictatorship of 1939–1975 (see Unit 1) meant censorship or voluntary restraint, and to read some of the pro-Franco papers of the time is to look into an introverted, bigoted world which now seems curiously quaint. However, after 1966, when censorship was abolished, and with the increasing liberalization of the late Franco years, the nature of the press changed considerably and new, freer publications appeared.

The total freedom of the period immediately after Franco's death led to the phenomenon of *el destape*, literally meaning 'undressing', a term referring to the liberalization of Spanish society, manifested with particular vigour in the press ... and the flood of pornography unleashed gave the term *destape* added significance.

The new daily newspaper *El País* (first appeared 1976) was very influential in the early days of transition from dictatorship to democracy, earning international respect for the responsible stance it took, encouraging moderation and enlightened progress to a new order. Another new publication of the time was the weekly news magazine, *Cambio16*. Excellent and well balanced in terms of its content, and of equally high quality in its design and production, *Cambio16* was one of the key Spanish publications which had considerable influence in South America, encouraging the people of Chile to vote the dictator General Pinochet out of office in the referendum of 1988.

The *quiosco* (newspaper kiosk), so typical of Spanish streets, has a full range of mostly good-quality publications. These publications are now mainly politically independent and tend to be better than some British papers at reporting news from around the world, and not just from Spain. This also applies to regional and local newspapers; there is no Spanish equivalent of the British 'tabloid press', consisting of entertainment rather than enlightenment. However, there have always been satirical publications like *La Codorniz* and *El Jueves* (*Thursday*, which actually comes out on Wednesday!); *Hermano Lobo* was popular in Franco's day; Spanish children enjoy a full range of comics – *tebeos*. Here are some of the most useful publications:

National daily newspapers
El País (politically independent)
ABC (monarchist)
La Vanguardia
El Correo Español
El Mundo

Current affairs magazines
Cambio16 (politically independent)
Tribuna
Interviú (politically independent)
Tiempo

Satire
La Codorniz

Women's magazines
Dunia
Cosmopolitan
Elle
Telva
Marie Claire

Young women's magazine
Mía

Fashion
Vogue

Gossip/society magazines
Hola! (Spanish version of *Hello*!)
Semana

Parents' magazine
Ser Padres

Motor magazines
Autovía
Top Auto
Coche actual (Spanish version of *AutoExpress*)

Regional newspapers
La Voz de Galicia
Heraldo de Aragón
Diario de Andalucía

Radio and TV

Spain has many independent and local radio and TV stations in addition to the national, government controlled company: TVE (*Televisión Española* – Spanish Television) and RNE (*Radio Nacional de España* – Spanish National Radio). Some of the other TV channels and radio stations that are available to Spanish viewers are foreign owned.

As regards radio, *Radio Barcelona* was the first radio station in 1924, typical of this ever 'modern thinking' city. *Radio Nacional* has four stations, numbered rather like the British BBC Radio stations, plus *Radio Exterior de España* which broadcasts to the rest of the world. The SER network has the most listeners, and among the other popular broadcasters are, *Onda Cero*, *Antena 3* and *Cadena Cope*. Of over 1500 radio stations in Spain, about half are private and about half publicly owned. Many of the autonomous regions have their own local radio stations, among them vehicles for the languages of Catalonia, the Basque Country and Galicia.

The quality of material broadcast on television – including a profusion of glamorous games shows and a large number of

South American soaps and dubbed American soaps and films – is patchy, although there are some good programmes. Here are some of the main TV channels available, including some local stations:

A further wide range of programmes is available on Via Digital (Digital TV) and Canal Satélite (satellite TV).

SPANISH TV CHANNELS	
TVE-1	National TV
La 2	National TV, channel 2, also known as TVE2
Antena 3	National TV
Tele 5	National TV
Canal+	National TV
Telemadrid	Madrid and central Spain
TV3	Catalonia
Canal 33	Catalonia
ETB-1	Basque Country
ETB-2	Basque Country
Canal 9	
Canal Sur	Andalusia and southern Spain
TVG	Galicia

Telecommunications and IT

Spaniards are great fans of the *teléfono móvil* (mobile phone): the telephone has for many years offered a good way to keep in touch in this country, in which distances are considerable and families often live far away from their 'real' home. The major Spanish telecommunications company Telefónica is a significant player on the world stage in the field of telecommunications, with very important market shares in Latin America as well as Europe. The Spanish are very 'switched on' to computers and Internet, and even have a nickname for e-mail – Emilio, as in '*Te voy a mandar un Emilio*' ('I'll send you an e-mail').

Cinema

Films are in a sense an additional literary medium of the 20th century, one which was taken up enthusiastically in Spain and which is still very popular, with many new cinemas being opened in recent years. This country has had and still has several great names in the cinema, and some of the greatest creations of Spanish literature have been produced in film. Franco made the most of cinema as a useful propaganda medium, and censorship stifled any balancing of the one-sided nature of political and social and religious references; the only 'true' Spanish cinema was that being produced abroad by people like Buñuel (below).

Few people are aware that Franco himself was very keen on the cinema and was even an amateur producer: he wrote and produced a film which glorified the *Reyes Católicos* ... against whose yardstick of nationalism he wished to be judged.

Ironically, until recently Spanish films, directors and actors were not as well known outside Spain as the many so-called 'Spaghetti Westerns' by Italian producers often shot in the desert-like landscapes around Almería in south-eastern Spain. With its reliable climate and, in those days, a plentiful supply of cheap film extras to play the characteristic hordes of 'Red Indians', Almería became the centre of the Spanish film industry in the late 1960s, especially for the making of Westerns. However, the film industry has moved a long way since then and the list of the most significant Spanish film producers and actors is extensive.

Buñuel

Luis Buñuel (1900–1983), one of the masters of cinema, was a great friend of surrealist artist Salvador Dalí and poet Federico García Lorca when they were students in Madrid. He then studied cinema in Paris in 1925, and in 1929 collaborated with Dalí on his first creation, the surrealist film '*Un chien Andalou*' ('*An Andalusian Dog*'). His best films, several of which won prizes, are '*Nazarín*' (1950), '*Viridiana*' (1961), '*The Exterminating Angel*' (1962), '*Belle de Jour*' (1967), '*Tristana*' (1970), '*The Discreet Charm of the Bourgeoisie*' (1972) and '*That Obscure Object of Desire*' (1977). Several of these are based on novels by Spanish novelists such as Galdós (see Unit 3).

Erice

Victor Erice, born in 1940, was responsible for poignant and beautiful films such as his first, '*El Espíritu de la Colmena*' (1973, '*Spirit of the Beehive*') and '*El Sur*', (1983, '*The South*'), both of which are set in the period just after the Civil War (see Unit 1). More recently, he made '*El Sol De Membrillo*', (1992, '*The Sun of the Quince Tree*'), about a Spanish artist.

Saura

Carlos Saura was, before Almodóvar, Spain's most established director. Among his best-known films are '*Cría Cuervos*' (1975, '*Raise Ravens*'), a study of childhood memories. He also directed '*Bodas de Sangre*' (1983, '*Blood Wedding*'), a *flamenco* version of the Lorca play (see Unit 3), '*Carmen*' (1983, the opera) and '*Ay, Carmela!*', (1990, '*Oh, Carmela*'), the touching story of a small group of travelling players during the Spanish Civil War. Another film focusing on dance is '*Tango*' (1998), set in Argentina.

Camus

Mario Camus made several films, among them '*La Colmena*' ('*The Beehive*') based on the novel by Cela (see Unit 3) and '*Los Santos Inocentes*' based on a story by the writer Miguel Delibes (see Unit 3). He also made a film version of Lorca's play *La Casa de Bernarda Alba* ('*The House of Bernarda Alba*') (1986) (see Unit 3).

Aranda

Vicente Aranda's film '*Amantes*' ('*Lovers*', 1990) was based on the true story of a young man torn between his love for a young serving girl and his lust for an older widow who seduces and captivates him, eventually persuading him to murder her rival for the sake of her money. Another film by Aranda, '*La Pasión Turca*', was very successful abroad, and a more recent film of his is '*Celos*' ('*Jealousy*').

Luna

Bigas Luna directed '*Jamón, Jamón*' (1992, '*Ham, Ham*'), the story of an amazingly tangled web of love and lust set near Zaragoza, and '*La Teta y la Luna*' (1994, '*Tit and Moon*'). More recently he directed '*La Camarera del Titanic*' (1998, '*The Waitress of the Titanic*').

Trueba

Fernando Trueba directed one of the most charming of Spanish films, '*Belle Époque*' (1993, '*Beautiful Age*') the story of a group of young people in love in rural Spain. Another of his films, '*Too Much*', was made in English in the USA, starring Antonio Banderas and Melanie Griffiths.

Amenabar

Alejandro Amenabar wrote '*Abre los Ojos*' ('*Open your Eyes*') in 1997, of which an American version, '*Vanilla Sky*', was produced in 2001 by Tom Cruise.

Almodóvar

Pedro Almodóvar was born in 1951 in a village in La Mancha. His father was a worker on some of Franco's grand building projects (see Unit 1) and the family moved around a lot. Almodóvar was educated in a seminary, but in 1967 ended up as a clerical worker in Telefónica (the Spanish telephone company) in Madrid. Having been fascinated as a child by the Hollywood epics often shown in village halls, he became an amateur film maker, as well as playing in a rock band, writing comic strips and joining an avant-garde theatre group. He did everything for his early films, writing scripts, operating the camera and using his own voice to record the soundtrack, and from an early stage he identified himself with the era of *destape* (see Unit 8). His early feature films, '*Pepi, Luci, Bom*' (1980) and '*¿Qué He Hecho Yo Para Merecer Esto?*' (1985, '*What Have I Done to Deserve This?*') are engagingly outrageous and ironically humorous. '*Mujeres al Borde de un Ataque de Nervios*' (1988, '*Women on the Verge of a Nervous Breakdown*') is chaotically hilarious, portraying the difficulties of women coping with new-found freedom. Women and their problems often feature in his films, and for a number of years he had a group of favourite actresses; he has also written parts for his own mother into his films, and almost always appears himself at some stage.

Always courting controversy, Almodóvar's themes in '*Matador*' (1986), '*Laberinto de Pasión*' ('*Labyrinth of Passion*') and '*La Ley del Deseo*' (1987, 'Law and Desire') '*¡Atame!*' (1990, '*Tie Me Up! Tie Me Down!*'), '*Tacones Lejanos*' (1991, '*High Heels*'), '*Kika*' (1994), are satirical and provocative, while his larger-than-life kitsch style is balanced by intriguing plots and characterization. Later films like '*La Flor de mi Secreto*' (1995, '*The Flower of My Secret*') and '*Carne Trémula*' ('*Trembling Flesh*'), are more conventional in some ways, but display his mastery of cinematographic technique.

Almodóvar is one of the most popular Spanish film directors outside Spain, and in recent years has often worked in Hollywood, fulfilling his childhood dream. His 1999 film '*Todo sobre mi Madre*' ('*All About My Mother*') has been hailed by critics as 'grown-up' Almodóvar. More recent films include '*Hable con ella*' ('*Speak to her*', 2002) and '*My Life without me*' (2003), his first film in English.

Rey

Fernando Rey (1917–1995) made a name for himself in the films of Luis Buñuel such as '*Viridiana*', '*Tristana*', and '*Ese*'

Oscuro Objeto del Deseo' ('*That Obscure Object of Desire*') in which, typically, he played the part of the archetypal elegant and well-educated Spanish gentleman.

Abril

Victoria Abril, for many years a well-established Spanish actress, is known for being not just a good actress but also glamorous and impishly seductive, as in her rather erotic leading role in '*Amantes*'. She is now often seen on film and television; still a popular actress, among her recent films was '*Tu Nombre Envenena Mis Sueños*' (1998, '*Your Name Poisons My Dreams*').

Torrent

Ana Torrent was one of the two child stars of Victor Erice's '*The Spirit of the Beehive*' in 1973, and then in Carlos Saura's film '*Cría Cuervos*' in 1975. After a teenage career mostly in television, she has since become a very successful actress, one of her best films possibly being '*Sangre y Arena*' (1989, '*Blood and Sand*').

Belén

Ana Belén is another actress who started very young. She had a starring role in the Mario Camus film version of Lorca's play '*La Casa de Bernarda Alba*' (1986) (see Unit 3) and among her other major films is Vicente Aranda's '*La Pasión Turca*'.

Maura

Carmen Maura was born in Madrid in 1946 and studied at Madrid University. She owned a small art gallery in Madrid but decided in 1971 to become an actress. It was when she was a member of an avant-garde theatre group in Madrid that she met Pedro Almodóvar in 1976. She starred in '*Pepi, Luci, Bom*' (1980), and in five more Almodóvar films, becoming Spain's most popular actress. Along with Bibi Andersen, Cecilia Roth, Rossy de Palma and others, she was one of the group of actresses called *Chicas de Almodóvar* (the Almodóvar Girls), who usually featured in this director's films. Carmen Maura worked with Spain's most established director, Carlos Saura, in '*¡Ay, Carmela!*' (the name of a popular song of the Spanish Civil War, in which the story is set), for which Maura won the 1990 best actress Felix Award, the European equivalent of the Oscar.

Banderas

Antonio Banderas also began working for Almodóvar, playing leading male roles in several films in which his Latin masculine good looks were exploited to the full. After a supporting role in '*Interview with the Vampire*', be became a Hollywood heartthrob, later marrying Melanie Griffiths and starring in other American films like '*Zorro*'.

Bardem

After a supporting role in '*Edades de Lulú*' ('*Ages of Lulu*'), Javier Bardem came to the fore in the early 1990s, winning prizes early in his career for '*El Detective y la Muerte*' and '*Días Contados*'. He then moved on to star in Almodóvar films such as '*Carne Tremula*' (1999, '*Trembling Flesh*'). Among his latest films is '*Tu Nombre Envenena Mis Sueños*' (1998, '*Your Name Poisons my Dreams*').

Cruz

Penélope Cruz began work as a dancer, but her best films include '*Jamón, Jamón*' ('*Ham, Ham*', 1992), '*Belle Époque*' ('*The Age of Beauty*', 1993), '*Todo sobre mi Madre*' ('*All about my Mother*', 1999) and '*Abre los Ojos*' ('*Open your Eyes*', 1997), produced as '*Vanilla Sky*' in 2001.

Fashion

Spain has been a late starter in terms of its influence on world fashion, though there has been a handful of top names. Significantly since the death of General Franco, Spain's new-found prosperity and cultural importance had led to the growth of Madrid as an exciting new fashion centre in the 1980s and 1990s. Not only is there a new generation of exciting and innovative young fashion designers: even foreign designers often take their shows to Madrid, considering it an important venue, and making use of the large number of excellent Spanish fashion models. Here are a few of the great names of Spanish fashion.

Cristóbal Balenciaga was born in 1895. Inspired by the art of El Greco and Goya (see Unit 4), his designs were quite revolutionary and spectacular when he started. Gaining a solid reputation as a traditional Spanish couturier, he is quoted as saying that no woman can make herself appear chic if she is not chic in herself. He retired in 1968.

Antonio Castillo, born in 1908 to a noble family, left for France at the outbreak of the Spanish Civil War (see Unit 1) in 1936, where he trained with Chanel. He exploited the risqué potential of black lace, but his classic designs were characterized by dignity and regal elegance, neatness and tradition.

Adolfo Domínguez could be said to be the Spanish equivalent of the Italian designer Giorgio Armani. He was not traditionally trained, but was a film maker and author as well. He introduced his first men's clothes collection in 1982, and his first women's collection in 1992 in Madrid. In the 1980s he was often known as the 'king of the wrinklies' because of his use of wrinkly fabric for his designs of men's clothing.

John Galliano, strictly speaking not a Spaniard, being from Gibraltar, was greatly influenced by French couturiers, having been a designer with Givenchy and Dior.

Paco Rabanne was born in San Sebastián and studied architecture in Paris. Turning to fashion, he opened his fashion house in 1966 and is known for space-age fashion and using experimental materials.

Jesús del Pozo trained as an engineer, and then became an artist and designed interiors. He opened his own menswear shop in 1974, then began catering for women in 1980.

Other modern Spanish fashion designers to watch are: *Vittorio y Luchino* (from Seville, even though their names seem Italian), *Vera Medem*, *Roberto Verino* and *Agatha Ruiz de la Prada*, who has a reputation for being rather eccentric.

Mango is, essentially, a complete fashion business, consisting of the whole enterprise from designer and dressmakers through to the retail outlets. The first shop opened in Barcelona in the early 1980s, and Mango now has shops not only all over Spain, but also abroad: indeed, sales abroad in the late 1990s began to exceed those in Spain, making Mango the second most important exporter of clothes in Spain. The company's success is attributed to the fact that almost all of the employees are young, average age 25, and 75 per cent women, and to the fact that it produces its own clothes in line with its own characteristic image.

Food and drink

Spain exports a wide range of produce, particularly fruit and vegetables. Thanks to its favourable climate and position in south-western Europe, Spain is able to provide many types of fruit and vegetables earlier in the season, exporting them to more northerly European countries. In southern Spain particularly, there are acres of plastic greenhouses under which tons of tomatoes, melons and peaches and other products are grown. Spain is a major world producer of olive oil, wine and seafood. Thus, many Spanish culinary products figure in the larders and refrigerators of European homes.

However, although most tourists and even people who have not visited Spain know the names of a few Spanish dishes, the tourist trade has in some ways prevented Spanish cuisine from becoming well known. This is because so many large tourist hotels tend to serve 'international' buffet food, to ensure that all of their clients will find something 'safe' to eat. One shudders to think of the number of tourists whose only experience of Spanish dishes and drinks has been sanitized *paella* and *sangría* (see later in this section) served up on an excursion to a *flamenco* and bullfighting show. The more adventurous tourist who ventures into the old town centres, and follows the locals into restaurants in side streets or in the back room of bars will be rewarded with a much more interesting – and usually cheaper – gastronomic experience.

La cocina española: Healthy eating

The typical diet in most areas of Spain is a very healthy one, as proved by the fact that Spaniards have a higher life expectancy than almost any other country. The elements which figure strongly in the Spanish diet, olive oil, garlic, red wine, and good-quality fruit and vegetables coupled with the popularity of fish and seafood, all contribute to healthy eating.

Platos típicos

Here is a brief description of a small selection of traditional Spanish dishes: it should be borne in mind that the details of any recipe vary from region to region, and according to personal taste! These are given as examples only. For more details and more dishes, a good Spanish cookbook is essential (one is recommended at the end of this chapter):

- *albóndigas en salsa*: meat balls cooked in a delicious sherry sauce
- *calamares fritos*: squid rings fried in light batter, best served with a drop of lemon juice
- *churros*: thin, slightly crispy doughnuts, ideal for 'dunking' in coffee, or better, hot chocolate; can be ordered in cafés and bought in special shops (*churrería*) at breakfast time or at stalls during *fiesta* time

- *cocido de garbanzos*: a very basic dish – chickpea and vegetable stew
- *cocido de lentejas*: another basic but nourishing stew, this time of lentils
- *gazpacho*: this is a chilled vegetable soup, most popular in Andalusia
- *fabada asturiana*: a delicious, almost earthy bean stew, typical of Asturias in north-western Spain; available in tins in Spanish supermarkets
- *huevos al plato*: eggs baked in an earthenware dish with tomato and vegetables, simple but tasty
- *pollo al ajillo*: chicken roasted with garlic
- *riñones al jerez*: tiny, tender kidneys cooked in a delicate sherry and tomato sauce
- *tortilla española*: Spanish omelette, made with potatoes, often eaten cold, cut into cubes or slices
- *paella*: essentially, this is a dish based on rice (best with Spanish rice grown in the Valencia region) flavoured and coloured yellow with saffron, with seafood and/or possibly chicken and a few vegetables

Paella

There are many different versions of paella, varying from region to region, but most contain seafood such as squid and prawns, and shellfish, for example mussels and clams. Don't be put off by the shellfish in their shells which usually decorate the paella when served up, but beware of crunching your teeth on broken bits of shell! Paella should be cooked in a proper *paellera*, a heavy iron pan with handles on the sides, and is often cooked in the open air at barbecues, *fiestas* and beach parties, and there are competitions for cooking the biggest and best. *Paella valenciana* is the best known and most typical, made with rice, chicken, prawns, peas, mussels, red peppers, tomatoes, onion and garlic ... and, of course, the obligatory *azafrán* (saffron). This flavouring is from the autumn-flowering crocus, large fields of which are cultivated in La Mancha.

Miscellaneous

Eating habits

Spaniards always eat with bread, the style of which varies from region to region: bread usually in one hand, fork in the other. Meals tend to be quite substantial (but see also *tapas*).

Many Spaniards take breakfast on the way to work, one of the reasons why Spain has more bars and cafés per person than any other country in Europe.

Tapas

The Spanish almost always eat as they drink, so most bars have a range of *tapas*. There is an infinite variety of these snacks, ranging from meats and cheeses to seafood and olives; many bars have particular specialities, and Spaniards love to go from one bar to another sampling the *tapas* rather than having a full meal. *Pinchos* are usually *tapas* on cocktail sticks, while *raciones* are larger in quantity, and served on oval dishes.

The word *tapa* means lid: it is said that this arose from the habit of Spanish barmen years ago of covering customers' glasses with a thin slice of bread to prevent flies falling into their drinks. Customers would nibble the bread, so toppings were added, and thus the custom of serving and eating *tapas* developed.

Fast food

Apart from *tapas* and *churros*, there are no obviously Spanish types of fast food; however, spit-roasted chickens are often bought in shops or supermarkets to take away; in recent years, pizzas have become popular, and *pizzerías* have sprung up in many places. Telepizza is one of the fastest growing Spanish companies, its home delivery mopeds being a common feature in Spanish towns. Of course, *hamburguesas* are the most fashionable fast food: there are branches of several well-known companies in most large towns and cities in Spain.

Cooked/cold meats

Spain has a range of cooked and cold meats, often served as *entremeses* – starters; the best known and most widely available are:

- *jamón serrano*, cured ham, the best being cured in the mountains (*serrano* is based on *sierra*); always served in paper-thin slices
- *chorizo*, a large red sausage, made from chunky pork highly spiced with paprika and garlic, usually served in thin slices, and can be used in cooking
- *salchichón*, a pork sausage, not spiced

Cheeses

Although not known particularly for cheeses, Spain has a variety of regional cheeses, the best known among them being *manchego*, a subtly flavoured cheese, sold either fresh or matured, when it is harder, tasting a little like Italian parmesan cheese. There is a wide variety of good local cheese in northern Spain, where there are far more dairy cattle.

Sweets and cakes

A Spanish *pastelería* is a mouthwatering shop to visit with a surprising variety of sweets, pastries and cakes. Here are a couple of well known examples:

- *palmeras* are made from coiled flaky pastry covered with a sweet, sticky coating
- *turrón* is the Spanish version of nougat popular especially at Christmas. Sold in blocks, it can have all sorts of flavours and textures, many based on almond paste; the best comes from Xixona near Valencia, where almonds are cultivated (see Unit 6)

El vino

Spain is one of the world's greatest wine producers – and Spanish wines have been gaining a good reputation in recent years; in some cases, improvements and modernization have been introduced by the so-called 'flying wine makers', foreigners who have moved into the Spanish markets. This is not new, given that the Rioja wine region was established by French *vignerons* and that several British families became involved in sherry production and helped make sherry internationally popular. Here are a few of the best Spanish wines, region by region:

- *Cariñena*: basic but lovely reds from southern Aragón
- *Cava*: the Spanish version of champagne – cheaper and most enjoyable, from the Penedés region
- *Jerez*: the English word 'sherry' comes from the Arabic version of the name of this town in Andalusia which produces its range of 'fortified' wines using the *solera* system, blending the wine from barrel to barrel. Best loved in Spain are *fino*, pale and very dry, served lightly chilled, and *manzanilla* – a sherry with a 'salty' finish, produced near the sea
- *Montilla*: similar to sherry, but from a region near Córdoba, also in Andalusia
- *Rioja*: full-bodied reds from this area in northern Spain, very similar to the wines of Bordeaux in France … hardly surprising, since the vineyards and wine production were set up by wine producers who came from Bordeaux at the end of the nineteenth century
- *Penedés*: fruity, light whites from Catalonia in north-east Spain

- *Ribeiro*: fruity reds and whites from Galicia
- *Valdepeñas*: fruity, basic but pleasant wines from La Mancha

Beer

Spain has a range of brands of *cerveza* (beer), but all are light, lager-type beers; in bars one can ask for a bottle of 1/5 or 1/3 litre or a *caña* – a draught beer in a slender, straight glass.

Cider

Sidra is produced in considerable quantities in Asturias, where it is traditionally poured from a great height, bottle held high in one hand, glass held low in the other: the purpose of this is to 'bring the cider to life'.

Among stronger drinks and spirits, there are dozens of liqueurs, popularly taken in a *copita* (small stemmed glass) with coffee, especially *anís* (aniseed); the Jerez region produces brandies, the better ones of which are of very good quality – ask for a *coñac*.

Other drinks

Agua mineral: With or without wine, most Spaniards drink mineral water with meals and most regions of Spain have their own mineral water, available either *con gas* or *sin gas* (sparkling or still).

Café: One of the high spots of a stay in Spain is the consistently good quality of the *café*, whether taken as straight *café solo*, or as *café con leche* (white coffee).

Té: Tea is almost always taken as *té con limón*, often to settle the stomach.

Chocolate: Hot chocolate is very popular, and is thick and sticky, ideal for dunking *churros*; you will sometimes see a bar which specialises in chocolate – *chocolatería* – well worth a visit.

Horchata de chufa is a drink made from tiger nuts, a sort of milky liquid tasting a little of peanuts and coconut, originating from south-east Spain.

Batidos de leche (milk shakes) are popular all over Spain and come in a variety of flavours.

Recipes

Here are four lesser known dishes which you might like to try. The recipes have been simplified a bit, and like any others, they vary from region to region and family to family.

ALBÓNDIGAS EN SALSA

1lb of minced beef and pork	oil
breadcrumbs	1 onion
milk	garlic
1 egg	sherry
flour	saffron

Mix the meat with the breadcrumbs soaked in milk; season and shape into small balls. Cover in flour, and fry in oil. Fry chopped onion and garlic, add flour to thicken, then a glass of sherry and some water. Pour sauce over meatballs, and cook for 3/4 hour.

CHURROS

flour	salt to taste
water	sugar

Make a paste, the consistency of toothpaste, with water and flour and squeeze through an icing bag, squirting loops or spirals into a pan of hot oil. Fry until golden and crisp. If in a spiral, break into lengths of a few inches. Sprinkle with sugar and serve with coffee or hot chocolate.

GAZPACHO

breadcrumbs	1 chopped onion
crushed garlic	4 tomatoes
olive oil	half a peeled cucumber
vinegar	pepper
1 green pepper	salt to taste

Soak the breadcrumbs and garlic in water, then blend with all other ingredients in a blender. Dilute with water, and chill for several hours before serving.

HUEVOS AL PLATO

1 egg	asparagus
tomato paste	a few peas
ham	olives or whatever you fancy

Lightly oil an earthenware oven dish, lay a slice of ham on the bottom, cover with tomato paste, surround with asparagus and vegetables. Crack an egg into the middle, bake for 15 minutes.

GLOSSARY

la tecnología	technology
la industria	industry
la empresa	company, firm, business
el coche	car
conducir	to drive
(no) sé conducir	I can/cannot drive
el permiso de conducir	driving licence
la carretera	road
la autopista	motorway
la moto	motorbike
el escúter	scooter
el tren	train
la estación	station
viajar en tren	to travel by train
ir en tren	to go by train
el avión	aeroplane
el barco/el buque	boat/ship
el diario/periódico	newspaper
la revista	magazine
la radio	radio
la televisión/la tele	television/TV
el programa	programme
la emisora	channel
el cine	cinema
la película	film
el director de cine	film director
el actor/la actriz	actor/actress
la moda	fashion
estar de moda	to be fashionable
estar pasado de moda	to be out of fashion
cocinar	to cook
comer	to eat
beber	to drink
el gusto	flavour
la receta	recipe
el plato	plate, dish (including in culinary sense)

Taking it further

Reading

Cinema
Spanish Cinema, Peter Evans (ISBN: 019818414X)

Films
All of the films mentioned are well worth seeing, and many of them are available on video.

Spanish TV and radio
Several Spanish TV and radio stations are available on the Hotbird/Eutelsat satellite: TVE Internacional, Canal 24 horas (24-hour news), Radio Exterior, Radio Clásica, Radio 1, Radio 3, Radio 5.

Spanish fashion
Spanish fashion in *The Fashion Book* (Phaedon).

Spanish food
Easy Spanish-style Cookery, Australian Women's Weekly Home Library.

Websites

There are many websites available on subjects covered in this unit. If looking for film stars or directors, look out for the word **filmografía** – list of films made.

www.elpais.es
www.elmundo.es/
www.abc.es/
www.vanguardia.es/
www.cambio16.es/

08

present-day political structures and institutions

In this unit you will learn
- about the end of Franco's dictatorship
- about King Juan Carlos
- about Spain's royal family

One cannot fully understand or appreciate the present day political and social situation in Spain without reference to the last quarter of the 20th century. This is because, almost uniquely among the major nations of Europe, Spain has achieved much of its current political status, and therefore an enormous degree of social development, in this brief period.

In Unit 1, we left Spanish history somewhat up in the air in 1975. This was not just because the end of general Franco's dictatorship marked the end of one era and the beginning of a new era in politics. It also marked the dawn of a new age in almost every facet of life in Spain.

Certainly, Spain has been transformed politically since 1975. From being a political anachronism, a tightly reined military dictatorship in an almost entirely democratic western Europe, Spain has transformed itself into a prosperous modern democracy. Thirty years ago, this would have seemed impossible; Spain's transition has been one of the great successes of 20th-century democracy. Therefore, we have to examine this transition in some detail to understand how Spain has got to where she is now ... and who the heroes of this evolution have been.

Death of a dictator

Francisco Franco died during the night of the 19–20th November 1975 after a battle on the part of his doctors to keep him going; it is one of those strange mathematical facts that if one adds together the dates of the start (18.7.36) and finish (1.4.39) of the Spanish Civil War, one ends up with the date of Franco's death. Even ignoring this weird coincidence, there was a sense of foreboding both in Spain and abroad ... would Spain manage to maintain her political stability or would she degenerate into a new civil war? It was surely too much to hope that there would be a peaceful transition. The one element of hope stemmed from a decision made by Franco in 1948: he declared that Spain was once again a monarchy (King Alfonso XIII had abdicated in 1930/31). He went even further than simply announcing this decision: Franco brought back to Spain Alfonso's 10-year-old grandson, Juan Carlos de Borbón, to be educated and 'trained' by him to take over the running of the country.

How strange this must have been for this young boy: having been born and having lived in exile, suddenly to be told that he would one day be king. Even stranger to be uprooted from his family and to leave behind his own father, himself exiled as a young prince and destined never to be king, and to be 'adopted' by a much hated dictator who apparently wished to groom him as his successor. Franco formally named Juan Carlos his successor in 1969.

The role of Don Juan de Borbón

Nobody knows for certain how much Franco influenced the young prince in those early years, and many assumed that he would merely be a puppet, a mere pale copy of the dictator himself. According to Juan Carlos himself, Franco simply told him that when he took over the running of Spain: 'You will have to do things differently.' In 1978 the magazine *Interviú* published what purported to be an interview with Franco recorded some time before his death. In it Franco says much the same sort of thing, admitting that it would be time for major change. That interview was no more than a spoof resulting from the fertile – and perhaps wishful – imagination of a journalist.

In fact, Juan Carlos had remained strongly influenced by his own father, who had good reason for wanting his son to become king; as a young officer in the Royal Navy, having completed his naval training at Britannia Royal Naval College, Dartmouth, in 1932, Don Juan de Borbón y Battenberg was confronted with a momentous decision: he was serving aboard HMS *Winchester* when he learnt that both of his brothers had renounced any claim to the throne of Spain, leaving him as sole heir. He had to decide whether to abandon his naval career and accept this position, or to remain in the Royal Navy and leave Spain without an heir to the throne. Of course, he chose the former, but Franco never contemplated giving way to him. Don Juan concentrated on bringing up Juan Carlos to love Spain and to accept responsibility for her future. The Admiralty made him an honorary lieutenant in the Royal Navy, a rank he held until his death. Don Juan, later the Count of Barcelona, maintained his affinity with the navy and the sea; he was an accomplished ocean-going sailor, and spent much time in later life living aboard his yacht *Giralda*, a converted Scottish fishing boat, which he donated to the Spanish Naval College a couple of years before his death in 1995.

It now seems certain that Don Juan influenced his son more than Franco did. Yet Spaniards were unsure of the true nature of their king when he came to the throne at the age of 37 – on 22 November 1975.

The new king

On the one level, we have the Basque woman in Madrid who stated in April 1976 that Juan Carlos was at best worthless, and of no interest to her. On another level, the leader of the Spanish Communist party in exile, Santiago Carrillo, gave him a nickname – all Spanish monarchs have had one – which reflected the feeling of many at the time: Juan Carlos *el Breve* – the short lived – writing him off as a king who would not survive for more than 24 hours. The only conclusion one could draw was that this king was going to have to earn a secure position and the affection and respect of his people the hard way – more so than almost any of his predecessors, because he was not only a new monarch with a hard act to follow, but one who lived in an age and a country where the very idea of a monarch was anathema to many.

He inherited a country in which at last the cork was coming out of the political bottle: the aspirations of the people had been fermenting for a very long time.

A choice for change

One of Juan Carlos' first duties was to choose a suitable man to introduce political change: one with not only the know-how but also the charisma to carry it through. The one thing such a man could not have, given the nature of Spain's status beforehand, was experience. Juan Carlos made a successful choice in July 1976, selecting Adolfo Suárez to replace the Francoist Arias Navarro, who had been a sort of caretaker prime minister since the dictator's death. Suárez himself had been one of Franco's bright younger-generation politicians, and had been appointed by Franco to the post of Director of Spanish Television. This had not been a role too close to the heart of Franco's regime, but one that gave him an awareness of public relations issues, just what he would need to carry the people with him in his search for a democratic solution for Spain.

The cork leaves the bottle

In the last months of 1975 and the early months of 1976, in spite of the uncertainty, a political ferment had started to bubble to the surface: a sense of coming political freedom could be observed, with youngsters from Catalonia and the Basque Country making the most of their new-found freedom to sing nationalist songs in their own languages, even when on holiday in southern Spain. (Politics would remain the key subject of conversation in schools, colleges, bars and in the streets for a number of years afterwards). More importantly, in the ensuing months of 1976 the opposition parties united and the Socialist party and the Trades Unions Congress met legally for the first time in 40 years. Suárez's interim government held a referendum in December 1976, in which 95 per cent of the Spaniards who voted approved the Law of Political Reform, paving the way for a new Constitution. In April 1977 the seemingly impossible happened, when the Communist party was legalized: the sight and sound of a convoy of cars driving around the centre of Madrid, horns blaring and with Communist party flags waving out of their windows, was quite something, and General Franco, who so hated *Los Rojos* (the Reds), must have been spinning in his grave!

Democracy arrives

On 15 June 1977 the first democratic elections for 41 years were held: the outcome was a victory for the UCD (*Unión Centro-Democrático*), a remarkable coalition of several moderate centre parties led by Adolfo Suárez, with the new *cortes* (parliament) opening on 22 July. Two months later, the *Generalitat* (self-government of Catalonia) was reinstated, and in October the Moncloa Pact was signed between the government and opposition. During the course of 1978 the new constitution was drawn up, and later approved by the nation in a referendum, and by the king. However, within a couple of years the cracks began to show in the UCD coalition, leading eventually to the resignation of Adolfo Suárez in January 1981. In society, the *destape* had made many people feel uncomfotable, the boom in crime and illegal drugs had made them feel insecure. The expression '*Bajo Franco vivíamos mejor*' ('Under Franco we lived better') was often heard, even among some people who were not Francoists: Francoists themselves longed for a return to the certainties of the old days. Still, this period of painful political wrangling was a necessary part of the process at a time when the fledgling democracy was still fragile and untested: a more traumatic event was still to come.

El 23F

Suárez was succeeded as prime minister by a rather lugubrious figure, Leopoldo Calvo Sotelo; he totally lacked the charisma of Suárez, and under his weak leadership, the coalition began to collapse rapidly. The traditionalists on the right of the coalition felt that change was too rapid, while those on the left wanted more reform and sooner, accentuating the feeling of instability. So it was that on 23 February 1981, the final assault on democracy was attempted, when Lieutenant Colonel Antonio Tejero, with his droopy moustache and shiny black leather tricorn hat, burst into the Congress, the Spanish parliament, with a contingent of civil guards. Various military garrisons around Spain had been expected to join in the uprising, as in 1936, under the control of the generals involved in the plot. Tanks came onto the streets of Valencia, but most supporters of the plot preferred to bide their time and hedge their bets, waiting to see how successful Tejero was. As his men fired their guns at the ceiling of the Cortes, he shouted to the *diputados* (members of parliament) '*todos al suelo, coño*' ('All lie down on the floor, …'). As he hid between the benches, Santiago Carrillo, by now a Communist *diputado*, thought he would be lined up against a wall and shot. It was to be the man whom he had ridiculed that would save him and prevent Spain from descending into the abyss.

Meanwhile, Spaniards and Spain's friends abroad feared – and Francoists hoped – that the country would return to military dictatorship, or worse, disintegrate into another civil war.

Juan Carlos earns his throne

King Juan Carlos heard news of the attempted coup while playing squash. He immediately dressed in his uniform as Commander-in-Chief of the Armed Forces and drove himself to a television studio in the centre of Madrid, whose streets by now could have been a very dangerous place to be. He demanded to make a radio and television broadcast immediately. Those who heard the King's speech live were moved and impressed, their spirits uplifted by his obvious bravery and resolution. As for the military rebels, their Commander-in-Chief laid down a challenge, stating that the will of the people, enshrined in the Constitution, was sacrosanct.

An extract from the King's speech during the night of 23 February 1981 reads as follows:

> *La Corona, símbolo de la permanencia y la unidad de la Patria, no puede tolerar en forma alguna, acciones y actitudes de personas que pretenden interrumpir por la fuerza el proceso democrático que la Constitución votada por el pueblo español, determinó en su día a través de referéndum.*

> (The Crown, symbol of the permanence and unity of our Country, cannot tolerate in any way actions and attitudes of people who attempt to interrupt by force the democratic process which the Constitution, approved by the Spanish people, brought into being at that time by means of referendum.)

Juan Carlos' fortitude paid off, and the units which had actually rebelled returned to their barracks. As for Colonel Tejero, he and his men, who had occupied the congress building and kidnapped the *diputados*, beat a retreat through a rear window and skulked off. Tejero himself was subsequently tried along with other key figures such as General Milans del Bosch, commanding officer of the Valencia garrison: they were imprisoned for 30 years. A day or so after the 23F (*veintitrés F,* 23 February) as it is often known, a huge crowd walked in silence through the centre of Madrid in silent protest at the arrogant insolence of the plotters of the coup, and to express

Tejero takes over Congreso

solidarity with their King. Five days after the '*tejerazo*', as the attempted coup also came to be known (a rather disparaging play on the name of the most visible plotter), the King made a speech which was even more specific in putting the armed forces in their place: he made it at the Military Academy in Zaragoza, whose Director in the early 1930s had been a certain Francisco Franco.

Juan Carlos: *Rey de Todos los Españoles*

As a result of this potentially tragic event, the King gained enormously in affection, respect and prestige both in Spain and abroad. The greatest accolade paid to him was that of Santiago Carrillo, so impressed and grateful that he renamed him 'Juan Carlos, *Rey de Todos los Españoles*' ('King of all the Spaniards'). Not only that, the new Constitution had been threatened, invoked and thus strengthened by the very event that had threatened it. It is, perhaps testament to Juan Carlos and the peaceful transition, even to the '23F' episode itself, that most younger and even middle-aged Spaniards are no longer interested in the Civil War/Franco era, reflecting their confidence in the current status of Spain, and a determination to look forward, not back.

The Constitution

The major element of the Spanish Constitution of 1978 which should be underlined is that it is based on consensus: it was the result of 17 months of negotiation, agreements and compromise, all of which reflected public opinion. The lengthy document which resulted consists of 169 articles under 10 headings. It owes much to the constitutions of several other European countries as follows: Italy, in the way political powers and responsibilities are defined; France provided the blueprint for formulating specific laws; Germany for certain aspects of parliamentary procedure. The Spanish Constitution, being born in the last quarter of the 20th century, has interestingly original elements too, such as protecting the individual from the worst excesses of the use of computer data.

It is also very detailed in defining and guaranteeing the rights of the individual. Perhaps more importantly, the Constitution resolved age-old problems such as doing away with the close relationship between Church and State, establishing the principle of autonomy for the regions of Spain and consolidating and delimiting the Crown. This last aspect of the Constitution makes the Spanish State a constitutional monarchy very similar to that of the United Kingdom. As Head of State, the King is defined as symbolizing the unity and permanence of the state, precisely the status Juan Carlos invoked successfully on the 23F.

The Spanish parliament, *las cortes generales*, is based, like the British one, on a two-house system: the *congreso de los diputados*, or lower house, is that of the 350 elected members of parliament; the *senado*, or upper house, has 208 elected members and 46 appointed by the parliaments of the 17 autonomous communities (see later). The *diputados* are elected by proportional representation; both houses have a maximum term of four years, and while the lower house is responsible for political debate leading to new law, the upper house provides a moderating influence. The executive, or government, consists of the *presidente del gobierno* who, once elected, selects the members of the *consejo de ministros* (council of ministers, or cabinet). All of this operates in much the same way as in other European democracies.

A couple of further laws have been passed since 1978 which have refined the Constitution still further in respect of the actual system of election and referenda.

The main political parties

Partido Socialista Obrero Español (PSOE) (Spanish Socialist Workers' Party)

Spain's oldest political party, it was founded in 1879; moderately left wing, but Communists split off in 1921, and Marxist principles were abandoned in the late 1970s to bring the party into line with other European socialists and to make it electable. Felipe González, Secretary General from 1974, won power in local elections in 1979, then won the general election in October 1982, finally losing the general election in 1996.

Partido Comunista de España (PCE) (Communist Party of Spain)

The Communists split away from PSOE in 1921; survived in exile during Franco's regime; leader Santiago Carrillo from 1960, returned to legitimacy in 1977. Although never very influential, Santiago Carrillo was a national figure largely because of his comments on Juan Carlos (see earlier); current leader Julio Anguita.

Partido Popular (PP) (Popular Party)

Founded as Alianza Popular (AP) (Popular Alliance) in 1977 by an ex-Franco minister, Manuel Fraga Iribarne; poor showing in 1977 elections, better in 1982, 1986 and 1989; won general election in 1996 under new leader, currently President, José María Aznar.

Unión de Centro Democrático (UCD) (Central Democratic Union)

Coalition of minor centrist parties concocted by Adolfo Suárez which won the first general election of the new democracy; it lasted for five years before collapsing. Suárez tried to revive the idea under a new name *Centro Democrático y Social* (CDS) (Democratic and Social Centre), but it failed in the 1982 elections; the UCD served an essential purpose in giving a political focus to the atmosphere of compromise, consensus and moderation of the transition to democracy.

Convergencia i Unió (CiU) (Convergence and Union)

Led by Jordi Pujol since 1980, this is the major Catalan party, controlling the parliament of the autonomous region and with substantial representation in national government. It refers to itself as a 'moderate national party', being a coalition of several smaller democratic parties, and has been very influential in Spanish national governments of both PSOE and PP.

Partido Nacional Vasco (PNV) (Basque National Party)

The leading Basque party, among several others such as *Euskadiko Ezkerra* (EE) (the Basque left) and *Herri Batasuna*

(HB), the latter being the most radical of them – the political wing of ETA.

Public interest in politics

The parties listed above are only the main ones; there is also an enormous range of parties in each region. Although the novelty of democracy seen in the late 1970s and 1980s has worn off to a certain extent, the Spanish still take their politics very seriously, and newspapers and news magazines are always full of the latest political scandals and wrangling.

The return of Socialism

In the late 1970s a young lawyer from Seville called Felipe González stood out in the *Partido Socialista Obero Español* (PSOE) (the Spanish Socialist and Workers' Party). As an articulate and persuasive leader of the party, he was destined for great things. He built up the party and his own reputation to such an extent that they easily won the general election of 28 October, 1982. After the increasing levels of incompetence of the UCD coalition government, and its virtual collapse before and after the events of 23F, many Spanish voters were eager to see reform and felt that PSOE now had the strength and maturity to achieve it. In the event, PSOE was in government for almost 14 years. It still seems incredible that, less than seven years after the dictator's death, Spain had a strong Socialist government. One cannot help feeling that the events of 23F had been just what Spanish democracy needed, strengthening the position of the King, asserting the sanctity of the democratic will of the people, and proving that the armed services could, indeed, be kept under control, at the service of the nation rather than controlling it.

Social reforms

In its first few years in power, the Socialist government undertook a number of major reforms as well as implementing two major decisions in relation to Spain's position internationally (see EU and NATO in Unit 12). Here are a few examples of those which have had most impact on the daily lives of Spaniards.

Amnesty

After a series of changes to the relevant laws, complete amnesty was granted in 1977 for all political offences committed up to that point. (See the Basque problem later in this unit.)

Legalization of trade unions

After Franco's death there was a boom in strikes and demonstrations once trades unions were legalized in 1976, giving vent to years of pent-up frustration. This activist fervour died down once democratic elections offered another means of expression to working people, and as social justice began to be improved.

Divorce

Up to the 1990s for a woman trapped in an unhappy marriage there was no possibility of escape; what is more, a woman could be imprisoned for adultery, but there was no such punishment for a man. However, the new democracy quickly responded to this problem, and the new Divorce Bill was passed in July 1981.

Women's rights

This was a major area of reform in the 1980s. One of the major elements of social injustice in Spanish society had been the low status of women: for example in Franco's day, women could not obtain work or a passport without permission from their father or husband, and it was difficult for a woman to study at university. The new democracy quickly reacted to this situation, and in addition to various articles in the Constitution of 1978, a number of other measures were introduced. In 1987, the *Plan para la Igualdad de Oportunidades de las Mujeres* (Plan for Equal Opportunities for Women) began the fight against sexual discrimination, for equality of opportunity and in support of women's rights. A similar measure, El Segundo Plan para la Igualdad de Oportunidades de las Mujeres introduced in 1993 took progress still further, concentrating on the more general aspects such as equality at work and in education and the positive image of women.

Many other measures were introduced to improve the position of women, and economic pressures coupled with new job opportunities led to a vast increase in the number of married women with a job. However, the persistence of *machismo* (based on the word *macho* – the male of the species) meant that few husbands helped their working wives around the house or took a fair share in the upbringing of their children. Recognizing that modern women often actually had harder lives than their mothers, the Spanish government introduced a publicity campaign in the late 1980s to encourage men to play their part in the home. By the late 1990s, the new generation of husbands were, on the whole, much more helpful to their working wives, though *machismo* is still a problem.

The press

After the censorship of the Franco régime, press freedom was gradually introduced and then completed in 1977 when RTVE (Radio Televisión Española) was freed from state control. During the period of liberalization known as *el destape*, the use of nudity in the press and on the screen became almost a political symbol, being seen at first in political magazines like *Interviú* and then growing to a flood of pornography in the late 1970s. (See press and media sections in Unit 7.)

Las autonomías

One of the most significant changes wrought in Spain under the new constitution was the devolution of considerable powers to the autonomous regions, which came into effect in 1984.

This contrasts starkly with Franco's principle of unity, enshrined in the words which appeared on coins of his era: *Una*, *Grande*, *Libre*, (One, Great, Free). The order of priority of the three principles by which he said Spain should be governed, revealed that unity was paramount in order to achieve greatness ... freedom only came as an afterthought. He achieved that unity by maintaining an iron grip on Spain, stifling any manifestations of regional distinctiveness or separatist aspirations. The new Constitution does the opposite, acknowledging and valuing regional characteristics, and giving the regions a sufficient degree of autonomy to minimize any separatist aspirations to a certain extent.

But what exactly are the *autonomías*? As we saw in Unit 1, the division of Spain into regions was the result not just of its physical geography, but also its history: most of them correspond to the old kingdoms into which the land became divided during the Reconquest. With some alterations and redrawing of borders, these ancient regions have become the *autonomías*. Almost all are subdivided into *provincias*, most of which are named after their capital cities. (NB The first letters of the name of the province or its capital appear on the registration plates of cars from those provinces.) Each *comunidad autónoma* (autonomous community) has its own parliament, with between 33 and 135 seats, depending on the size of region, and all have elections every four years. Each has a president, a budget and control over certain aspects of life. Within them are the 8000 or so municipalities, with elected *concejales* (councillors) and *alcaldes* (mayors), also feeding into the system of provincial government. There are also 60 constituencies represented since 1987 in the European Parliament.

Here are the 17 *autonomías*, along with some information specific to each region:

Andalucía

The largest *autonomía*, in the south, the last area to be freed from the Arabs, associated most with *flamenco* and bullfighting; very influential, having such a large voting population, high levels of rural and urban poverty, and high rates of unemployment; now becoming more prosperous.

Aragón

In the north-east, from the Pyrenees south across the Ebro valley to the Iberian Mountains; Aragonese people are known as *maños*; formerly a kingdom (see Unit 1): capital Zaragoza.

Asturias

In the north-west, the most ancient kingdom, never overrun by the Arabs; the local dialect, *bable*, had all but disappeared, but is now being revived; capital Oviedo.

Baleares

In the Mediterranean, east of Catalonia; consisting of Mallorca, Menorca, Ibiza and a couple of other tiny islands; language is *Mallorquín*, related to *Catalán*; popular tourist venue.

Canarias

A group of islands off the west coast of Africa, the main ones being Gran Canaria, Tenerife, Lanzarote, Fuerteventura; very popular with tourists, warm and sunny all year round.

Cantabria

The middle region of the north coast of Spain, centred on Santander; very green, although coast popular with (mostly Spanish) holiday makers; capital Santander.

Castilla-La Mancha

Formerly Castilla la Nueva, the large agricultural region south of Madrid which was part of the kingdom of Isabel la Católica.

Castilla y León

Made up of the old kingdoms of Castilla (la Vieja) and León; formerly Castilla la Vieja and León (two separate regions); agricultural region going north from the Sierra de Guadarrama mountains.

Cataluña/Catalunya

Once independent region in north-east Spain, with strong identity, own language and culture; a prosperous agricultural and industrial region, some inhabitants have separatist aspirations; capital Barcelona, and region often known by its legal/political name, la Generalitat.

Comunidad Valenciana

Region stretching along coast of south-east Spain; *Valenciano* language an off-shoot of Catalan; agricultural region, with several tourist resorts; capital Valencia.

Extremadura

Region in west of Spain along Portuguese border; agricultural area, home of *conquistadores* (see Unit 1).

Galicia

North-west corner of Spain with own culture (very Celtic, like Scotland and Wales or Ireland) and language (close to Portuguese); capital Santiago de Compostela.

Madrid

The capital, and centre of a growing nexus of consumer industry, as well as of commerce, financial services, national administration, etc.

Murcia

Region in south-east Spain, including several tourist resorts; capital Murcia.

Navarra

Region between Aragón and the Basque Country; ancient kingdom, northern half Basque; capital Pamplona.

País Vasco (Euskadi)

Area inhabited by this ancient people, consisting of three provinces in Spain and two in France (see Unit 1 re the Basque race); has own culture and language (unlike any other in Europe); unfortunately, best known for Basque terrorism.

Rioja

Tiny region in the north, between the Basque Country, Navarra, Aragón and Castilla y León, best known for its wine production; capital Haro.

The current political situation

After a number of years of financial scandals and accusations of corruption, Felipe González's PSOE government of almost 14 years came to an end in 1996 when the *Partido Popular* under José María Aznar won power. At the time, some people feared a return to Franco-like conservatism, but Spanish democracy is too mature for that. Besides, Aznar has consolidated on the progress González made in gaining for Spain her rightful place on the international stage, quickly becoming a respected figure in Europe. At home, however, there are sectors of society which would welcome a return to Socialism, and in 2003/4 antipathy towards Aznar and his government increased; in other words, Spanish democracy now means a healthy balance of views across the political spectrum, in which a succession of governments of opposite but fairly moderate political views provides for stability and continuity. Extremism and injustice are things of the past.

Other elements of the establishment

197
present-day political
structures and institutions
08

The Church

Traditionally a major influence on Spanish society, the Church had been shocked by the wilder excesses of reforms attempted in the early 1930s; therefore, it supported the military rebellion which led to the Civil War in 1936, consequently becoming tainted in the eyes of many Spaniards. In the later years of Franco's regime, however, the elderly bishops began to lose prominence as many hard-working parish priests gained respect, particularly for their charitable work among the poor. In the 1970s, this generation of clergy began to replace Francoist bishops, and worker priests, doing everyday jobs during the week, increasingly took the church's message out to the laity rather than waiting for them to come to Church. The disestablished Church nowadays is more respected than when it was associated with Franco's regime.

Church-goers now practise their Catholic religion through genuine conviction rather than mere traditional observance. Although churches are not as full as they used to be, most Spaniards still retain some sort of belief; many only attend church at special times such as Christmas, Easter and family rituals such as baptisms, weddings and funerals. Other religions also exist, both Christian and non-Christian, but they are in the minority.

The military and *la mili*

As with the church, the *fuerzas armadas* (armed forces) had been a force for tradition and conservatism up to and including the Franco era. This unwillingness to change with the times along with the feeling that the Army had the right to determine the future of the nation reared its ugly head again in 1981 at the time of the 23F. However, as with the Church a new enlightened generation of officers has occupied the senior ranks, a generation brought up with democracy. So, the armed forces are no longer feared as they once were as enemies of the will of the people; such resentment as there is focuses on the question of why the nation should fund armed forces at all.

In the 1980s, with the new-found freedom of expression, there were demonstrations and protests at the fact that so much of the time and energy of Spanish youth were wasted in the compulsory 18 months of military service, and in Spanish cities one often saw graffiti with the slogans '*No a la mili*' ('No to military Service') and '*Mili KK*' ('military service is s***', KK, being pronounced 'caca', is the name of an anti-military service organization). Youngsters would try anything to gain exemption on medical grounds, such as bedwetting, smoking heavily and attempting to ruin their eyesight. Families protested when their sons were sent to military garrisons hundreds of miles away from home, and some young men never returned home as a result of the frequent unexplained accidents involving guns or motor vehicles.

Responding to all this pressure, the government of the early 1990s began to plan for change: first, almost all young conscripts would be guaranteed places at garrisons near home; second, there would be a gradual reduction in the length of military service and a commitment to its total abolition, which was finally achieved in the late 1990s. The only trouble was, of course, that to replace one of the largest armies in Europe, manned largely by conscripts, with all-professional armed services is an extremely expensive business. The change has also added to the number of unemployed and unskilled young people. During their military service, most youngsters at least learnt a trade of some sort.

Two other aspects of the armed services have attracted attention in recent years: first, the Spanish public has become concerned at the danger faced by its men in uniform when Spain contributes contingents to international fighting forces or peace-making missions such as in the Gulf, Bosnia, Kosovo, and Iraq. However, they are generally proud of their '*cascos azules*', Spaniards in the pale blue helmets of the United Nations. Second, there is the issue of women in the armed services. During the 1990s ambitious young women began to be admitted, albeit in very small numbers, to the military academies, but they still find it extremely difficult to progress up through the ranks. Still, Spain's close involvement with other NATO countries (see Unit 12) is helping to create a less *machista*, more open, culture in *Las FAS* (*fuerzas armadas*).

Police forces

For decades, there were three police forces in Spain, although special local forces were introduced in the 1980s in a couple of regions; all are armed at all times.

Policía municipal/local

These are mostly town traffic police, seen directing traffic and enforcing traffic laws in towns and cities. Their uniform is dark blue, usually with white pith helmets.

Guardia civil

The civil guard is a militarized police force living in garrisons; known for their olive green uniforms and shiny black *tricornio* (patent leather tricorn hat), belts and shoulder harnesses; mostly responsible for law and order in country areas, security at borders and road patrols and traffic policing (*guardia civil del tráfico*). Unfortunately, they used to have an awful reputation for brutality against gypsies and protesting peasants, and were hated by the rural poor in the 1930s. The poet and playwright Federico García Lorca attacked them in the *Romancero Gitano* (see Unit 3): it was members of the *guardia civil* who murdered him outside Granada in the early stages of the Civil War. They were themselves often victims of Basque terrorist violence, being considered legitimate targets because they were, as far as the terrorists were concerned, 'foreign occupiers'. They are now quite respected and accepted and rarely wear the *tricornio*, preferring a more normal cap.

Policía nacional

These used to be called *policía armada* in Franco's times, when they wore smart grey uniforms with a red trouser stripe; however, they gained a reputation for violence when dealing with student demonstrations in the late 1960s and early 1970s, when they were nicknamed *los grises* (the greys). As a result, their uniform was changed to a sort of khaki colour, and its style actually looked more military, which was undoubtedly not as intended. Their role is crime detection and prevention and security of public buildings.

Ertzainza

The Basque police force was re-introduced in the 1980s to take over the former roles of the *guardia civil* in the Basque Country, the idea being that they were less likely to be targeted by ETA (see following section) because they are local, and highly distinctive with their blue uniforms and red berets, already well-established regional symbols.

Mossos d'esquadra

Similar to the *Ertzainza*, but in Catalonia; they wear blue berets.

Guardia civil, policía nacional, policía municipal

The Basque problem

The most ancient race in Spain (see Unit 1), the Basques also
have had the strongest separatist ambitions. Having suffered
terribly at the hands of the Nationalists during the Civil War,
and repressed by Franco, the Basque Country was fertile ground
for terrorism. *Euzkadi Ta Askatasuna* (ETA) (Basque for Basque
Homeland and Liberty) was formed by extremists in 1959 to
engage in violent protest against the forces of Franco's
repression. After many other assassinations of police, soldiers
and civil guards, their most spectacular crime was the
assassination of Franco's Prime Minister Admiral Carrero
Blanco, in December 1973. Five terrorists were executed against
a background of international protest in 1975, provoking more
murders of policemen.

One ETA faction declared a truce after the 23F attempted coup,
but others continued through the 1980s and early 1990s. A
major accusation against Felipe González's government in the
early 1990s was of collusion with an anti-terrorist group which
had assassinated several terrorists: GAL – Grupo Antiterrorista
de Liberación. With the return of democracy to Spain, the
French government began to cooperate with the Spanish in
combating ETA. In the mid- and late 1990s, the Spanish

government has tried to negotiate an end to ETA terrorism, using the Algerian government as a mediator, but this did not stop ETA planning an assassination attempt on the King in 1997 when he was on holiday in Mallorca. Fortunately, the plot was detected in time. The problem of Basque terrorism rumbles on, but the hope is that with passing generations it will fade away.

The royal family

Juan Carlos married Princess Sofía of Greece, a cousin of the Duke of Edinburgh, and they have three children: Elena, Cristina and Felipe. Juan Carlos chose to live in a small palace, more like a country house, *el Palacio de la Zarzuela* outside Madrid, rather than in the huge *Palacio Real* in the capital. The family spends its annual holiday in the *Palacio de Marivent* as guests of the people of Mallorca, and they often eat out in local restaurants there. The Spanish royal children all attended local state schools, although Felipe has also attended all three military academies, a Canadian boarding school and various universities in preparation for succession. His sisters have careers: one is a civil servant, the other a teacher, and both have married commoners. At the time of writing, the King and Queen have two grandsons, one born to each princess.

An 'ordinary' royal family

There have been many anecdotes over the years which show how down to earth the Spanish royal family is. Here are a couple of them:

> The King often rides around Madrid on his motorbike. One day he gave a lift to a hitchhiker, insisting on taking him right to his door. The man offered profuse thanks, and asked who his chauffeur was, whereupon Juan Carlos took his helmet off, and his passenger was more than a little surprised to see who had given him a lift.

> Princess Cristina stopped her car at a traffic light in Madrid and was accosted by a vagrant selling packets of paper tissues. She gave him the price asked for, but did not take the tissues. The vagrant was then amazed when a policeman standing nearby told him who his 'customer' had been.

Felipe is Crown Prince with the title of Príncipe de Asturias, and will succeed his father even though he has two older sisters, owing to the operation of the Salic Law in Spain (which forbids female succession to the throne). Felipe was until recently one of the most eligible bachelors in the world: intelligent, educated, handsome and very tall (not for nothing is he addressed as *Su Alteza* (Your Highness)! In November 2003 Felipe's engagement to the Spanish TV journalist Laetizia Ortiz was announced. The couple are to wed in May 2004.

The monarchy and the press

Far from being critical of their King, the Spanish press is generally very supportive. A few years ago newspapers expressed concern when Juan Carlos, a great sportsman, had a skiing accident: the feeling was that the King should not take such risks, especially if there was no bodyguard on hand to protect him. The press also expressed indignation when the King's motor yacht, a gift from an Arab sheikh, kept breaking down during the family's usual holiday in Mallorca: then the press expressed admiration when the King chose an off-the-shelf and very modest replacement cruiser rather than a tailor-made floating palace. Generally, the attitude of the press, reflecting that of the people, is one of pride in their King and the Spanish monarchy.

The Spanish royal family

The future

The future of Spain in the new millennium seems rosy: a prosperous, democratic country with an intelligent and enlightened King, a country which plays its full part in the world (see Unit 12). It should also not be forgotten that Spain is now a mature country which has come to terms with its past, and not just the tragic episodes of recent history. Among the various events and celebrations of 1992 (see Unit 7), one escaped almost unnoticed: *Sefarad 92* (the word *Sepharad* refers to Jewish Spain). This was a major cultural festival in which Spain celebrated the Jewish contribution to its heritage and welcomed back the Jews who have settled in Spain over recent decades, 500 years after their ancestors were expelled (see Unit 1).

Many descendants of those expelled came to Spain for the occasion. One family from London still had the key to the house their ancestors had to abandon 500 years before: they found the house in Toledo, and not only had the lock not been removed from the main door – their key still worked! Juan Carlos gave the keynote speech at the *Sefarad* festival; apologizing for the injustice done by his forebears to the Jews, he welcomed them back, rejoiced in their shared heritage and declared that only by coming to terms with its past in this way could Spain consider itself to be a truly mature nation.

GLOSSARY	
el dictador	dictator
el régimen	regime
el rey	king
la reina	queen
el príncipe	prince
la princesa	princess
real	royal
heredar	to inherit
la corona	crown
el trono	throne
el presidente	president
el primer ministro	prime minister
la democracia	democracy
votar	to vote
el voto	vote
la política	politics

el político	politician
el partido	party
de izquierda(s)	of the left, left wing
de derecha (s)	of the right, right wing
pronunciar	to pronounce, declare
el discurso	speech
el golpe	coup
el ejército	army
la armada	navy
la fuerza aérea	airforce
el soldado	soldier
el marino	sailor
el oficial	officer
la policía	police
el policía	policeman
vigilar	to watch over
patrullar	to patrol
atacar	to attack
el asesinato	assassination
asesinar	to assassinate, murder
el terrorista	terrorist
la guerra	war
la paz	peace
la amnistía	amnesty

Taking it further

Reading

Transition: *Spain: Dictatorship to Democracy*, Raymond Carr and Juan Pablo Fusi (Allen & Unwin, ISBN: 004 9460145); *Spain after Franco*, Juan Kattán-Ibarra and Tim Connell (Stanley Thornes, ISBN: 0 85950 152 3); *The Triumph of Democracy in Spain*, Paul Preston (Methuen, 0 416 36350 4); *Spain – A Portrait after the General*, Robert Elms (Heinemann, 0434 22824 9).

Society: *Fire in the Blood*, Ian Gibson (BBC Books/Faber & Faber, 0 563 36194 8 – accompanied TV series); *The Spaniards*, John Hooper (Penguin, 0 14 009808 9).

Websites

A useful site on historical information in Spanish, era by era, is: **www.docuweb.ca/SiSpain/spanish/history/.html**. In the US, try **www.spainembedu.org/** or: **www.spainemb.org/information. indexin.htm**. This last site has some fascinating web pages in Spanish on the royal family (for which see also **www.casareal.es**), and many other topics and documents of current interest in Spain.

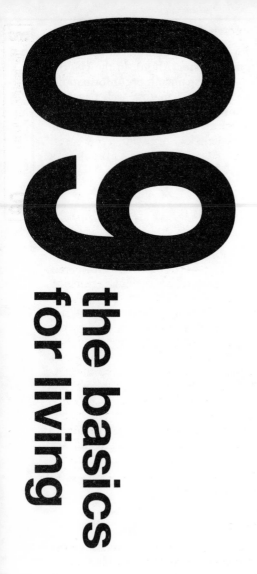

09

the basics
for living

In this unit you will learn
- about education in Spain
- about the health service
- about housing and transport

One refreshing aspect of observing contact between nations, particularly in the case of children, is the realization of how alike we all are behind the barriers of culture and language. There are differences in the way of life, structures and institutions, yet all citizens have the same basic needs.

The way of life in Spain is fairly typically European, and the structure of most institutions which provide for basic needs is similar to that in neighbouring countries: indeed, in a few cases, Spanish institutions are modelled on those of Spain's neighbours.

Education

Provision

Spain's education system has always been a mix of private and state provision. In the case of private education, the major provider has always been and still is the Catholic Church; most private schools are religious schools in that they are either run entirely by a religious order or are predominantly staffed by lay teachers but with a number of priests or religious (monks or nuns) on the teaching staff and strong religious ethos; religious private schools are usually called *colegio*, and they take children between the age of 6 and 18. There was a spell when this church control was suspended during the period of reform in the early 1930s, but during the 1990s the typical ratio of private education to state education was about 30 per cent private to 70 per cent state provision. Education costs Spain almost 5 per cent of its gross domestic product, which is less than most other countries of the European Union, but expenditure has been increased dramatically over the past decade.

The control of education

Through the Ministry of Education, central government retains control of education all over Spain in respect of basic legislation, regulation of educational qualifications and regulation of qualification levels required for transfer to higher levels, length of school year, minimum educational content, regulations on school standards and general planning. However, most other aspects of education are under the control of the local autonomous government, and particularly in the regions with separate languages, where the teaching of these languages is a particular local responsibility. (These regions are the Basque Country, Navarra, Catalonia, Valencia, Baleares and Galicia.) There is a move away from the teaching of pure knowledge and towards acquisition of skills; the general philosophy of education is to give pupils a knowledge of Spanish culture in the broadest sense and to prepare them for life.

Legislation

Over the past 30 years there have been several major educational reforms.

Ley General de Educación y Financiación de la Enseñanza Obligatoria (LGE) 1970 (General Law of Education and Finance of Compulsory Education)

Up to the 1960s, education was very selective in both private and state sectors and, indeed, up to 1970 there was insufficient state provision of secondary education anyway. In some places, two schools had to share the same building: one operating in the morning, and the other in the afternoon. The LGE changed all that, putting state educational funding onto a firmer footing, and setting up the structural basis of the education system in terms of the types of school and examinations (see later).

Ley de Reforma Universitaria (LRU) 1983 (University Reform Law)

Up to the 1970s, university education had been available on the basis of family fortunes rather than academic merit, but with the boom in courses and student numbers of the new democratic era, this law was needed to regulate the university sector.

Ley Orgánica del Derecho a la Educación (LODE) 1985 (Organic Law on the Right to Education)

This law consolidated all children's right to education.

Ley Orgánica de Ordenación General del Sistema Educativo (LOGSE) 1990 (Organic Law on the General Organization of the Education System)

The evolutionary implementation of the LOGSE was begun in 1990, working its way up through the system until completed towards the end of the decade. The structure of education after the LOGSE reforms is seen most clearly in the chart, but the major new developments were:

- extension and regulation of pre-school/nursery education
- compulsory education extended from ages 6–14 to ages 6–16

- splitting compulsory education into primary (6–12) and secondary stages (12–16)
- reorganizing secondary education into two phases: 12–14 and 14–16
- more freedom of choice of subjects in secondary education
- the *bachillerato* course (leading to exams usually taken at 18) shortened to two years (16–18)
- access to university gained by a *prueba de madurez* (test of maturity)
- improved vocational/professional education to prepare students for work

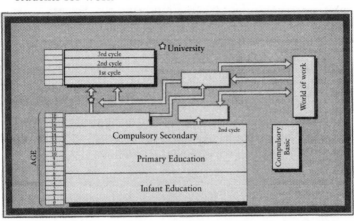

Progression through the Spanish school system

Enseñanza Secundaria Obligatoria (ESO) 1999 (Compulsory Secondary Education)

This legislated for compulsory secondary education up to age 16, and also introduced more subject choice for pupils.

Ley Orgánica de Calidad de Educación (December 2002) (Organic Law on the Quality of Education)

This law addresses issues of quality in education in order to improve results, reduce the drop-out rate and to make quality more consistent. It establishes the rights and duties of both parents and pupils, and norms for grants and academic awards. It also sets out principles not just for compulsory education (up to 16) but also for pre-school and nursery education, adult and vocational training and special educational needs. It lays down standards for teacher-training and assessment, and for the governance and inspection of all educational institutions.

Pre-school education

Since the early 1970s, a high proportion of Spanish children have experienced some sort of pre-school education; Spain compares favourably with most European countries in this regard, and the proportion of children benefiting from this is much higher than in the UK for example. Various types of private and state provision exist, ranging from the *guardería infantil*, which is little more than a creche, to the *jardín de infancia* or *parvulario*, which are proper, structured nursery schools. Almost all children of the 4–5 age group receive *educación preescolar* (pre-school education), the compulsory age for starting primary education being six. Spanish parents are, for the most part, very ambitious when it comes to their children's education, and keen to get them started.

Primary education

The first phase of compulsory education is from the age of 6 until 12. The *escuela primaria* is organized in three stages of two years each; children are generally taught by their class teacher who will be a trained *maestro* or *maestra* except for the following subjects (most need no explanation):

- *lengua y literatura* – Spanish language and literature
- *matemáticas* – mathematics
- *conocimiento del medio* – environmental knowledge
- *educación artística* – artistic education (music and arts and crafts)
- *educación física* – physical education
- *lengua extranjera* – foreign language (from age eight)
- *religión* – religious education (must be offered, but attendance not compulsory for pupils)

Secondary education

For state school pupils secondary education schools used to be called *instituto*; now they are officially referred to as *centro de educación secundaria*. The four-year course is divided into two, each of two years, during the second of which the pupils have an increased level of *optativas* (optional subjects). Eventually, all secondary level teachers will be *licenciados* (university graduates), and the schools will take pupils up to the age 18, including for professional/vocational subjects. Spanish parents have to pay for children's schoolbooks and stationery. The subjects taught are arranged as follows:

- *ciencias de la naturaleza* – natural sciences
- *educación física* – physical education
- *expresión plástica y visual* – arts and crafts (plastic and visual expression)
- *geografía, historia y ciencias sociales* – geography, history and social sciences
- *lengua extranjera* – foreign language
- *lengua y literatura* – Spanish language and literature
- *matemáticas* – mathematics
- *música* – music
- *religión* – religious education (must be offered, but attendance not compulsory for pupils)
- *tecnología* – technology

About five times a year, pupils are given an assessment – *evaluación* – in each subject, sometimes after a test. They have to pass every subject or do a *reválida* (resit). At the end of the year, if they have not passed, they may be able to do an overall *examen de reválida* (resit exam). At both primary and secondary levels, a pupil who has not achieved the established objectives may have to *repetir* – repeat one year of the stage he/she is in. At the end of their four years, pupils receive a certificate enabling them to proceed to a *bachillerato* or vocational training course.

¡Hay que repetir!

Bachillerato

The term (meaning bachelorship) actually refers to the major external examinations taken by Spanish school pupils at about 18; the two-year *bachillerato* course is usually taught at the same school as compulsory secondary education, and there are several streams available according to subjects studied:

- *humanidades y ciencias naturales* – humanities and natural sciences
- *ciencias de la naturaleza y de la salud* – natural and health sciences
- *artes* – arts

There are essentially three groups of subjects for each student: those common to all students, those for his/her chosen stream and optional subjects.

Formación profesional

General professional training is given during basic secondary education and the *bachillerato*, but specific professional training after compulsory education consists of *módulos profesionales* (professional modules) leading to European Community Level 2 and 3 qualifications. They contain a large input of practical experience in work placements.

University

A university course used to be the preserve of the wealthy, and prior to the 1960s very few Spanish women benefited from university education – now more women than men go to university. Nowadays, a higher proportion of Spain's population has studied or is studying for a *licencia* (university degree) than in most other countries of the developed world; all too often, however, many *licenciados* (graduates) are unable to obtain employment appropriate to their qualifications. The *exámenes de selectividad* (university entrance exams) are a major hurdle for many. In recent years there has been a general trend on the part of students away from the traditional degrees such as humanities and social sciences towards more modern courses, particularly in subjects such as business management, science and technology. The range of courses available is much as in any other developed country, though the *carrera* (university course) is usually longer than in the UK, consisting of three years of *comunes* (common studies) before specialization.

Generally speaking, Spanish students attend their local university, and many remain living in their family home; for some specialized subjects, they have to go to a university or college far away from home. Few students receive any financial support other than what their families can afford, and many have part-time jobs; for them, the problem is combining work with their studies.

In addition to the universities and faculties all over Spain, the *Universidad a Distancia* (UNED), rather like the Open University in the UK, is the means of university study for over 100,000 adults, mostly aged over 30.

The health service

Article 43 of the Spanish Constitution of 1978 establishes the right of all Spaniards to health treatment. Here are the main stages leading up to the current situation:

Seguro Obligatorio de Enfermedad (SOE) (Compulsory Insurance against Sickness)

Established in 1942, ensuring that all workers were covered for periods away from work due to illness, in return for contributions deducted from their wages at source.

Ley de Bases de la Seguridad Social (Law of Basic Social Security)

This set up the system whereby 84 per cent of Spaniards were covered for medical attention by doctors and in hospitals. A greater proportion of doctors came within this national health system, and more hospitals were built; however, patients still had to present their health insurance certificate to prove their entitlement for treatment, and many used private provision.

Instituto Nacional de la Salud (INSALUD) (National Institute of Health)

Set up in 1978, and by 1982 86 per cent of Spaniards had entered the INSALUD scheme.

Ley de Sanidad (General Health Law) establishes the *Sistema Nacional de Salud* (National Health System), within which 98.9 per cent of Spaniards are entitled to free treatment.

El Plan de Consolidación del Sistema Nacional de Salud (Plan of Consolidation of the National Health System) improved the efficiency of the system.

Characteristics of the Spanish National Health Service

Compared with other developed countries, particularly within the European Community, Spain has:

- a high number of doctors per 100,000 inhabitants
- a low number of dentists per 100,000 inhabitants
- a relatively low number of nurses
- an average number of hospital beds
- about one-third of hospital provision in the private sector
- relatively low use of hospitals, partly because the elderly are usually cared for by family
- an improving picture in terms of the levels of health of its population
- a low rate of infant mortality
- the highest life expectancy or among the highest – about 80 for both men and women
- cardiovascular diseases and cancer as the major causes of death
- about 15 per cent suffering some sort of limiting medical condition
- a quite high annual number of injuries and death as a result of traffic accidents
- a high number of accidents at work and work-related illnesses

Other aspects of the health service and social security

All Spaniards are covered by the social security system, although pensions and unemployment benefit are related to contributions. However, *el paro* (unemployment) is still a big problem in Spain: unemployment rates are very high, and unemployment benefit only covers the first few months out of work.

Since the days of dictatorship, when there were even prizes for *familias numerosas* (large families), and concessions for families in areas such as transport, families have always been quite well catered for. Spain looks after its children well, and the incidence of child abuse is low.

Spanish doctors and other health practitioners are generally held in quite high regard, although nurses are not particuarly well paid. Most ambulances in Spain are provided by *La Cruz Roja Española* (Spanish Red Cross); helicopter ambulances are used quite extensively owing to the large distances between towns.

Public attitudes to health

Smoking

Although generally Spaniards are reasonably careful about their health, and far more so than once was the case, an alarmingly large number of people smoke, especially youngsters. Cigarettes and tobacco are still extremely cheap compared to other countries, being mostly produced in Spain, making them easily accessible to everyone, even the young. There have not yet been the concerted anti-smoking campaigns as seen, for example, in the UK and US, although regulations are now being introduced to restrict smoking in public places.

Drinking

Spain has never really had a major problem with alcoholism, and not all Spaniards drink as much as foreigners might think; however, like tobacco, alcoholic drinks are very cheap – often cheaper than proprietary soft drinks – so the major area of concern is excessive drinking by young people. Beer is the cheapest and most easily accessible means of getting drunk, and the practice of passing a *litrona* (a litre bottle or glass of beer) around a group of youngsters used to have cult status. A similiar cult is the fashion for weird, exotic cocktails: for some the ultimate kick is to lean backwards onto the bar, for the barman to mix a highly intoxicating cocktail directly in the mouth, to be gulped down in one go.

Drugs

Because of its geographical location – near Africa – and its ties with Latin America, Spain has for decades had major problems with the sheer quantity of illicit drugs smuggled in on boats or by airline passengers. The increased flow of such drugs, coupled with the greater freedom of post-Franco Spain, led to a boom in drug taking in the 1980s and early 1990s. Such phenomena as the open peddling of drugs, *drogadictos*, *toxicómanos* and *yonquis* (drug addicts and junkies) injecting themselves in public places, syringes littering beaches and tourists being frequent victims of drug-related petty crime, led to a clean-up campaign, partly to reduce the negative effects of the drug problem on tourism.

Moreover, major campaigns have been waged successfully against not just the *camellos* (drug pushers) and *traficantes* (drug traffickers and smugglers), but also against the drug barons. The civil guard and the customs service were equipped with fast launches and helicopters: particular blackspots were the coast around Gibraltar and the *rías* (river inlets) of Galicia, ideal havens for coastal smuggling. Powerboats confiscated from the arrested smugglers could be seen in the grounds of the *Escuela Naval Militar* (Naval College) in Marín, Galicia, taken there to rot; yachts, in contrast, were given to the college for use by the cadets. One judge in particular, Judge Baltasar Garzón, made a name for himself in the mid-1990s for his successful pursuit of drug barons. Detoxification and re-education programmes had some success, such as that of *Proyecto Hombre* (Project Man).

In some senses, the drug problem has diminished, and depenalization and partial legalization of soft drugs for use in private, although controversial, have at least reduced the profile of the drug problem. One remaining factor which grabs the headlines is that of the *Carretera del Bacalao*: youngsters in Madrid, especially, get high on drugs and drink, then drive to nightclubs in the Levante (south-east) coast, sometimes using the wrong carriageway of the motorway, often with violent and tragic consequences.

Health for visitors to Spain

All nationals from European Union countries are entitled to free medical treatment in Spain; however, to claim it, it is advisable to carry form E111, which in the UK, can be obtained from a post office. It is also advisable to have travel insurance which includes additional health and emergency cover; medicines prescribed by a doctor have to be paid for at the chemists, and reimbursement claimed on return home. Chemists are always indicated by a large green or red cross, and they are usually able to offer advice on minor medical complaints. For emergencies, call the *Cruz Roja* (Red Cross) ambulance service; at hospitals, look for *Urgencias* (Emergency Department); in some towns, the *Cruz Roja* have emergency treatment centres.

Housing

Generalizations are always dangerous, but one normally thinks of the Spanish as living in flats in towns and cities. While this is true of most Spaniards, the spectrum of housing type is far broader than most people realize.

In the country

In Unit 4 we looked at the traditional types of rural housing typical of some regions of Spain. Whatever the style of housing, there are a few general points one can make:

- Most rural housing is owner occupied rather than being rented.
- Rural dwellings in Spain often house the animals as well as the people.
- Farming people tend to congregate in large villages rather than live in scattered small clusters of houses; many travel quite a distance away from the village to farm their land.
- Rural houses usually have two floors; village houses usually have a large yard and outbuildings for storage.
- Most rural dwellings have quite small shuttered windows to keep out the extremes of heat and cold, and most have terracotta-tiled roofs; except where local stone is used, many have rendered and whitewashed exterior walls.
- Houses in villages near towns and cities are often bought and renovated by city dwellers, either as permanent homes or as weekend and holiday retreats.
- Large, modern housing developments, consisting of two-storey houses, are springing up around villages all over Spain, especially where it is possible to commute to work in nearby towns and cities, and this type of development is becoming widespread as prosperity increases.

In towns and cities

Most Spanish people prefer to be city-dwellers, to make the most of 'life on the streets', in the bars, cafés and restaurants; if you telephone a Spaniard and he/she is out, you will be told '*Está en la calle*' (He/she is in the street') rather than 'out'.

Flats

- Most town/city housing is rented rather than being owner occupied, as so many working families live in rented tenement flats.

- Town flats range in size from the tiniest *piso* (flat) or *apartamento* (apartment) to the largest *ático* (penthouse); the latter are popular because they are quieter, up and away from noisy streets, and with no noisy neighbours above the ceiling.

- Noise pollution is often a real problem, from neighbours or sometimes nearby bars, discos, etc.

- Most bathrooms have a bidet and some have a shower but no bath.

- Few flats have more than a balcony or two, so an important feature of a town are its parks and public gardens, especially for children.

- Large blocks of flats usually have a *patio interior* (interior yard) or *patio de la luz* (yard of light), a shaft or open space down the middle to let light and air into interior rooms. Each flat will have windows and balconies giving onto this interior *patio*.

- Increasingly, good-quality flats are in well-appointed buildings or clusters of buildings with gardens, swimming pools and basement car parks.

- Flats have a *trastero* (storage room) allocated to them, usually in the basement of the building.

- Air-conditioning is considered essential in modern flats in cities like Madrid, and large awnings often shade windows and balconies to keep out the heat.

- The ambition of many Spaniards is to own a flat in the town centre.

- The next step up the ladder of housing status is to move to a *chalet* on the outskirts of town.

Houses

- Houses are more likely to be owner occupied than flats.

- Some towns and cities have districts with older individual houses, either terraced or detached; they range from small houses with a *patio* (yard) to palatial houses with large gardens.

- Most towns and cities have 'fringe' districts of self-build houses constructed by their owners with no planning or building standards, extended as need arises and space permits; tighter controls now make this less possible.

- There used to be a lot of *chabolas* (shanty houses) on the outskirts of big cities, constructed out of any material available, such as wood and corrugated iron, by families seeking work, but unable to find cheap housing, or by gypsies, always a marginalized social group. These dwellings have disappeared in most areas as living conditions have improved.
- In certain areas where rock formations are suitable, cave dwellings used to be popular, being cool in summer and warm in winter, usually with electricity and all other amenities; a few are still inhabited, notably at Guadix, near Granada, Andalusia, in the Sacromonte district of Granada, and in the Ebro Valley.
- Nowadays modern developments of *chalets* (individual houses) are springing up all over Spain, especially in affluent areas, although many are of terraces of houses (*una hilera de casas sin interrupción* – an unbroken row of houses!).

Transport in Spain

Road travel

Spaniards love their independence, and car ownership levels are quite high. There is an enormous contrast, however, between the sheer pleasure of driving across country on wide-open roads, with sweeping and often dramatic panoramas, and the agony of town traffic. Most cities and towns are very congested: the narrow streets were not designed for modern day transportation: major *atascos* and *embotellamientos* (traffic jams), and the problem of finding a parking place are the most stress-inducing aspects of the life of most Spanish drivers. The parking problem is intensified by the fact that Spanish urbanizations are more densely packed than, for instance, those in the UK, because such a high proportion of Spaniards live 'vertically' in blocks of flats. Bus and taxi lanes are useful for speeding the flow of public transport, but not for the private motorist. Driving standards are no worse than in any other European country, although there are blackspots, such as the notorious N340 coastal road south from Málaga, where many accidents involve tourists in unfamiliar hire cars trying to cope with bad traffic conditions on an intrinsically unsafe road. Drink-driving is a problem, and the law is quite strict. The *guardia civil de tráfico* (see Unit 8) use breathalysers and the penalties for infringement are suitably high.

Another 'hazard' faced by Spanish drivers concerns air pollution: in Madrid patrolmen with vivid green vehicles can perform spot checks on the exhaust emission from any motorist's car; the penalties for this sort of pollution can be fines or even impounding of the offending vehicle.

One consolation of driving a car in Spain is that fuel prices are considerably lower than they are currently in the UK, although nowhere near as low as in the USA (unleaded fuel was about 70–75 per cent of UK prices at the time of publication). Whereas all *gasolineras* (petrol/gas stations) once only sold fuel made by the nationalized fuel company, CAMPSA, Spain now has petrol stations owned by a wide range of fuel companies: therefore there are far more of them on cross-country routes than used to be the case. Among other Spanish companies are Cepsa and Repsol, which now have petrol stations in other European countries such as the UK, and most brands seen elsewhere in Europe are now common in Spain.

Roads are numbered as N (*Nacional* – national main roads), C (*Comarcal* – district roads), and local roads usually shown in red, green and yellow, respectively, on road maps. *Autopistas* (motorways) are coloured in orange and *Autovías* (dual carriageways) are shown in purple, both being shown as A. Only the *autopista* is subject to *peaje* (payment of tolls), and the tollbooths are situated at the beginning or end of a stretch of motorway, at other entrances and exits, or as one passes from a stretch of motorway run by one company onto one run by another. One usually takes a ticket when joining a motorway, paying the toll when leaving. Although tolls are an additional expense on the motorist, the fee is often less than what one saves in fuel and wear and tear on the car as compared to using

Road rage affects parking

normal roads. All motorists pay the *impuesto de rodaje* (road fund licence or road tax) but it is less than half what it costs in the UK.

Public transport

Metro
Three Spanish cities have a *metro* (subway or underground system); the ones in Barcelona and Valencia are fairly modern, and the one in Madrid is a mixture of a system dating back many decades and a couple of much more modern lines built within the past 20 years. In each case, fares are cheap, and one generally pays a single price within a zone, encouraging use for longer distances.

Buses
Town bus services are efficient and very cheap: fares are at a fixed price, whatever the distance, and buses nowadays are manned by one person, the driver collecting fares as passengers get on. One important thing to remember, both on full-size *autobuses* and *microbuses*, is that passengers get on through the door at the front of the bus and off at the rear.

Long-distance buses
The **autocar** (coach) or *coche de línea* (regular service coach) is a cheap and efficient way of travelling between towns; large towns usually have their *estación de autocares* (coach station).

Railways

Rail travel in Spain is cheap and generally efficient. In fact in 1999, Spanish railways had the record of being the safest in Europe. Most of Spain's rail network of 15,000 kilometres is run by *Red Nacional de los Ferrocarriles Españoles* (RENFE) (Spanish National Railway Network). The Spanish *ancho de vía* (railway gauge) is wider than that of the rest of Europe, because when the network was built in the 1840s, there was a need for bigger, heavier steam locomotives with larger boilers, due to the steep inclines necessary in such a mountainous country. Most trains – rolling stock and locomotives – are conventional, and traction is provided by a mixture of electricity, via overhead cables, and diesel. The name of a particular type of train is often descriptive, such as TRD – *Tren Regional Diésel* (diesel train), or *Intercity*. However, *expreso* is anything but, this usually being a slow, long-distance stopping train as opposed to an intercity fast train. The unique Talgo trains and the modern AVE trains are described in Unit 7, but a major problem faced by RENFE is how to adapt all of its network and rolling stock to the European gauge, to enable easy movement of long-distance trains between Spain and France.

A few preserved railways in Spain run old steam locomotives, but the most significant non-RENFE railway is the FEVE – *Ferrocarril de Vía Estrecha* (narrow-gauge railway) which runs on narrow-gauge tracks across the north coast of Spain from the French border to Galicia and from Alicante to Denia on the Costa Blanca, serving Benidorm.

Air travel

Owing to Spain's geographical size and often difficult terrain, air travel is popular among those Spanish people for whom time is money, and there are over 40 airports. A high proportion of foreign tourists arrive by air.

Shopping in Spain

Increasingly, as in other countries, Spanish people drive to out of town hypermarkets and shopping malls rather than entangle themselves in town traffic with its attendant parking nightmare: it is hardly surprising that in 1999, hypermarkets controlled 32 per cent of the retail market. Most hypermarkets have a shopping mall on the same site or other specialist stores such as sports shops or furniture showrooms. In most places there are fast-food outlets, and in some even entertainment in the form of cinemas or discos. Hypermarkets are typically open from 10am to 10pm.

Among the most popular are:

- *Continente*
- *Al Campo*
- *Pryca*
- *Mercadona*
- *Eroski*
- *Hipercor*, part of the *Corte Inglés* empire, city centre department stores

Town centre shops are generally best for specialist items such as clothes, music, books and so on, and some of the shop names will be familiar to foreign visitors, such as Laura Ashley, Virgin, Benetton and Body Shop in the largest cities. Opening hours are usually 10am–2pm and 5–8pm. There is also an abundance of smaller *supermercados* (supermarkets) such as Spar, Froiz and Dani, and little 'corner shops'; as elsewhere, at the time of writing the cost of a basket of shopping is considerably lower than in the UK, even comparing favourably with other European countries. Every town has its open-air or covered *mercado* (market) – a good place to buy produce. (There is a list of names of specialist shops in the glossary at the end of this unit.)

Banks

Most banks – *bancos* – open only in the mornings from 8am–2pm. Visitors needing Spanish currency should remember to take their passport and go to the desk with the sign *cambio* (change) or *extranjero* (foreign business). People who have a credit card or banker's card showing the Mastercard, Visa, Cirrus or Maestro symbols, will find it more convenient to use a *cajero automático* or *cajero 24 horas* (cash dispenser). The *euro* was introduced in 2002 and is now the sole currency, although *pesetas* are sometimes used in informal discussion of house prices.

Post offices

Spanish post offices – *Correos* – offer the usual range of services and are open 8am–9pm; nowadays the stamps they sell are self-adhesive. Stamps can also be bought at an *estanco* (state-run tobacconists) and post boxes used to be yellow, as are post office vehicles. Most post boxes nowadays are stainless steel, with a red and yellow band (the colours of the Spanish flag). The post is delivered by the *cartero/cartera* (postman/woman), but the postal service tends to be rather slow.

Telephones

Public telephones are plentiful, because, as well as call boxes (*una cabina telefónica*), most bars, cafés, restaurants and petrol stations have a pay phone. Some still take coins, and some operate with prepaid cards, but one can go to a *locutorio* (public telephone office) in a town centre where one pays the receptionist after making the call. Most public phones are operated by Telefónica, the Spanish telephone company. Large numbers of Spaniards use a *teléfono móvil* (mobile phone).

GLOSSARY

el alumno	*pupil*
el pupitre	*desk*
los deberes	*homework*
estudiar	*to study*
el boletín	*school report*
sacar notas buenas/malas	*to get good/bad marks*
aprobar	*to pass*
ser suspendido	*to fail*
la beca	*grant*
el médico	*doctor*
la enfermera	*nurse*
la consulta	*doctor's surgery*
la clínica	*clinic*
la receta	*prescription*
pedir hora	*to ask for an appointment*
hacer un reconocimiento médico	*to examine*
el paciente	*patient*
el dentista	*dentist*
el hospital	*hospital*
el farmacéutico	*chemist*
el medicamento	*medicine*
el jarabe	*syrup*
la pastilla	*pastille*
el comprimido	*pill*
la tableta	*tablet*
el sobre	*sachet*
tomar	*to take*
repetir la dósis	*to repeat the dose*
cada ... horas	*every ... hours*
la cucharada	*spoonful*
alquilar	*to rent*
vivir en	*to live in*
ir a casa	*to go home*
la habitación/el cuarto	*room*
el dormitorio	*bedroom*

el salón/cuarto de estar	*lounge*
el comedor	*dining room*
la cocina	*kitchen*
el cuarto de baño	*bathroom*
el vestíbulo	*hallway*
los muebles	*furniture*
el coche/el auto	*car*
conducir	*to drive*
el permiso de conducir	*driving licence*
aparcar	*to park*
esperar	*to wait for*
la parada de autobuses	*bus stop*
la estación de ferrocarril	*railway station*
el andén	*platform*
la vía	*track*
el billete de ida	*single ticket*
el billete de ida y vuelta	*return ticket*
de primera/segunda clase	*first/second class*
el horario (de llegadas y salidas)	*timetables (of arrivals and departures)*
el aeropuerto	*airport*
el avión	*aeroplane*
el piloto	*pilot*
la azafata	*air hostess*
volar	*to fly*
despegar	*to take off*
aterrizar	*to land*
la tienda	*shop*
el mercado	*market*
comprar	*to buy*
vender	*to sell*
el pan/la panadería	*bread/baker's shop*
el pastel/la pastelería	*cake/cake shop*
la leche/la lechería	*milk/dairy*
la carne/la carnicería	*meat/butcher's shop*
la fruta/la frutería	*fruit/greengrocer's*

Taking it further

Reading

Any good tourist guide should have useful general information on services in Spain, such as *Spain, Eyewitness Travel Guides* (Dorling-Kindersley, ISBN 0 7513 0106 X), in the section called 'Survival Guide'.

Websites

You will not find much information on any subject covered in this unit on English websites. If you can read Spanish, there are plenty of articles on education, health and transport on: **www.sgci.mec.es/uk/Pub/tecla.html**. There are Spanish websites available on some of the subjects covered in this unit, but this will be a problem if you cannot read Spanish. Here are some interesting ones:

Education
   www.cabildofuer.es/cabildo/con_educacion.html

Health
   dgsp.san.gva.es/SSCC/Salud_Infantil/Index.html

Transport
   fi.uba.ar/deptos/68/68.html

Business
   www.business-spain.co/index.htm

10 the Spanish at work and play

In this unit you will learn
- about industry in Spain
- about tourism
- about leisure activities

Spain now is quite a different country politically from what it was only three decades ago, and the same is true if one compares the economic situation and lifestyle now with what they were then. Of course, there is a strong relationship between them all, and in Spain's case, considerable influence from abroad has been a major factor in the changes which have occurred. Before looking at the Spanish at work and play, it is useful to take a look at the relevant recent historical background to provide some appropriate context.

As we saw in Unit 1, General Franco had to attract investment from abroad to rebuild Spain's economy after the ravages of the Civil War. Tourism was a useful source of income, but it also had the effect of exposing the Spanish to a freedom of thought which would threaten the hold Franco had over the people. Still, Spain certainly gained in economic strength, and some areas of economic activity advanced rapidly, although the totalitarian nature of the regime and tight controls largely restricted growth to what suited the state. To a certain extent, growing economic prosperity kept most Spaniards reasonably content in the later days of dictatorship, but the way this prosperity was shared out among the people reflected the old social structures: essentially the rich were getting richer, the middle classes were doing quite nicely, but the working classes were still comparatively disadvantaged, not helped by the fact that proper trades unions were banned. After Franco's death, tight controls on Spain's economy relaxed, but competition from abroad increased; it was clear that Spain could never again be the protected market it had been, but how could the country maintain economic development, catch up with its neighbours and yet achieve stability at the same time? A further aspiration also needed to be satisfied: having been an isolated, pariah state a generation before, Spaniards anxious to 'belong' in the sense of wanting international respectability were enthusiastic supporters of the country's application to join the EEC as it was then. The country realized that although membership would bring difficulties to some sectors of Spain's economy, only the stability and security it could provide would guarantee continued progress, and it was therefore essential for Spain's economy to adapt to open competition. January 1986 was thus a significant turning point in Spain's development: Spain has now become one of the most committed members of the EU, and arguably has benefited more than most from membership.

Spain is one of the most committed members of the EU

Industry

Fishing

Spain's 2500-mile coastline and the population's love of fish and seafood inevitably mean that the Spanish fishing industry is extremely important. This industry was the one for which EEC membership was most traumatic, the fishing fleet having to be halved to meet European Community requirements. This traditional industry is wide in its scope, ranging from the Basques who hunt whales far from home, to the Mediterranean coastal fisherman who catch sardines and those who cultivate mussels in the *bateas* (platforms) moored on the *rías gallegas* (inlets of Galicia). Spaniards spend almost as much on fish and seafood as they do on meat, consuming about 30 kg of fish or seafood a year per person, twice as much as the average European, and they only buy the best. It used to be said that a housewife in any town in Spain could buy fresh fish, thanks to refrigerated transport. Of course, all this fishing and fish consumption means that the processing and canning industry is of major importance too, and the fishing industry in general employs over 100,000 people. In the UK the Spanish fishing sector is misunderstood, and all too often accusations of contravention of UK fishing limits are unfounded, as so many British fishermen have sold their quotas to the Spanish. In fact the Spanish also buy most of Britain's crab production, sending refrigerated lorries to the UK to fetch cargoes of crab and other seafoods that are not as popular in the UK as in Spain.

Food processing

Given Spain's high level of agricultural productivity, the food processing and related industries are an extremely important sector (see agriculture, later in this unit), employing something approaching half a million people. Most of its products are exported, in particular canned fish and seafood, olive oil (Spain is the world's greatest producer) and wine. Of course, this industry is spread all around Spain in areas whose agricultural produce needs to be processed.

Power generation

Franco had over 1000 dams built, largely to power Spain's industrial regeneration with cheap electricity. Nevertheless, Spain is too dependent on external sources of energy, in particular imported oil, which provides two-thirds of its energy needs. Natural gas is on the up, while home-produced coal is still extremely important. Nowadays the development interest is focused increasingly on renewable energy sources such as wind and solar power. The electricity and gas industries are being deregulated to increase competition and improve performance.

Heavy industry

Much of Spain's heavy industry, based mainly in Asturias and the Basque Country, was set up with the involvement of British companies; an example is Babcock Wilcox, a heavy engineering company in Bilbao, a branch of the Scottish company of the same name. In the 1970s and early 1980s. Spain was one of the world's most important shipbuilding nations, rivalling Japan and South Korea, and usually exceeding the tonnage of any other European country; this is still an important sector (see also Unit 7) but to a lesser extent. Spain still produces much of its own steel, for example at Avilés and Castellón, although in general terms, Spain is moving towards more high-tech, high-value industries.

Engineering

The Spanish motor industry is described in Unit 7, where it can be seen that since the 1960s most cars produced in Spain are actually foreign makes: for example BMC/British Leyland, as it was then (until they withdrew from Spain in the 1970s), Citroën, Renault, and Seat versions of Fiats. In the 1970s, Ford and General Motors invested heavily in Spain, and were largely responsible for introducing more intensive working hours to the Spanish labour scene. More recently, Volkswagen took over Spain's 'own' marque SEAT, investing not only money but also a share in its reputation for quality and reliability, exactly what SEAT needed in order to market its products abroad successfully. Spain has moved from being a country used by foreign manufacturers for cheap labour to being a more proactive and innovative country in this field: SEAT now offers a distinctive range of cars which are rapidly gaining a reputation for original and elegant lines and for being well engineered. SEAT has also notched up notable successes in the World Rally Championships. What is more, SEAT's parent company, the Volkswagen-Audi Group, has relocated its design department to Catalonia, so Spain is now involved in the designing and styling of all of the group's products. In fact, not only does Spain produce more cars than the UK, the automotive industry has become Spain's major manufacturing industry. It has been boosted in terms of home sales by government incentive schemes intended to encourage people to buy new cars, but it relies heavily on exports, making it rather vulnerable to the whims of the international market. Still in this field, two companies building motor coaches have been successful: Caetano established a factory in the Midlands area of the UK in the 1980s, and the Basque firm Irízar not only exports its buses to 44 countries, but also has factories in China, Morocco, Mexico and Brazil. While Spain's railways were mostly built by British companies in Victorian times, her prowess in railway engineering since the 1950s has been notable (see Unit 7). Spain's CASA aerospace company is a member of the increasingly successful European Airbus Industries, along with France, Germany, and the UK, building airliners which have captured hundreds of sales from Boeing and the USA.

Chemicals

Spain is quite active in the chemical and petrochemical sector, although most of the companies involved are European multinationals such as BASF, Bayer and Hoechst, or US companies including Dow Chemical, DuPont (in Asturias) and Procter & Gamble. The national petroleum company, CAMPSA, is now no longer in a monopoly position (see Unit 9) and Spain's other major oil company, Repsol, has a chemicals offshoot: Repsol Química Spain also has an active plastics industry such as GE Plastics at Cartagena.

Other products

It is a curious fact that Spain ranks fifth in the world in book production, amazing since half of all Spaniards never read a book. Spain also still has a very active industry producing traditional crafts, some of its production being dedicated to the tourist industry, and much of it exported. The leather industry is significant with products ranging from shoes to embossed leather work (see Unit 7). Some areas of Spain are famed for their embroidery or lace, while Andalusia, in particular, is famed for inlaid woodwork. Spanish porcelain, such as that of Sargadelos and Lladró, is only one part of a ubiquitous ceramics industry: each region has its own styles, and some local ceramics factories date back to Arab times. Toledo, once famed all over Europe for its swords, still produces decorative *damasquinado* (inlaid gold) jewellery and ornamentation. Finally, of course, Spain produces what are regarded as the world's best guitars, much of the production being in small workshops in the cities of Andalusia.

Planning for the future

The Spanish government of the 1990s set up a number of schemes to promote a shift in Spanish industry from traditional industries towards new, high-tech industries. The *Centro de Desarrollo Tecnológico Industrial* (CDTI) (Industrial Technological Development Centre) fosters the participation of Spanish companies in major international technology programmes, such as particle research, radiation research, the European Space Agency (ESA), and others, including Airbus Industries, already mentioned. The *Plan Nacional de Calidad Industrial* (National Plan for Industrial Quality) and the *Plan de Promoción del Diseño Industrial* (Plan for the Promotion of Industrial Design) and other organizations have been working towards improving the quality of Spanish products and to foster progress among small and medium-sized companies. The *Escuela de Organización Industrial* (EOI) (School of Industrial Organization) established its base on part of the site of EXPO 92 in Seville, where it runs courses to promote industrial success. An element of economic policy espoused particularly by the *Partido Popular* government in the late 1990s is that of deregulating or privatizing nationalized or publicly owned companies in order to improve their efficiency; even Spain's flagship airline, Iberia, passed into private ownership at the end of 1999.

Agriculture

Spain has the good fortune to have an enormously varied climate and therefore scope for a very wide range of agriculture. (See Unit 1 for climate.) Until the upsurge of tourism, this was an important element of the economy, and indeed it is still a major money earner. However, this has in the past been a troubled area of the Spanish economy.

Ownership

Two words have in the past been crucial in explaining Spanish agriculture: *latifundio* and *minifundio*. *Latifundio* is the term used to refer to the norm of land ownership in the south and south-west of Spain: enormous estates owned by wealthy landowners who often spent most of their time away in Madrid, living off the profits earned by the sweat of the *jornaleros* – landless peasants who worked for them, often employed by the day (hence the name, daily workers). In the early 1930s, such peasants could hardly wait for the slow progress of land reform intended to redistribute land in their favour: some of them took the law into their own hands, massacring wealthy families and seizing their land.

Nowadays, more enlightened policies of land redistribution have been introduced. *Minifundio* is at the opposite end of the land ownership spectrum: small farms in the north and north-west would often be split up among several children to provide each with an inheritance; after a few generations of such fragmentation, a son or daughter might inherit a few scattered strips of land which were difficult and even uneconomic to farm. In more recent times, partial solutions to this problem have been found by encouraging exchanges of land or cooperative farming. Certainly, the number of identifiable 'farms' has dropped and their size increased. One remaining problem, however, is that of how to retain rural populations (see Unit 12), and how to maintain sufficient numbers to farm the land, given that the number of people working the land has fallen from 50 per cent in 1940 to less than 10 per cent of the population.

Characteristics of Spanish farming

Add to the problems mentioned the fact that of Spain's 50 million hectares of territory, only 20 million hectares of land can actually be cultivated, 17 million of which are unirrigated; and add another fact, that the terrain often makes farming difficult, and one begins to understand why agriculture in Spain is often precarious. Whatever the patterns of ownership and the local conditions, mechanization has turned farming in Spain from being an often soul-destroying and arduous business into a rather more efficient process. In addition to the 20 million hectares of cultivated land, about six million hectares are used for pasture and about 18 million are under forest. In addition to vast areas given over to cereals production, Spain has large areas of 'industrial' agriculture – that is products like sugar beet, sunflower and cotton. Spain ranks second in the EU in livestock production other than cows, third in beef production and sixth in dairy production. Forestry produces wood, resin and cork, the latter principally in the far south-west. Of its overall agricultural product in terms of value, about 60 per cent is from agricultural produce (30 per cent approximately in vegetables, 15 per cent in fruit, 10 per cent in cereals); the remaining 40 per cent is from the livestock sector of which about 70 per cent comes from meat and 30 per cent from dairy produce and wool. Although Spain does import a considerable amount of produce, her agriculture exports slightly exceed the value of imports, the bulk of trade being within the EU. All produce is quality controlled by regulatory councils.

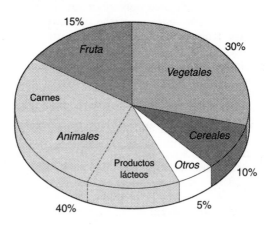

The breakdown of Spanish agricultural production

The money earners

As well as being self-sufficient in several areas of production, Spain is a major exporter of a range of agricultural produce, the following being the greatest money earners.

Olive oil
Produced all over central, southern, eastern and south-eastern areas; Spain is the world's top producer.

Fruit
Mostly in the south and east; Spain ranks third in the world for fruit production and first in Europe for citrus fruits, having the great advantage of a very early season, and therefore capturing the market early in the year.

Wine
The Spanish wine industry occupies fourth place in the world rankings; although not rated as highly overall for quality as French or Italian, Spanish wine has a great range of types (see Unit 7).

Vegetables
A huge variety is produced all over the country; Spain is notable for tomatoes, peppers and salad produce, the Canaries have the advantage of a very early season; a huge acreage of land is devoted to cultivation under plastic, particularly in the south-east of Spain where there is ample sunshine. Much of the labour is provided by Moroccan immigrant workers, willing to endure the incredibly hot conditions in the greenhouses.

Agriculture, region by region

Of course, variations in climate have a lot to do with what grows where in Spain, and the country therefore benefits from the ability to produce a wide variety of products; what follows is a description of the agriculture typical of the major climatic regions of the country.

The north and north-west
Much of Galicia and Asturias are given over to small-scale farming: some farmers have other work, and one sees many families who use large allotments either to be self-sufficient in produce or as a secondary source of income. They cultivate any sort of fruit and vegetable which will grow in the mild, wet climate, including citrus fruits. Cattle, sheep and pigs are also

reared. The *Ribeiro* wines are produced in Galicia, while Asturias is famous for its cider. Cantabria and the Basque Country also have a damp, mild climate, and the agriculture is mostly similar, except that there is more emphasis on dairy farming. The Rioja region just south of the Basque Country produces some of the best wines in Spain: their similarity with those of Bordeaux is not accidental: *vignerons* (wine growers) from Bordeaux came to La Rioja to start afresh when their vines were ravaged by the phylloxera pest during the 19th century.

The north-east

Generally drier, the centre of Aragón produces mostly cereals – wheat, barley and corn – while well-irrigated areas and the mountainous valleys of the north and south have a more varied range of mostly vegetable produce. Catalonia is similar, but in the coastal area the *Penedés* wines (including *Cava*) are produced; *Cariñena* wines come from the south of Aragón, where olives are also cultivated.

The centre

The continental climate – cold, dry winters and hot, dry summers – is such that the most widespread cultivation across wide prairies is of cereals, although irrigation is now enabling a wider range of crops to be produced. Sheep are more frequent than cattle, their milk producing *Queso Manchego* (cheese from La Mancha). Also in La Mancha, south of Madrid, the lilac-coloured autumn-flowering crocus is cultivated for the production of that most prized condiment, saffron, such an essential ingredient of a good *paella*. Towards the south are the vineyards of Valdepeñas and as one heads for Andalusia, one sees the beginnings of olive cultivation.

The south and south-west

Cork oak is the most notable product of the dry lands of Extremadura, much of which are given over to cereal production; sheep, pigs, goats and cattle are raised – including fighting bulls. Andalusia has an incredible range of produce: citrus fruits, vines and olives almost everywhere (Jaen province in the north produces a phenomenal amount of olive oil); the west is notable for cotton, rice, fighting bulls and the wines of Jerez; the coastal areas produce more exotic fruits such as dates, apricots, peaches and melons; the acres of plastic greenhouses around Almería in the east produce valuable crops of early fruit and vegetables.

The south-east

The Huerta de Valencia (vegetable garden of Valencia) is renowned for its fertility, producing all sorts of fruit and vegetables, particularly any that need plenty of water and sun. *La tomatina* (the tomato fight) is celebrated at the end of August at Buñol, near Valencia, and the area produces much of Spain's citrus fruit; around Albufera, a huge lagoon south of Valencia, rice is cultivated, and further south, the area around Alicante is covered with olive and almond trees.

The Islands

The Balearic Islands are thought of mostly as tourist traps, but Menorca and Mallorca still have a varied agriculture, while the Canaries are renowned for high-value crops such as bananas, pineapples, and early salad produce.

Working practices and the unions

In Franco's time, the only *sindicatos* (trade unions) were the official ones, which were vertical in structure – covering all employees of an enterprise at every level – rather than the typical horizontal uniting of all workers with common concerns and interests. Once legalized, genuine trade unions became very vocal during the transition to democracy. However, Spain's high unemployment rate in the 1990s, of around 20 per cent, translated as 3 million people out of work, has meant that the unions have had to be fairly moderate in their demands; by 1999 the unemployment rate had fallen to about 15 per cent. An enthusiastic member of the EU, Spain has adopted all the employment legislation including the minimum wage. Working hours have changed somewhat: traditionally, Spanish workers started early and finished late in the day, having two or three hours off in the middle of the day. Increasingly, they have moved to a more intensive working day. Safety at the workplace was a major problem in the overtly capitalist society of the Franco regime, and even in the late 1990s this remained a matter of national concern, with cases of neglect on the part of some employers.

There is now a full range of trades unions, of which some of the main ones are:

- *Comisiones Obreras* (CC.OO) – in the past had Communist connections, largest membership in Madrid and Andalucía
- *Confederación Nacional del Trabajo* (CNT) – the anarchist union of the pre-Civil War years, largely based in Catalonia

- *Sindicatos Unitarios* (*SU*) – mostly covering the construction industry
- *Solidaridad de Trabajadores Vascos* (*STV*) – a Christian trade union peculiar to the Basque Country
- *Unión General de Trabajadores* (*UGT*) – the Socialist union, with the greatest following in the north of Spain
- *Unión Sindical Obrera* (*USO*) – Socialist union with large membership in the east of Spain

Women in the workplace

Given the restrictions placed on women in Franco's Spain, when virtually the only working women were those employed in the health and service sectors, major changes were needed. Indeed, of the million plus extra workers who joined the market in the late 1980s, almost one million were women. Consequently, in spite of over 2 million extra jobs created in those years of economic boom, unemployment remained high. Nonetheless the proportion of women in work rose considerably, although many are not particularly well paid and the process of change is not without problems (see Unit 8).

Tourism

There have been visitors to Spain for centuries, of course, but one of the manifestations of the increased levels of prosperity – and peace, at least in western Europe – of the second half of the 20th century was the phenomenon we know as tourism. In fact, there were several factors which favoured tourism after the Second World War: the relatively rapid return to prosperity of the countries of northern Europe, along with increased leisure time; the taste for foreign travel acquired by Second World War military personnel; rapid, cheap air travel resulting from the development of jet aircraft. Franco (see Unit 1) was able to capitalize on tourists' taste for sun, sea and sand at exactly the time when Spain desperately needed foreign money.

By the 1960s, Spain was receiving 6 million visitors each year; with the growth of new tourist developments in places like Torremolinos and Benidorm, this figure had reached 24 million ten years later, almost 40 million in 1980 (the same as Spain's population!), and over 50 million in the 1990s. Most of the visitors are from other EU countries, including about 5 or 6

A 'typical' tourist to Spain?

million British tourists. In 2003, Spain was for the first time the most popular holiday destination for British tourists, overtaking France. The most popular areas are the Costa Brava (Wild Coast) and Costa Dorada (Golden Coast) in the north-east, the Costa Blanca (White Coast) in the east and south-east, and the Costa del Sol (Coast of the Sun) in the south – and, of course, the Balearic and Canary Islands.

All of this has brought money to Spain and work to Spaniards, to such an extent that about 60 per cent of Spain's gross domestic product is in the service sector, of which a high proportion is related to tourism. However, welcome though all this is, there have been drawbacks: first, the effects of unrestrained development (see Unit 11); second, the inherent instability of the tourist market, always hit badly in times of recession; third, the fact that Spain was very conscious that mass-market tourism did not always attract the tourists Spain wanted (we have all heard of the 'lager louts'), or those with most money to spend. Therefore, in the 1990s, much time, effort and imagination were invested in trying to switch Spain's tourist market to higher quality cultural tourism and 'green' tourism: genuine tourists (as opposed to beach loungers) travel around Spain visiting sites of architectural and artistic interest, while others make the most of Spain's natural beauty. In both cases, this has the effect of spreading tourist money more evenly around the country. This policy has already had some success, with the added benefit to Spain's image abroad that at last visitors see that the country has more to offer than sun, sea and sand!

One example of a city which is benefiting from cultural tourism is Bilbao: the dramatically styled Guggenheim Art Museum, which became a major tourist attraction overnight, is drawing large numbers and has given this previously rather gloomy industrial city a new-found self-confidence.

One should not, of course, forget internal tourism: while it is true that most Spaniards used to shun the bright sunshine, and women considered it essential to maintain as pale a complexion as possible, nowadays they are just as sun loving as the rest. In fact, well-to-do Spaniards used to take their holidays on the north coast, and resorts such as Zarauz, San Sebastián and Santander were popular in the nineteenth century. Indeed, the Palacio de la Magdalena situated on a promontory overlooking the harbour entrance in Santander, used to be the summer residence of the royal family (it now houses the university). Santander and San Sebastián in particular are full of grand, stately hotels beloved of these early Spanish holiday-makers, such as the elegant Hotel Sardinero close to La Playa del Sardinero (the sardine-fisherman's beach) in Santander. San Sebastián has its casino, also dating from the era. Nowadays, Spaniards generally take their holidays away from the heat of the cities, favouring the sea or the mountains. Madrid is almost deserted in August, with temperatures in the high 30 and low 40s (Celsius). The expression '*estar de Rodríguez*' ('to be a Rodríguez') refers to the situation of any bachelor husband remaining in Madrid when wife and family are away on holiday: the story goes that a telephone rang in a Madrid nightclub and when the waiter called Señor Rodríguez to the phone, several men stood up – all of them using this common surname as an alias to fool the young lady they were with … without the wife's knowledge, of course!

'Estar de Rodríguez'

Leisure pursuits

The Spanish have always been keen on sport as spectators: bullfighting (see Unit 6) is not a true sport as such, and if there is one spectator sport above all others in Spain it is football. The Spanish league is somewhat smaller than those in Britain, but the value and quality of the players is comparable. Among the great internationally known clubs are Real Madrid, Atletic de Bilbao and Barcelona; the two best-known football stadia in Spain are Santiago Bernabeu (Real Madrid) and Nou Camp (Barcelona), appreciated for their design as well as for their size. Football, of course, is ubiquitously practised and played, popular at school and at neighbourhood level. In the Basque Country, *pelota vasca*, a unique ball game played by two or four players in a *frontón*, or two-sided court, retains its appeal as an exciting sport to play or to watch, major games being the focus for a great deal of betting. Basketball and volleyball are popular spectator sports all over Spain, and cycling has a great following, reinforced by the incredible international success over a number of years of the great Miguel Induráin. Similarly, golf and motorsport gained in popularity as a result of the prowess of Severiano Ballesteros and Carlos Sainz. Always a popular participation sport, tennis has been boosted by the likes of Arantxa Sánchez Vicario, Conchita Martínez and Carlos Moyá. Perhaps most significantly, the surprising successes of Spanish athletes at the 1992 Olympic Games in Barcelona encouraged many more Spaniards to take their physical health seriously: all over Spain now one sees people of all ages running, walking or exercising. A more leisurely sport often played in parks and on beaches is *petanca*, a sort of bowls game also played in France and Italy.

The more violent sports of hunting, shooting and fishing are quite popular: generations of Spaniards have enjoyed shooting at anything which moves, which partly accounts for the relatively low number of songbirds. Political correctness and concern for fauna and the environment in general have led to a reduction in the number of active hunters; although fishing is less popular than it is in the UK and the USA, it is still practised to an extent, especially on the fast-flowing rivers and streams of northern Spain.

A major growth industry in Spain is that of theme parks: for decades there had been large permanent funfairs on the edge of large cities, such as in the Casa de Campo, west of Madrid, and in the Parque Primo de Rivera in Zaragoza. Then, beginning with so-called water-parks in the Costa areas in the 1990s, theme parks of all sorts began to spring up, always with the regulation white-knuckle rides which are every bit as popular in Spain as elsewhere.

At home Spaniards watch a great deal of TV, having a wide choice of channels, although what they offer may not always be of particularly good quality. Almost all homes have at least one television set, and, as elsewhere, children often have one in their bedrooms. Over 20 per cent of homes have computers, and the Internet is an increasingly popular source of information and entertainment.

TV family

However, it will be a long time before Spaniards are weaned off their favourite source of leisure and entertainment. It is said that Spain has more bars than the whole of the rest of Europe put together, but that is not to say that their customers are alcoholics. Quite the contrary, the Spanish like to linger over a drink, preferably on the *terraza* (open-air terrace) of a café, chatting or watching the world go by. The evening *paseo* (walkabout) is a favourite time for this: families come out in droves to parade in the cool of the early evening, taking the children to local parks and gardens, then repairing to their favourite café. Games such as draughts, dominoes, and cards are popular among the regular customers, and bars are a favourite place to read newspapers or join in the communal watching of a TV football match. Later on, couples and groups will spend the evening out, tasting the *tapas*, *raciones* and *bocadillos* (see Unit 7) in one bar after another: try el Tubo, a couple of adjoining alleys in Zaragoza, or the student town of Pontevedra (Galicia), each with dozens of bars offering *tapas* of every type.

Restaurants range widely in price and quality, but the two factors do not necessarily go hand in hand, especially in tourist areas. There are plenty of very reasonably priced restaurants and eating places in Spain where the quality is excellent. Children are always welcome in bars and restaurants. Visitors are recommended to follow the locals: they are more likely to end up in a back-street restaurant, or in a *comedor* attached to a bar or café. There may not even be a printed menu, but the cooking will be good, honest home-produced fare, and the wine will be equally pleasant and inexpensive. The point is that Spaniards love eating out; a high proportion of them go out to lunch every day from their workplace, often to the same local eating place. Consequently, low-priced restaurants abound; larger cafeterias usually serve a range of full meals as well as *tapas*, *raciones* and *bocadillos*. These are often in the form of *platos combinados* (combined dishes), with several items all served on one large plate. Eating and drinking out rank among the greatest pleasures of Spain. Indeed, this is a major factor in making the Spanish lifestyle one of the most pleasant in the world.

GLOSSARY

trabajar	*to work*
la industria	*industry*
la pesca	*fishing*
la presa	*dam*
la electricidad	*electricity*
el petróleo	*crude oil*
la empresa	*company, firm*
la fábrica	*factory*
la ingeniería	*engineering*
la tierra	*land*
cultivar	*to grow, cultivate*
crecer	*to grow*
la granja	*farm*
el granjero	*farmer*
el campesino	*peasant*
el aceite	*olive oil*
el vino	*wine*
la fruta	*fruit*
las legumbres	*vegetables*
el turismo	*tourism*
el turista	*tourist*
visitar	*to visit*

jugar al fútbol/tenis	*to play football/tennis*
correr	*to run*
pasearse	*to go for a walk*
ver la tele	*to watch the TV*
tomar algo de beber	*to have a drink*
el parque	*park*

Taking it further

Reading

Economy, work and industry: *Living and Working in Spain*, David Hampshire (Survival Books, ISBN: 0951980424); *Contemporary Spain*, Christopher J. Ross (Arnold Paperback); *The Modern Spanish Economy*, Keith Salmon (Pinter Paperback); Agriculture: A good tourist guide will have information on regional cooking – and therefore agriculture – such as: *Spain, Eyewitness Travel Guides* (Dorling-Kindersley, ISBN 0 7513 0106 X); *Wines of Spain*, Jan Read. Entertainment: Good guidebooks such as that mentioned earlier usually have ample information on entertainment and leisure possibilities.

Websites

You will not find much information on any subject to do with business covered in this unit, on English websites, but try

www.business-spain.co.uk/index.htm.

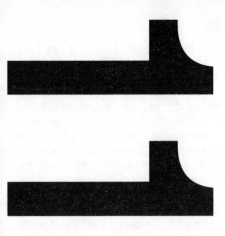

11

Spanish people

In this unit you will learn
- about population trends
- about the family
- about immigration

Population trends

The population of Spain has for the past decade or so been nudging 40 million, having doubled since 1900. From the high level in the first quarter of the 20th century of almost 4.0 (average number of children per woman), the Spanish birth rate fell quite drastically, overall, to the end of the century. From being around 2.5 in 1950, it rose to 2.9 in the 1960s when Franco was attempting to encourage population growth by giving additional financial assistance to *familias numerosas* (large families); it then fell quite drastically in the 1980s with the advent of birth control and greater freedom for women. It has continued to fall as Spain has become more prosperous and material considerations have become more important to Spanish couples; the present rate of around 1.2 – one of the lowest in the world – has given rise to concern in some social circles, since it falls short of the rate needed for the Spanish to reproduce themselves and maintain the current population.

At the other end of the scale, life expectancy has more than doubled from one end of the 20th century (34 for men and 36 for women) to the other (80 for both men and women), now being – along with Italy and France – the highest in Europe and among the highest in the world. This reflects improved living standards and health provision – and perhaps even a healthy diet and lifestyle. These two factors together bring problems for Spain: the 'population pyramid' is changing its shape and in danger of becoming top heavy. The knock-on effect of this, of course, is that there are more elderly people to support and for longer – a greater financial burden for the wage-earning population.

Population movement

Spain used to be very much an agricultural country, its population being spread around the landscape, although it has always tended to be the case in central Spain that people live concentrated in large villages, rather than scattered around in smaller villages. In his attempts to water down the separatist aspirations of the Basque Country and Catalonia, General Franco actively encouraged people to move from poor rural areas to work in the factories of the north and north-east: the population of these areas is now much more cosmopolitan than it was 60 years ago. In addition, Franco's policy for economic regeneration tended to rely on the development of a few industrial centres around Spain such as the huge refineries of

Campo de Gibraltar and Huelva. The theory was that prosperity would spread out from these centres, but in fact they simply sucked into themselves the available finance and the most talented people. This had the effect of depriving rural areas of the energy and drive of the most able young people. Thus an increasingly ageing population would gradually die off, leaving some villages completely abandoned.

This process has continued in the more prosperous era of democracy: the problem is that of how to retain rural populations (see Unit 10) at levels sufficient to work the land. In 1999, the Spanish government signed an agreement with Morocco, allowing more Moroccans to do seasonal agricultural work in Spain to make up for the shortfall in available agricultural labour. Against this background, the irony is that the size of villages near major population centres has actually increased owing to the increasing tendency for the affluent middle classes to move away from cities and commute to work.

The family

Traditionally, the family unit has been extremely important: in the past the husband/father figure reigned supreme, the wife/mother figure, although somewhat idealized, also had a very clear role, and children were the focus of more care and attention than in other countries. Marriage, therefore, was of paramount importance, its major purpose being procreation. However, couples generally married somewhat later than elsewhere, especially among the middle and professional classes: the system of *oposiciones* (competitive exams for entry into a profession) meant that some couples had to wait for years to get married, not being permitted to do so until the prospective husband had managed to become established in his intended profession. In those days, marriage tended to be at around 30, and young men and women continued to live with their parents until married.

As already mentioned, General Franco actually had policies to encourage large families. Divorce was not possible except in extreme circumstances, family planning was unheard of; although single parent families existed, they were few and far between, having a considerable stigma attached to them. Abortion was prohibited; back-street abortions were possible but fraught with danger, and once abortion was legalized in Britain, many Spanish women travelled to the UK for this purpose.

All of this has changed since the return of democracy in Spain, and over the past 20 years or so, Spanish society has evolved into much the same mould as that of other developed countries. Greater levels of social freedom, more open and tolerant attitudes and the prevalence of a more materialistic outlook on life have changed Spanish society almost beyond recognition in a relatively short space of time. It is now barely distinguishable from its neighbours in respect of its attitude to marriage and the family. The modern husband is prepared to listen to and respect his wife's opinions, and the modern father plays a full part in the upbringing of the children.

The typical Spanish city-dwelling middle-class family of today consists of a working mother and father trying hard to fit in time with their children and to have them cared for when both are busy at work, with a good standard of living, but suffering from the typical stresses and strains of modern life.

If there are characteristics peculiar to Spanish society, they are that children are still very much the focus of attention of parents, relatives and friends. Spanish parents are still very ambitious for their children, take a close interest in their education, and are willing to make sacrifices for them. The elderly, as always, are usually cared for in the family home, playing an active part in the home and valued and respected for it. In fact, these features are actually prevalent in other southern European countries too, and although the importance of the family as a social unit is not what it once was, it is still very considerable.

The modern Spanish husband

The role of the sexes

One of the most striking aspects of recent social change has been the transformation in the role of women (see Unit 8). In fact, 52 per cent of the population are women, and although there is still a way to go, they are far better represented in most walks of life. Over the past three decades there have been a number of very successful women in Spain who have stood out as having achieved a lot in fields previously almost inaccessible to them. There is not room to do any more than mention a few names here. Nuria Espert was easily Spain's best and best-known actress in the Spanish theatre in the 1970s and 1980s, and is now a director of considerable repute; Carmen Maura (see Unit 7) was arguably Spain's greatest cinema talent in the 1980s until Antonio Banderas came to the fore; Pilar Miró attracted a lot of media attention in the 1990s as director of TVE, and then moved on to direct films like '*Tu Nombre envenena mis Sueños*' (1998, '*Your Name Poisons My Dreams*')

Significantly, the wives of prime ministers, Spain's 'first ladies', now attract considerable attention: Felipe González's wife Carmen Romero went so far as to become a *diputada* (member of parliament) herself, while Ana Botella is known as the glamorous wife of the current (at the time of writing) prime minister, José María Aznar. There have been prominent women politicians, and even bullfighters such as Cristina Sánchez, but these have been few and far between.

There have been and still are problems for women wishing to be in the armed services, and there are still areas of life and work which are virtual no-go areas as far women are concerned. However, one only needs to look back to the Franco era for comparisons to realize how much positive progress has been made, and how remarkably quickly. It is amusing to recall that in the early 1990s, in a British television series on modern Spain, a couple of elderly women were asked what they thought of the new-found sexual freedom of Spanish women. They gave an unexpected answer – instead of saying how awful and immoral it was, they replied how unfair it was that they had not been able to enjoy such freedom themselves! As mentioned in Unit 8, it is men who still need educating to change the sometimes still prevalent *machista* attitude.

Immigration

Although much invaded in the past by races who settled there, Spain has never had a large-scale problem with immigration in modern times. However, in the past three decades there have been minor waves of immigration. The first type of immigration came from Latin America in the 1970s: political or intellectual refugees seeking sanctuary from repressive, dictatorial regimes – in a sense the return flow of a similar exodus from Spain in the early Franco years. In a way, these immigrants served as an ongoing reminder of what Spain herself had escaped from with Franco's death in 1975, leading to the active involvement of the Spanish press in campaigns to oust South American dictators such as General Augusto Pinochet of Chile. It might even be said that they helped to stabilize the process of reinstating democracy.

Interestingly, such immigrants also made a positive cultural contribution: musicians exiled or fleeing from Chile and elsewhere continued writing and recording material which represented the plight of their homeland. One such was Quilapayún, a Chilean folk group popular in Spain in the late 1970s and early 80s: their LP '*Santa María de Iquique*' told the story of the massacre by the authorities of over 3600 peasants and mineworkers protesting about their plight in 1907, exploited, underpaid and oppressed by rich foreign companies.

This musical history lesson was clearly making a statement of political protest at the bloody overthrow of the democratic government of Salvador Allende in 1973 by Pinochet. His coup was supported by the CIA and capitalist interests anxious to reverse Allende's nationalization of mining and other companies, by which he had tried to ensure that Chileans and not foreign shareholders would benefit from the country's natural resources. Given the novelty and excitement of political freedom at the time, this sort of music held great appeal to the idealistic Spanish youth, at exactly the time when Spain was preparing itself to elect its first socialist government for almost 50 years.

The second type of immigration in recent times is illegal immigration from two directions: a trickle of political refugees from Latin America – mostly from Castro's Cuba – attempting to find freedom and prosperity in Europe. A much larger flow of illegal immigrants from the late 1990s has been from Africa. The close proximity of southern Spain to North Africa makes

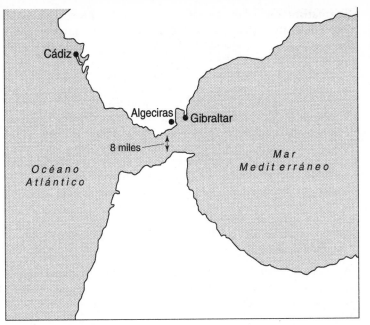

The Straits of Gibraltar

the Straits of Gibraltar a favourite crossing place for African refugees seeking a new life in Europe. Some are indeed from North African countries, but many are from further afield, for example political refugees from Rwanda and Liberia, and economic refugees from famine-stricken countries. All too often such people have attempted to reach the coast of Andalusia undetected in makeshift rafts known as *pateras*, coming to grief in the treacherous waters of the Straits of Gibraltar. In the later years of the 1990s, 101 corpses were washed up on Spanish shores, and almost 300 other illegal immigrants disappeared attempting the crossing. Numbers of prospective immigrants drowned in 2003 broke even these records.

Those who have made it to Spain and remained have added to the considerable numbers of homeless in the streets of large cities: some have found work and Spain has been tolerant enough to allow them to stay, but others have not been so fortunate. Generally speaking, Spain treats illegal immigrants in a reasonably compassionate way, and manifestations of out-and-out racism, though occasional, are rare. Indeed, one measure taken in 1999 reveals an interesting level of political pragmatism: one of the target destinations for Moroccan illegal immigrants over the years has been the market gardens along the south coast – labouring in sweltering conditions under plastic greenhouses. Aware that a high proportion of these seasonal workers were in fact illegal immigrants – poorly paid and living and working in poor conditions – the Spanish government signed a pact in 1999 with Morocco to 'import' thousands of Moroccans legally for up to nine months a year. In fact, the Spanish government is also responding to the chronic shortage of labour in the agricultural sector: Spain apparently needs up to 350,000 extra workers in agriculture to do work which, in spite of the 15 per cent unemployment rate, Spaniards themselves are unwilling to take on. Such immigrants seem not to be involved in any racial friction, since they simply work hard, saving their earnings to send home to their families, and keeping themselves to themselves. 'Tourist' immigration is discussed in Unit 12.

Internal migration by Spaniards to other towns and areas of Spain continues, but nowadays only to the extent of the level of mobility common in developed countries: prosperous towns continue to attract those seeking work, and given the possibility of rapid transportation the professional middle classes are quite happy to move with their jobs away from their original homes and families. The effect of all of this is to reduce regional prejudice and 'internal racism'.

However, there remains one social underclass which is still marginalized to a certain extent: the *gitanos* (Spanish gypsies). These people, who are not travelling gypsies as elsewhere in Europe, have always lived on the edge of civilization in Spain, for example in the caves of Sacromonte in Granada. Nowadays, most are much better housed, and although some still make a living selling garlic or *claveles* (carnations – the national flower of Spain) in the streets, many have prospered, particularly in Andalusia; some thanks to their talent with horses – running riding schools for tourists – and others from their artistic skills in *flamenco* culture, thereby gaining a greater degree of respectability and integration for all *gitanos*.

Spanish gypsies have made *flamenco* very much their own, and many have become world famous. In the 1980s and 1990s, *flamenco* music and dancing became fashionable in clubs and discos in Madrid – thanks partly to the fact that Prime Minister Felipe González (1982–1996) and some of his ministers were from Andalusia – then spread to Paris and London; singers and guitarists such as Camarón de la Isla and Habichuela, and dancers such as Joaquín Cortés have become icons of this most Spanish of art forms.

The environment in Spain

The Spanish have in the past had an ambivalent attitude to the environment, ranging from the high degree of care and interest in nature that prompted the establishing of some of the world's earliest and finest nature reserves, to the careless attitude seen in the wanton pollution of land, air and sea, and the unregulated building boom of the Franco years. The dictator's economic regeneration of Spain was all too often achieved at the expense of the environment, as one still sees today in the ugly refinery complexes and chemical factories which still belch out pollution in places like Huelva, Algeciras (Campo de Gibraltar) and Portugalete near Bilbao.

With the return of democracy, Spain has become much more conscious of environmental issues at a national, governmental level: pollution is controlled or prohibited by legislation on building, management of industrial waste and so on, and concerted efforts are now being made to reduce air and water pollution from industry.

The *Instituto para la Conservación de la Naturaleza* (ICONA) (Institute for the Conservation of Nature), the organization which monitors nature conservation all over Spain, is now a respected body, always consulted in the media on any environmental issue or item of news. Public awareness of Spain's nature heritage was also raised in the 1970s by Dr Félix Rodríguez de la Fuente, a naturalist who made a stunningly beautiful television series about Spain's wildlife; when he was tragically killed in a helicopter accident while filming, young people all over Spain mourned his death and a song in tribute to him was popular in the record charts. Another environmental icon is José Antonio Valverde, the prime mover behind the establishment of the Coto Doñana in Andalusia (see Unit 1) in the 1950s: still active in the field, his current project is for a museum of the sea to be established on the coast near the Coto Doñana.

The work of such people, allied to government publicity on environmental protection, has brought about a more enlightened attitude in Spain, reflected in the popularity among Spaniards of their nature reserves. In large numbers they visit the dunes of the Coto Doñana in safari buses, or learn about the wildlife at one of several excellent visitors centres dotted around the area. One black mark, however, is that there are still many keen hunters in Spain: in some areas even small songbirds are considered fair game. However, government publicity campaigns, public pressure and the work of *ICONA* are changing attitudes: nowadays one sees less evidence of wanton, careless dumping of waste and litter.

Interesting proof of new attitudes followed a major pollution incident in 1998: waste water from a mine north of the Coto Doñana broke through a retaining dam and polluted a river which feeds into the Coto. Emergency measures prevented the worst of the damage, but more significantly the event gave rise to outrage among Spaniards that such a thing could ever be allowed to happen. Similarly, the Prestige disaster in 2002 attracted volunteers from all over Spain to the coastline to Galicia, bringing practical help as well as popular protest.

Safari bus in the Coto Doñana

In recent years, the environmental protection service of the Civil Guard, SEPRONA (SERvicio para la PROtección de la NAturaleza), has come to the fore.

The Spanish are also very conscious of traffic pollution in their cities, and this problem has been dealt with since the late 1970s by pollution patrols (see Unit 9). An associated problem is that of noise pollution, with Spain ranking second to Japan among the noisiest countries in the world. As well as noisy vehicles, particularly small motorcycles whose ear-splitting noise reverberates in narrow streets, there is a problem with the increasing numbers of discos and night clubs poorly situated in residential areas, this being particularly acute in city centres and tourist resorts; not to mention the eternal problem of noisy neighbours upstairs or the volume of other people's televisions and stereos. Again, the only remedy is to increase public awareness of the problem to encourage people to be considerate; for most Spaniards, weekends and holidays away from the city bring the joy of escaping from noise and pollution.

The Spanish are also becoming very aware of the problem of water shortage as well as water pollution. The old adage 'The rain in Spain falls mainly on the plain' has always been a nonsense, being the opposite of the truth, which is precisely why Franco had so many dams built to control the water and channel it from the *sierras* with heavy rainfall to the arid plains (see Unit 1). Further to this, recent building of extensive pipelines enables water to be pumped from wet regions hundreds of miles to where it is needed: indeed, in 1999 the city of Cuenca, in its campaign to ensure that the new AVE (see Units 7 and 9) line to Valencia would pass through Cuenca, referred to the millions of gallons of water it had transferred to Valencia, insisting that it would only be fair exchange for Cuenca to be included in the planned AVE route.

In the summer months the media often mention these transfers of water to whichever region happens to be suffering drought that particular year, and one often hears public announcement broadcasts advising people to use water sparingly – all of which is helping to raise public consciousness of the problem. Tourism, however, consumes vast amounts of water – a particular problem in an area like the Coto Doñana: considerable public concern surrounds the development of the resort of Matalascañas along the dunes which separate the Coto Doñana from the sea, a resort whose need for water is having the effect of lowering the watertable in the marshes which attract migratory birds from far and wide.

Religious observance

Over the centuries since Pope Alexander VI granted the title *Reyes Católicos* to Isabel and Fernando (see Unit 1), Spain has often been considered the jewel in the crown of the Catholic Church. This was certainly the case during Franco's time: Franco himself had not been particularly devout until he decided to espouse religion in his anxiety to achieve political and social respectability for his regime. However, the fact that he associated the Church so closely with the regime caused a large proportion of Spanish people to lose trust in Catholicism, a shift of loyalties intensified by the dogmatism of senior clergy.

In the early days of democracy too, the Church's opposition to reforms in areas involving morality, such as birth control, abortion and divorce, lost it a lot of friends. As a consequence church attendance and worship are considerably reduced, yet Spain is still essentially a Catholic country, its culture and way of life reflecting its long history of religious influence.

The efforts of a new generation of more pragmatic clergymen, along with the passing of time and the dulling of unpleasant memories and associations mean that the Church is no longer regarded with such hostility by its opponents and by non-believers. Quite the contrary, the Church and its charitable agencies are now generally respected for their efforts to help the poor and marginalized at home and abroad. In fact, a recent survey found that religious belief is actually on the increase again, with 72 per cent of Spaniards believing in God, the greatest level of faith being concentrated in central Spain. About 70 per cent pray regularly, 34 per cent never do; more than 80 per cent claim to be Catholic, and about 5 per cent are of other Christian faiths while 1 per cent are Muslim, Buddhist or Jewish.

GLOSSARY

el pueblo	people, town, village
la ciudad	city, large town
el campo	countryside
rural	rural
vivir	to live
mudar	to move (house)
el habitante	inhabitant
la familia	family
el hombre	man
el marido/esposo	husband
la mujer	woman, wife
la esposa	wife
la madre	mother
el padre	father
el hijo/la hija	son/daughter
el hermano/la hermana	brother/sister
el abuelo/la abuela	grandfather/grandmother
nacer	to be born
casarse	to get married
morir	to die
el inmigrante (ilegal)	(illegal) immigrant
inmigrar	to immigrate

el medio ambiente	environment
cuidar de	to care for, look after
la polución medio ambiental	environmental pollution
la sequía	drought
irrigar, regar	to irrigate
cazar	to hunt
la religión	religion
la iglesia	church
el catolicismo	Catholicism
los fieles	the faithful
ir a misa	to go to mass
rezar	to pray
Dios	God

Taking it further

Reading

Spanish social trends: *Fire in the Blood*, Ian Gibson (BBC Books/Faber & Faber, 0 563 36194 8 – accompanied TV series; *The Spaniards*, John Hooper (Penguin, 0 14 009808 9); The role of the sexes, and women in society: *Constructing Spanish Womanhood: Female Identity in Modern Spain*, Victoria Loree Enders and Pamela Beth Radcliff (State University of New York Paperback, 1998); The environment: Good tourist guidebooks have useful information on nature parks, flora and fauna. Try the following: *Eyewitness Travel Guides* (Dorling-Kindersley, ISBN 0 7513 0106 X); Consejería de Educación y Ciencia: On certain specific topics the Consejería de Educación (Education Advisory Service) publishes booklets and work packs in Spanish on some subjects from this unit such as: *Las mujeres* (women), *juventud* (youth), *el Medio ambiente* (the environment), *la familia y las relaciones personales* (the family and personal relationships). Consejería de Educación y Ciencia, Embajada de España, Londres; Education and Science Office, Spanish Embassy, Peel Street, London W8 7PD. Tel: 0207 727 2462/0207 243 8535, Fax: 0207 229 4965.

Websites

You will not find much information on any subject covered in this unit on English websites, but it is worth trying the Consejería de Educación (Education Advisory Service) on

www.cec-spain.org.uk. If you can read Spanish, there are articles on women in society, the environment, *flamenco*, religion on **www.sgci.mec.es/uk/Pub/tecla.html**. There are Spanish websites available on some of the subjects covered in this unit. Here are a couple of interesting ones on the environment: **www.cofis.es/medio-ambiente**. For the latest information: the *Boletín Informativo de Medio Ambiente*, on: **www.mma.es:8088/GENERAL/sgnyci/**.

12

Spain in the wider world

In this unit you will learn
- about Imperial Spain
- about Spain and the EU
- about the future

Imperial Spain

Spain is one of a handful of countries which has had a genuine impact on the world in the sense of having spread its language and culture right around the globe. The Spanish language is truly a world language, and the story of how and why is told in the earlier units of this book. Yet this is not just a retrospective picture: arguably Spain has an influence overseas out of all proportion to its relatively modest size. While in the past it was men, resources and culture and ideas which Spain expended in the exploration, conquest and colonization of new lands, it is perhaps in the world of political influence that Spain has most to contribute to the world now.

Yet Spain's imperial past is not entirely a story of great glory: in certain areas of Latin America, virtual genocide was perpetrated in the name of Spain and its religion. While Spain was not as great a player in the slave trade as northern European countries, it shared in some of the guilt, and it must also be remembered that injustice and inhumane treatment were practised on religious minorities at home in past centuries. Much of what was done in the name of crown and cross was more the result of greed than of altruism, untold wealth being gathered in, supposedly for the benefit of the whole country.

Yet, as we have also seen in earlier units, in some senses Spain lost more than she gained in those imperial exploits: generations of people with drive and energy went to fight or settle abroad never to return, and the most skilled financiers and administrators were exiled for reasons of religion and race. All this left a country too weak to make the most of its increasing wealth, with the result that a great empire was gradually lost, and its wealth benefited other Europeans more than it did the Spanish.

Emigration and immigration in the 20th century

Although small-scale emigration to the Americas continued through the 19th century, it should also be remembered that a mass emigration took place in the 20th century: thousands of people fled from the Nationalist onslaught in the Civil War of 1936–1939, many remaining in voluntary exile rather than return to the new order set up by the victors. With the re-establishment of democracy, some have returned to Spain, particularly those who had settled in northern Europe, but others never did, forming a sort of Spanish diaspora. Here are just three examples of expatriate Spaniards (known personally to the author), who had to flee from the Civil War.

Two Basque sisters evacuated to the UK, taken in by a small private school, where they themselves later became teachers. Many other such Basque children were taken in by mining communities in South Wales and some of them stayed.

A Catalán girl who fled with her family to the Pyrenees, where they had to decide whether to go on up the mountain pass or to go through a railway tunnel. Hearing gunfire above them, they opted for the latter, escaping into France through the pitch-black tunnel ... others who continued up the road did not make it ...

A young farm boy from Extremadura who fled when he heard gunfire on returning to his village. He joined the Republicans, was twice captured by the Nationalists, and twice escaped ... the second time into France and then Britain, then fighting in the Second World War. He eventually settled in the UK, working as a painter and builder ... and his grandchildren persuaded him to write his story, listed in 'Taking it Further' in Unit 1.

Then, of course, there was the father of British politician, Michael Portillo, forced to escape from Franco's Spain or risk death for being a prominent republican.

Emigration from Spain to found the former colonies has never been balanced by subsequent mass immigration in the way this happened in the 20th century with the British Empire, but as mentioned in Unit 11, in the past 30 years there have been occasional incoming trickles of refugees from oppressive regimes in Latin America. There has been a curious though minor population inflow as described in Unit 8: small numbers of descendants of the Jews expelled in 1492 who have returned to live in Spain; in addition, many large properties on the Costa del Sol have in recent years been bought as holiday retreats, ironically, by wealthy Arabs.

More significantly, of course, in addition to the tens of millions of tourists who invade Spain annually, thousands of northern Europeans have settled in or retired to Spain, seeking a pleasant lifestyle and a kinder climate. A large proportion of them – particularly the British – are scarcely integrated into the community, preferring to live in little havens of Britishness.

A haven of Britishness for ex-pat settlers

Spain and the Hispanic world

Although Spain lost her last colony across the Atlantic over 100 years ago, she has maintained strong ties with all of them to a great extent. This is hardly surprising, since so many families in Spain have quite close relatives in Latin America.

Trade links are particularly important to Spain, and Telefónica is an example of a major Spanish company with a huge stake in the South American communications market – there are hundreds of others on a smaller scale. Politically, Spain tries to exercise a sort of benign, avuncular care over Latin America; however in 1992 there were voices in Latin America which expressed irritation at the celebrations of the 500th anniversary of Columbus' discovery, insisting that Spain should neither revel in such a disastrous era for indigenous American nations nor continue to try to influence affairs in its former colonies. In some cases, such as Chile, Spain has actually tried to exert a sort of moral authority and leadership.

Having been quite dynamic in 1988 in encouraging Chileans to oust their dicatator, General Augusto Pinochet, Spain attempted to extradite him from London to Madrid to face trial for the torture and murder of hundreds of Spaniards resident in Chile in the 1970s. Of course, Pinochet's supporters and many Chileans resented what they saw as interference in their affairs, but his opponents pointed to the fact that he was still influential at home and would never be tried there. Considerable numbers of Spanish grandparents are anxious to trace their grandchildren, given away to childless military couples in both Chile and Argentina when their parents were 'disappeared' without trace. Over the years the Spanish press has often carried articles criticizing oppressive or corrupt regimes in Latin America. Currently there is a great deal of interest in the future of Cuba – so isolated since the break-up of the Soviet Union – with questions like: 'What will replace Fidel Castro's communist regime? 'Will Cuba descend into anarchy?' 'Will the USA end its irrational economic blockade of Cuba and allow the country to integrate with the rest of the world?' 'Why can't the USA see that trade and aid will persuade Cubans to embrace democracy, not isolation.'

Culturally the ties have always been strong, with both Spaniards and Latin Americans benefiting from an enormous range and diversity of offerings in literature and music, having at their disposal the cultural products of over 20 countries. This shared cultural life was enhanced still further by the setting up in 1992 – in time for the Barcelona Olympic Games and EXPO 1992 – of the Hispasat satellite link, affording improved telecommunications and shared television programming. It was not long before the presenter of a Spanish word-based game show had to apologize to Latin American viewers for an embarrassing linguistic anomaly: his repeated instruction to contestants to 'take a letter' was causing offence to viewers abroad where the verb *coger* (to take) has the meaning of 'to copulate'! This only serves to underline how rich and varied the language is: Spanish is in the same position as English, spoken in a wide variety of forms in an enormous range of settings, belonging to all its speakers and not the preserve of Spain alone.

'Take a letter' on a game show!

However, the Spanish Academy took the lead in 1994, joining with equivalent bodies in the main Latin American countries to rationalize the Spanish alphabet (see Unit 2), and a subsequent conference acknowledged the importance of, and the valuable contribution made by, all the indigenous languages of the Americas and the other languages of Spain.

Spain and its other neighbours

Apart from its borders with France and Gibraltar, Spain's only other land border is with Portugal; its relationship with its smaller neighbour has always been a little strange, and there is no doubt that Portugal has in the past resented Spain, so often seeing Spain as a threat. Long gone are the days when Portugal turned to its oldest ally, Britain, for support: the relationship of these two EU countries is now a healthy one, with cultural and trade links reinforcing the bond of a shared history, just as Spain's relationship with France is very positive.

Spain's former colony, Morocco, has given rise to more problems over the years: when Spain was trying to give independence to its territory known as Spanish Sahara, Morocco had other plans – to take it over – and relations were distinctly frosty for a long time in the 1970s. In fact, Spain's two remaining outposts in North Africa – the cities of Ceuta and Melilla on the Moroccan coast – felt rather beleaguered, their borders bristling with barbed wire and Moroccan soldiers. In the late 1980s, however, largely thanks to the friendship between King Juan Carlos and King Hassan of Morocco, the icy relationship thawed to such an extent that the two countries began to plan a fixed link – bridge or tunnel – to link their countries and the two continents. As with Latin America, family ties resulting from the large numbers of Spaniards who settled in Moroccan coastal towns like Tangiers and Tetuan have meant that ordinary people maintained contact even though for a while governments did not.

As for Gibraltar – often referred to as a 'stone in Spain's shoe' – Spain has, perhaps understandably, resented this British enclave. This came to a head in 1969 when General Franco closed the border between Spain and the colony, furious that the British government would not discuss the issue of sovereignty. This was a disaster for the hundreds of Spaniards who crossed the border each day to work in Gibraltar; the border was reopened in 1985 in preparation for Spain's entry to the EEC, to avoid there being an ongoing conflict between two EEC members. Although there have been problems over the use of the airport and over the amount of drug smuggling carried on by Gibraltarians, relations are now quite good. Gibraltar attracts numbers of British and Spanish tourists from the neighbouring coastal resorts, curious to see British bobbies, drink English beer and eat fish and chips – all in the sunshine of southern Spain. The issue of sovereignty, however, rumbles on. The British Labour Government, from 1997 onwards, is prepared to consider shared sovereignty with Spain, but the Government and people of Gibraltar are not interested.

Spain and the EU

After years of ostracism and isolation under Franco, one of democratic Spain's priorities was to resume her rightful place on the international scene by joining the major international organizations to which other European countries belonged. In fact, Franco had tried unsuccessfully to associate with what was then called the EEC (European Economic Community), and the new, democratic Spain actually applied for membership for the first time in 1977. The EEC, however, wanted to be sure that democracy in Spain had been re-established firmly. January 1986 marked Spain's entry to the EEC. Since then, Spain's economy has adjusted well and become much more stable thanks to its position in the European context, as a result of which most Spaniards are committed Europeans and relationships with France are very good. There was little opposition to the *euro* during its planned introduction in 2002, and it is now well established.

Gone are the days when the Spanish – especially women – found it difficult to travel abroad: now they do not need a passport to travel across their borders to EU countries. Whenever Spain has held the presidency of the EU, it has earned credit because of the enthusiasm, commitment and sense of responsibility with which it has carried out its duties, and its prime ministers have been respected, key players in community decision making.

Spain and the UN

In the late 1940s, the United Nations Organization condemned the Spanish regime and recommended its members to suspend diplomatic relations with Spain. However, from 1951, Spain began to be admitted to some of the UN's peripheral

organizations and in 1955 was finally admitted to the United
Nations itself. In recent times, as mentioned in Unit 8, Spaniards
have been proud of the contribution made in various peace-
keeping missions by their very own '*cascos azules*', their
servicemen wearing the pale blue helmets of the United Nations
in zones of conflict such as former Yugoslavia, Angola, Namibia
and Central America. They have also been proud of the fact that
Spanish speakers from Latin American countries have occupied
key UN posts, such as the Peruvian Javier Pérez de Cuéllar,
Secretary General from 1982–1991. In October 1992, Spain was
elected to permanent membership of the UN Security Council.

Spain and NATO

Spain's negotiations for entry to NATO were being conducted at
a very awkward time in terms of internal politics: they spanned
the resignation of Adolfo Suárez as President of the government
in January 1981, the attempted coup of 23 February 1981, and
the weak government of Leopoldo Calvo Sotelo. In the event,
Spain finally became a member in May 1982, a matter of
months before the October elections which brought Felipe
González and his *PSOE* Socialist government to power (see Unit
8). They had declared their opposition to NATO membership,
and confronted with the *fait accompli* of membership, all they
could do was to promise a referendum to enable the people of
Spain to decide.

González had a major problem: the Spanish were generally anti-
NATO; the metro in Madrid and walls in Zaragoza near the
American airbase were littered with the slogans '*OTAN ¡NO!*'
and '*Yanquis go home*'. Yet Spain was about to apply for
membership of the EEC; it would not look very good if at the
same time as applying for membership of one international club,
Spain was leaving another. After delaying for as long as possible,
the referendum was eventually conducted in March 1986; in
spite of antipathy towards the USA and the very idea of NATO,
the Spanish, voted by 52 per cent in favour and 40 per cent
against remaining in NATO. What had happened was that
Spaniards had decided it was best to stay in NATO, having only
recently joined the EEC ... and that González had found a
confusing form of words in which to vote against NATO was to
vote '*sí*', and to vote to stay in was to vote '*no*', whereas all of
the anti-NATO compaigns had been shouting '*OTAN ¡NO!*' ...
(OTAN = NATO).

'OTAN ¡No!'? 'OTAN ¡Sí!'

Since then, Spain has gradually moved from a position of cautious membership, through being a member, but not a very active one, to a position of total participation. What is more, members of the armed forces of other NATO countries working together with the Spanish have learned to respect Spanish servicemen for their professionalism. A prominent politician of Felipe González's government – Javier Solana – was Secretary General of NATO from 1995–1999. Having done an extremely effective job in that role, his talents were recognized in 1999 when he was selected as Head of Foreign Policy and Security of the Western European Union, the military face of the EU, at a time when the EU's common defence policy was becoming increasingly important. Indeed, it may one day replace NATO's current European defence role as Europe takes on more responsibility for its own security.

Border control

Spain has had no major border problems in that her borders are well defined, but there have been border problems. The main one has been the smuggling into Spain of drugs and cigarettes (see Unit 9), but measures have been taken to deal with this problem. The second 'border' problem is that of illegal immigrants from Africa and Latin America (see Unit 11). In the late 1990s the Spanish government tried a new approach to this problem, one which should at least make the problem more manageable (see Unit 11). The coast of Spain is, of course, the southern 'border' for the whole of the EU.

The future

So: where is Spain now? The simplest answer to this simple question is: 'In a quite solid position'. Spain's economy is now well and truly settled, and in every political and social sense, Spain has largely caught up with its neighbours. It is now a respected participant on the international stage, and has gained the admiration of others for having achieved the transition to democracy peacefully. What is more, its new constitution has now experienced governments of opposite political persuasions and survived intact. The country has a reliable and popular monarchy which has earned its popularity, and what is more, the country has achieved a considerable level of political maturity. One can only say that the future looks very positive.

GLOSSARY

el imperio	*empire*
la colonia	*colony*
emigrar	*to emigrate*
inmigrar	*to immigrate*
el país	*country*
la influencia	*influence*
influir	*to influence*
las relaciones	*relations(hips)*
el comercio	*trade*
la política	*politics*
la cultura	*culture*
el vecino	*neighbour*
la Organización de las Naciones Unidas	*United Nations Organization*
la Unión Europea	*European Union*
la Organización de Tratado del Atlántico del Norte	*North Atlantic Treaty Organization*
el secretario general	*secretary general*
la seguridad	*security*
la contrabanda	*smuggling, contraband*
el contrabandista	*smuggler*
el inmigrante ilegal	*illegal immigrant*

teach
yourself

beginner's spanish

mark stacey & ángela gonzález hevia

- Are you new to language learning?
- Do you want lots of practice and examples?
- Do you want to improve your confidence to speak?

Beginner's Spanish is written for the complete beginner who wants to move at a steady pace and have lots of opportunity to practise. The grammar is explained clearly and does not assume that you have studied a language before. You will learn everything you need to get the most out of a holiday or to go on to further study.

teach yourself

quick fix spanish grammar
keith chambers

- Do you want to get to grips with grammar, *fast*?
- Are you looking for manageable chunks of learning?
- Do you want to check your understanding?

Quick Fix Spanish Grammar is a quick and easy way to fill the gaps in your grammar. There's one main point on each page, with exercises to help reinforce your learning. Either use the book as a dip-in/dip-out reference tool or work through it to reach a good basic level of competence.

teach® yourself